Skills for Bilingual Legal Personnel

Translating, Interpreting, and Cultural Fluency

Técnicas para el personal bilingüe en el área legal

Traducción, interpretación y penetración cultural

MARILYN R. FRANKENTHALER, Ph.D., J.D.
Associate Professor of Spanish
Coordinator for Paralegal Studies
Montclair State College
General Editor

CONTRIBUTORS:
Beatriz Valera-Schutz
Margarita González
John Zahner
JoAnne Engelbert

V68 **SOUTH-WESTERN PUBLISHING CO.**

CINCINNATI WEST CHICAGO, ILL. DALLAS PELHAM MANOR, N.Y. PALO ALTO, CALIF.

ISBN: 0-538-22680-3
Library of Congress Catalog Card Number 80-53395
1 2 3 4 5 6 7 8 9 0 D 1 0 9 8 7 6 5 4 3 2
Impreso en los Estados Unidos de América
(Printed in the United States of America)

ACKNOWLEDGEMENT

Materials for This Text Were Developed Through a

Grant by

Title I of the Higher Education Act of 1965

as amended

University Community Services

Funded through the New Jersey Department of

Higher Education

Project: Language Access to Legal Assistance

Hispanic Community Program Internship in Law

MONTCLAIR STATE COLLEGE

Upper Montclair, New Jersey

PREFACE

This text focuses upon all of the basic skills required by bilingual personnel serving the Hispanic community in the legal area. It may be utilized in advanced language courses which emphasize a specialization in translating and interpreting. The volume is also appropriate for use within an in-service training program for legal personnel. The approach followed throughout the materials additionally lends itself to individualized instruction and self-study, for the benefit of bilingual legal personnel who wish to improve their skills outside of the traditional classroom learning situation.

The ideas and principles contained in this volume are useful to all bilingual legal personel: paralegals, legal secretaries, court interpreters, attorneys, or administrative personnel. Persons using this book should be "bilingual" in the sense that they are fluent in both English and Spanish. This text is designed to furnish them with the specialized skills in translation, interpreting, and cultural awareness, for application within a legal system such as that of the United States.

These materials were originally developed as part of the Montclair State College Hispanic Community Program Internship in Law, to serve Hispanics who cannot afford the services of private attorneys and who seek legally-related services at public sector legal agencies. The project, entitled "Language Access to Legal Assistance," was funded through a grant by Title I of the Higher Education Act of 1965 as amended (University Community Services) through the New Jersey Department of Higher Education. The materials have been broadened in scope, so that they are useful to bilingual legal personnel working in a variety of situations. The presence of a number of examples in the text which relate to legal aid agencies is explained by the origin of the materials.

The text is divided into three parts: Cultural Fluency, Interpreting for Legal Personnel, and Translating for Legal Personnel. Part I deals with the necessary prerequisite to a study of the skills of translating and interpreting, "Cultural Fluency," where techniques to achieve communication across cultures are explored through exemplary situations and more generalized discussion. Parts II and III, Interpreting for Legal Personnel and Translating for Legal Personnel, stress the precision required in both oral and written communication. Both parts begin with the essential elements of theory and practice, including ethical considerations and regional differences. In Part II, interpreting is studied in the context of interview situations, telephone conversations, and the formal courtroom setting. In Part III, the special considerations involved in translating legal language are discussed in detail.

Examples of translations illustrate a wide variety of legally-related situations, from letters to clients through formal documents.

A companion volume to this text contains an advanced guide to Spanish/English Legal Terminology. Illustrative phrases are included, so that the translator may be guided by the use of words and phrases in proper context.

Through the different parts of this text, communication is approached from the standpoints of both culture and language. The objectivity required of the translator or interpreter is stressed throughout the materials, as an essential element in the accurate communication of ideas. Yet, bilingual legal personnel may also be able to play the role of advocates. An awareness of and a respect for cultural backgrounds and linguistic differences can breed comprehension and empathy, attitudes which should be encouraged among all legal personnel who serve Spanish-speaking clients.

Marilyn R. Frankenthaler
Montclair State College

ABOUT THE CONTRIBUTORS

MARILYN R. FRANKENTHALER, General Editor.

Ph.D., J.D., Member of New Jersey Bar. Coordinator for Paralegal Studies and Coordinator for Hispanic Community Program Internship in Law, Montclair State College. Author of books and articles dealing with literary criticism and legally-related subjects. Project Director for the Title I of H.E.A. Grant, Language Access to Legal Assistance, which sponsored the development of these materials.

BEATRIZ VALERA-SCHUTZ, Co-author, "Cultural Fluency."

B.A., M.A., Presently studying for J.D. at Rutgers University School of Law. Chief Linguist for the Hispanic Community Program Internship in Law, Montclair State College, 1979-80. Currently preparing articles dealing with several themes in Hispanic literature.

MARGARITA GONZALEZ, Co-author, "Cultural Fluency."

B.A., M.A. in Translation at the State University of New York, Binghamton. Served as translator and interpreter during 1978-79 academic year, as part of student staff of the Hispanic Community Program Internship in Law, Montcleair State College.

JOHN ZAHNER, Author, "Interpreting for Legal Personnel."

Ph. D., Coordinator for Grammar, Spanish/Italian Department, Montclair State College. Originator of courses in Spanish for Police Officers and Spanish for Hospital Personnel. Assistant Project Director for Community Outreach Courses, 1980-81, Title I of H.E.A. Grant.

JoANNE ENGELBERT, Author, "Translating for Legal Personnel."

Ph.D. Coordinator of Translator Training in Spanish, Montclair State College. Translator and author of books and articles on literary criticism. Contributing Editor to *Review*.

EDITORIAL STAFF

ANITA Y. AGINIAN, Contributing Editor.

Co-author of *Instructor's Manual for Skills for Bilingual Legal Personnel: Translating, Interpreting, and Cultural Fluency,* B.A., M.A., Linguist for Hispanic Community Program Internship in Law, Montclair State College, 1980-81.

MERYL FENSTER, Contributing Editor.

Co-author of *Instructor's Manual for Skills for Bilingual Legal Personnel: Translating Interpreting, and Cultural Fluency,* B.A., M.A., currently completing Ph.D., in Spanish at New York University. Linguist for Hispanic Community Program, Internship in Law, Montclair State College, 1980-81.

NANCY C. LÓPEZ-BALBOA, Contributing Editor.

Co-author of *Instructor's Manual for Skills for Bilingual Legal Personnel: Translating, Interpreting, and Cultural Fluency,* B.S., B.A., M.A., currently Adjunct Professor of Spanish at Montclair State College. Linguist for Hispanic Community Program, Internship in Law, Montclair State College, 1980-81.

TABLE OF CONTENTS

PART I

CULTURAL FLUENCY

Beatriz Valera-Schutz   Margarita González

INTRODUCTION

People communicate not only through language but also by responding or failing to respond to the cultural characteristics and expectations of others. In any personal contact situation the behavior of the persons involved is influenced by their cultural background, their roles in a given situation, and the particular circumstances in which they find themselves.

When cultural backgrounds differ, the same word or gesture may have an entirely different meaning for two individuals. A word or gesture may be interpreted as offensive — a result not intended by the speaker. Consequently, a misunderstanding can easily occur even though the speaker may not be aware of a negative effect. In a legal situation, because correct information is in itself so essential to the resolution of a problem, there is a special need to avoid any misunderstanding. In order to do so, a conscious effort is necessary on the part of legal personnel to be alert to any factor which might aid or interfere with effective communication.

The attorney, paralegal, receptionist — anyone serving the needs of a client in a legally-related situation — should have a basic awareness of a client's cultural background. This is especially true if a client is from another country or does not speak the language of the country in which he or she now resides.

The needs of this client can be easily appreciated by considering a hypothetical situation. Assume that you are a United States citizen and a native speaker of English; you know no Spanish; you find yourself in a Latin American country; and you need legal assistance. Certainly you would not only welcome but actually need the competent help of anyone who knew your language and who might also know some of your customs and personal background. In addition, there would be the need to adapt as quickly as possible to the unfamiliar surroundings in order to deal directly and effectively with the legal problem.

The unfamiliarity of legally-related situations in itself often hinders communication. This is true even when the client and legal personnel speak the same language. When language and cultural differences also exist, they create special requirements which must be considered because overall communication becomes more complex. These special requirements or needs must be dealt with by the person rendering assistance before the client and attorney can work together toward the resolution of the legal problem and throughout the period of necessary communication.

In striving for Cultural Fluency, we must consider the problems faced by the person seeking assistance, the client, as well as the difficulties encountered by legal personnel seeking to assist the client. The objective of this part of the text is to study these problems in a manner which will serve as a guide to an awareness of cultural factors, be they individual, familial or societal in their origin. This should provide an opportunity for the student to recognize and analyze their effect upon communication in a legal situation.

CHAPTER 1

THE PROCESS OF DEVELOPING CULTURAL FLUENCY

To illustrate the cultural factors which affect communication within the legal context, a legal interview situation is presented in this chapter. This legal situation is a composite of many actual ones. The persons involved are also composites. All of the factors involved —whether expressed by the client or legal personnel— are not likely to be characteristic of any one individual. Many exceptions to the type of behavior displayed in the situation can easily be cited. The situation is written to provoke conscious thought and analysis and is not intended as a positive or negative reflection upon the actual conduct of any one individual or group.

Composites are used to avoid the oversimplification of stereotypes which interfere with an accurate perception of individuals and their circumstances at any given time. The composites in this text indicate certain possible characteristics of a group as a starting point for the reader's own observations into a different culture in order that he or she may gain a more comprehensive view of the individual. A familiarity with certain practices accepted within a particular cultural group should not be utilized to try to make a member of that cultural group fit a generalized or preconceived pattern. Rather, a familiarity with certain cultural factors should help the reader to consciously think about their use in bringing about a favorable and positive reaction by the client. This is a part of a process which can help legal personnel to render the best possible legal services to the client.

As you read this part of the text, keep in mind that every actual situation is different and that each person is unique. It is not possible to take into account the great diversity of social classes, religions, and nationalities when one describes a particular situation. It must be emphasized that any negative trait described in this text is not meant to criticize or disparage any client, public or private sector attorney, or bilingual personnel.

The process of developing Cultural Fluency is divided into four steps which the reader is asked to follow in order to gain increased awareness of cultural factors which may influence communication in a legal situation.

Step 1. Focusing on an Interview Situation

A. Read the interview situation, which starts on page 5, for general content.
B. As you reread it, write down the particular characteristics which inhibit or enhance communication between the participants.

Step 2. Analyzing the Dialogue

A. Study the line-by-line analysis of the dialogue given in the text.
B. Compare it with your notes made in Step 1.
C. Summarize the behavior and reasoning of the participants in order to describe how each person views the same situation from his or her own perspective.
D. Suggest how the participants might improve the situation by omitting or altering specific words or actions.

Step 3. **Developing Cultural Fluency**

A. Read the summaries and suggestions for improving communication given in this section of the text.
B. Compare them with your summaries and suggestions.

Step 4. **Exercising Cultural Fluency**

A. Read the revised initial situation modified to show improvements which can be brought about through the exercise of Cultural Fluency.
B. Write down any additional changes you would make and why.

As you read the revised version of the dialogue, the objective of all the exercises should be apparent: to create the conscious awareness of and sensitivity to the cultural expressions, needs, and expectations of others. Even though the examples given in the text concern "legal situations," Cultural Fluency should be exercised in any situation in which members of different cultures are present.

STEP ONE: FOCUSING ON AN INTERVIEW SITUATION

When a person has a legal problem, the first step in attempting to deal with the problem is frequently a telephone call to a private attorney or a legal aid office. Although this call may be very important in establishing the basis for further communication, it is during the interview itself that the first personal contact occurs between the client and the client's legal representative. This is the time when client and attorney are least familiar with each other and also the time when each has most to gain or lose in terms of rapport and mutual confidence. For this reason we are focusing on an initial interview situation, where cultural factors come into play most clearly for the first time.

The client who perhaps requires the greatest help and understanding before and during the interview is the one who not only cannot speak and understand English well, but who also does not, at a given time, have sufficient funds to pay for necessary legal services. The client's lack of familiarity with the legal system is aggravated by the lack of familiarity with the cultural factors of a new environment. Although these circumstances may create special problems, they can be avoided if, (1) there is someone present who can easily recognize the probable cause of the problems, and (2) there is the opportunity for this person to work unobstrusively to anticipate or explain any possible misunderstanding. By creating the appropriate atmosphere, all concerned are better able to deal with the legal matter at hand.

In the following dialogue the client whose situation is similar to the one described in the preceding paragraph is Marta Fernández. Her full formal name is Marta Isabel Suero de Fernández. She is seeking a divorce from her husband who has left her with no means of supporting herself and her young son. She has been in this country for only a few years. She has never worked outside her home and is finding it very difficult to adapt to a lifestyle which is substantially different from that of the traditional Latin American culture in which she grew up. She believes that her family does not approve of her decision so she does not ask them for financial help to obtain her divorce. Since she is presently unemployed, she cannot secure the services of a private attorney.

The initial interviewer who obtains certain basic information in order to process the client's application for legal services is usually called an "intake worker." In this interview the intake worker is Frank Smith, who is bilingual and has some familiarity with the Hispanic culture. He has already taken the initial information from the client when the dialogue begins, so his role will be minimal.

Leonard Benson is a non-Spanish-speaking attorney employed by the legal aid agency. He has not had an opportunity to work with Spanish-speaking clients before and, although he would like to learn Spanish and know something about Hispanic culture, he has not yet been able to do so.

Ana Domínguez is a bilingual secretary who speaks both English and Spanish. She is occasionally called upon to interpret although she has not been trained as an interpreter. In the interview, because she is functioning as such, she is called the interpreter.

The interview situation which follows illustrates language as well as cultural difficulties. The language difficulties will be analyzed in the part of this text which deals with "Interpreting for Legal Personnel."

DIVORCE INTERVIEW AT A LEGAL AID AGENCY

A. READ THE ENTIRE DIALOGUE ONCE.

B. AS YOU READ YOU SHOULD BECOME AWARE OF HOW THE WORDS AND ACTIONS OF THE CLIENT, ATTORNEY, AND INTERPRETER INHIBIT OR ACTUALLY PREVENT COMMUNICATION BECAUSE OF CULTURAL BARRIERS.

C. AT THE SAME TIME, NOTE ANY WORDS OR ACTIONS WHICH HAVE, OR REPRESENT TO THE PERSON(S) USING THEM, ANY POSITIVE VALUE.

D. TRY TO DISTINGUISH THE THREE DIFFERENT PERSPECTIVES WHICH FORM THE BASIS OF THESE WORDS AND ACTIONS.

E. AT THE END OF THE DIALOGUE YOU WILL FIND AN EXERCISE WITH DIRECTIONS INDICATING WHICH ASPECTS OF THE DIALOGUE YOU SHOULD PAY SPECIAL ATTENTION TO WHEN YOU READ THE DIALOGUE FOR A SECOND TIME.

(Attorney Leonard Benson is seated at his desk, working. He is casually dressed in slacks and a plaid shirt — no tie or jacket. A Hispanic woman client, Marta Fernández, is led into the room by the intake worker, another member of the staff. This intake worker has already asked many questions of the client, and has noted much basic information on an "intake sheet" in order to determine that the client is in fact eligible for legal services. The attorney looks up briefly, smiles, but does not further acknowledge the presence of the client when she comes in.)

INTAKE WORKER: (Addressing the client as he indicates the attorney.) This is a person who takes care of divorce cases. (He puts the folder containing the intake sheet on the desk and leaves.)

ATTORNEY: Thanks, Frank. (Not looking up.) Be with you in a minute. (Keeps working. Finally looks up. Speaks courteously.) Just a few more things to get out of the way . . . Okay, Mrs. . . (Looking at intake sheet in folder. Baffled, he asks:) *What* is your name?

CLIENT: (Speech is heavily accented.) My last name is Suero Sánchez de Fernández.

ATTORNEY: Sorry, but I can't make head or tail of this. Your *real* last name.

CLIENT: (Looking at him quizzically.) My last name is Suero Sánchez de Fernández.

ATTORNEY: Well, it must be Fernández. (Pronounces name with English accent.)

CLIENT: Sí . . . yes. (Her tone indicating that she is willing to agree to this pronunciation to get on with the matter. Imitating English accent:) Fernández.

ATTORNEY: (Looking at her directly). Okay, now, you want a divorce.

CLIENT: Yes. (Looks at hands on lap.)

ATTORNEY: Do you speak English?

CLIENT: Yes, a little.

ATTORNEY: Well, that's a help. (Continues to look at client directly. Client does not look up but tries to listen intently to each word. Attorney looks over the intake sheet, sits back, then stretches a bit. Talking to no one in particular:) This should be pretty cut and dried.

CLIENT: I don't understand. "Cut?" . . . "Dried?"

ATTORNEY: Oh . . . nothing. Just let me read this over a bit more. (Reads for a few more seconds; then looks directly at client again.) Okay, please, tell me specifically, in your own words, why you want a divorce. What's the problem? What's up?

CLIENT: (Looks up briefly.) What you say? (Looks down again.)

ATTORNEY: (Patiently) I don't mean to be rude or anything, but I've got a lot to take care of. Please answer the questions directly.

CLIENT: (She is trying very hard to understand.) Yes.

ATTORNEY: (His voice begins to get louder.) You've got to do your part in order to help.

CLIENT: (Looks up briefly, then down again.) Help? Yes. I want help.

ATTORNEY: Great. I can see we're going to be here all day. (Sighs in attempted resignation.)

CLIENT: You no can help?

ATTORNEY: (Trying to "make the best of things.") Yeah, sure, I, yes can help. (Laughs lightly, trying to be humorous, yet he shakes his head.) Let's see . . . Question number one (Reading from a questionnaire, louder.) "Where do you reside?"

CLIENT: (Having trouble pronouncing.) I just want a divorce. My husband leave. (Obviously upset.)

ATTORNEY: (Calmly.) Well, I can see I'm not doing very well. (Calls out.) Ana. (Both wait a while in silence.)

INTERPRETER: (Ana enters.) Yes, Lenny. What is it? (Smiles at client.)

ATTORNEY: This woman doesn't speak English.

CLIENT: (Raises her voice, visibly perturbed.) Yes, I speak English.

ATTORNEY: (A bit louder but in a conciliatory tone.) Yes, Mrs. Fernández, you speak English, but we need some help.

INTERPRETER: (Addressing client.) Tienes que hacer lo que diga el abogado.

CLIENT: (Indignant and despairing.) Bueno, sea como sea, lo que yo quiero es mi divorcio. Hace más de una hora que estoy aquí esperando, y ¿para qué?, ¿para que me digan que no hablo inglés?

INTERPRETER: No es para tanto. Cálmate.

ATTORNEY: Come on Ana, let's get going. Ask her where she lives.

INTERPRETER: Él quiere saber dónde vives.

CLIENT: ¿Él es el abogado? Ya he hablado con otra persona en esta oficina.

INTERPRETER: Sí, y quiere saber dónde vives.

CLIENT: (Disheartened.) Ahí en la calle Grant.

INTERPRETER: ¿Qué número?

CLIENT: Quinientos sesenta.

INTERPRETER: She says she lives at 15-60 Grant.

ATTORNEY: Wait a minute. It says here 560 . . .

INTERPRETER: Yeah, that's what I said.

ATTORNEY: (Disregards comment. Continues normal line of questioning until he reaches one of the final questions.) Ask her whether there is any possibility of reconciliation.

INTERPRETER: ¿Te vas a juntar con tu marido?

CLIENT: (Completely taken aback.) ¿Qué? . . . ¿Qué? (Thinks a moment and then replies almost in a whisper.) No. (Shakes her head dejectedly.) Mi esposo se fue hace tiempo y no me ha mandado ni un centavo.

(The interpreter continues to interpret the attorney's questions in the same manner until the interview is completed.)

SECOND READING OF DIALOGUE

In reading the dialogue, you became aware that the atmosphere which was being inadvertently created was more likely to result in resentment or hostility than in better relations between the client and her legal representatives. The interchange between the attorney and client, which later included the interpreter, focused on the words said by each, but communication was strongly affected by cultural as well as by language factors.

The way in which each person perceives an entire situation is dependent upon much more than the words which are spoken. A personal contact situation includes not only *what* is said but *where* it is said, *why* it is said, and the particular circumstances of each member of the group. Without a sensitivity to all the important factors which comprise the total situation, it may appear that all is going well when in fact the very objective sought may become increasingly more difficult to attain. This objective is the creation of an atmosphere in which the client feels free to speak openly about all matters important to his or her case.

EXERCISE 1

Keeping this in mind, reread the dialogue carefully. As you read, list in the chart which follows, according to the number of the line of dialogue (column A), the cultural characteristic(s) and apparent misunderstanding(s) which affect communication between client and the agency personnel (column B), and the possible explanations for these (column C).

A LINE NUMBER	B CULTURAL CHARACTERISTIC OR CAUSE OF MISUNDERSTANDING	C POSSIBLE EXPLANATION
2	Too casually dressed for being a lawyer	Not the usual way in Latin America
9	Attorney is impolite. Should shake hands and show client to have a seat	Not well educated and no idea of other countries' customs
12	Should be adressed in a more proffesional way	
16/17	Totally uncourteous to the client	
18/19/20	Indicating client he has little time for her	
21	Asking unimportant questions	
24	Using vocabulary which is unfamiliar to client	
26/27	Client is not aware of US habits using names	
	Attorney is uncourteous to client, is not helpful at all and seems to have no intention to solve the problem of client. Instead, he is irritating her and she begins to be more nervous during her interview.	

Compare your answers with the dialogue and comments in the next section.

STEP TWO: ANALYZING THE DIALOGUE

In this section the perspectives of the parties are described as they are revealed through what is said and what is not said. This includes words as well as gestures, unspoken reactions, and silent justifications for reactions.

IN YOUR FIRST READING YOU WERE ASKED TO TRY TO DISTINGUISH THE THREE PERSPECTIVES AS REVEALED IN THE WORDS AND ACTIONS OF THE THREE PERSONS INVOLVED AND THE POINTS AT WHICH COMMUNICATION WAS INHIBITED OR PREVENTED BY CULTURAL BARRIERS. IN YOUR SECOND READING YOU WERE ASKED TO COMPLETE A CHART LISTING THESE AND POSSIBLE EXPLANATIONS FOR THEM. NOW AS YOU READ THE FOLLOWING SECTION COMPARE YOUR OWN OBSERVATIONS WITH THE DIALOGUE ANALYSIS. FOR REFERENCE, THE LINE NUMBERS AND TEXT OF THE ORIGINAL DIALOGUE ARE INCLUDED HERE.

(Attorney Leonard Benson is seated at his desk, working. He is casually dressed in slacks and a plaid shirt — no tie or jacket. A Hispanic woman client, Marta Fernández, is led into the room by the intake worker, another member of the staff. This intake worker has already asked many questions of the client, and has noted much basic information on an "intake sheet" in order to determinate that the client is in fact eligible for legal services. The attorney looks up briefly, smiles, but does not further acknowledge the presence of the client when she comes in.)

The attorney considers that there is no need to be more formally dressed than he is, primarily because there is a generally accepted casualness in this office. Further, since his clients are of limited financial means, he thinks he would make them feel uncomfortable by displaying his relative wealth and higher social and professional status by "overdressing." He is busy and he feels certain that a client who enters will appreciate this fact by seeing him at work. He believes there is no need to acknowledge those who have entered with anything more than a friendly smile, because he knows that it has to be a client brought in by the intake worker, Frank.

INTAKE WORKER: (Addressing the client as he indicates the attorney.) This is the person who takes care of divorce cases. (He puts the folder containing the intake sheet on the desk and leaves.)

The intake worker takes it for granted that the client knows whose office she is entering and considers an introduction much too formal a ceremony. He does not explain to the client at any time that it is his role only to take down certain information in writing and that the attorney will then take his initial information, check some of it over with her, and amplify it according to the particular need.

ATTORNEY: Thanks, Frank. (Not looking up.) Be with you in a minute. (Keeps working. Finally looks up. Speaks courteously.) Just a few more things to get out of the way . . .

The attorney is trying to "get a few things out of the way" so that he may give the client his full attention. The client, however, has already had to wait a long time in the waiting room before finally having her name called, being asked what her problem was, and then trying to explain the nature of her problem in some detail to the person who was filling out a sheet. At least, she believes, "the people here now know my problem. It's down in writing." But, she wonders whether the person asking the questions is an attorney. Mrs. Fernández did not realize that he was the intake worker. No one had explained the roles of any of the personnel to her. All that she understands is that someone at this agency is supposed to help her secure a divorce. Now she is being brought into another room, a third room. "Is *this* the attorney?" she asks herself. "No, an attorney wouldn't dress this way and he would surely be more respectful because of his education. Why didn't he stand up when I walked in? Is this the way he would dress to represent me in court?" She knows that at present she would be considered "poor," and that perhaps the poor are often overlooked and disregarded, but this agency is supposed to exist to help people like her. "Maybe," she thinks, "this isn't true."

Mrs. Fernández had not wanted to come. She had put off coming for a long time. She is not sure it's the morally right thing to do.

ATTORNEY: . . . Okay,
Mrs. . . . (Looking at intake sheet in folder.
Baffled, he asks:) *What* is your last name?

The attorney knows that Hispanics often have "a lot of names" but he's never found it necessary to figure them out. He believes that his job is helping the client legally, not trying to figure out all the social peculiarities.

Mrs. Fernández hopes that she doesn't have to repeat everything that she has already said to that person in the other office (the intake worker). Luckily she understands English . . . well . . . She doesn't understand complicated English, but she can surely understand or figure out anything that is said directly to her. She is surprised by the question, *What* is your last name?" It's there on the sheet. But, she may as well repeat it one more time.

CLIENT: (Speech is heavily accented.) My last name
is Suero Sánchez de Fernández.

The attorney, just by hearing the heavily accented speech, knows that the questioning will be more difficult than usual. He thinks, only half seriously, "Why don't these people learn how to speak English if they're going to live here?" At least, he believes, they should do things the American way and cut out all those extra names. He realizes his rhetorical question is irrelevant and tries to be as friendly as possible because he *does* want to help. He thinks: "One of these days I'm just going to have to learn Spanish."

ATTORNEY: Sorry, but I can't make head or tail of this.
Your *real* last name.

The client doesn't understand. She's not making up a name. What she said *is* her real name. Does he think she's trying to hide something? She feels that she is in a corner. She has used her full last name because she considers herself to be in a formal situation, the type in which it would be more appropriate to use her complete name than just a simple first and last name. If he can't even understand her name, how is he going to help her with her problem?

CLIENT: (Looking at him quizzically.) My last name
is Suero Sánchez de Fernández.

ATTORNEY: Well, it must be Fernández. (Pronounces name
with English accent.)

CLIENT: Sí, . . . yes. (Her tone indicating that
she is willing to agree to this pronunciation

to get on with the matter. Imitating English accent:) Fernández.

Upon hearing "Fernández" the answer "sí" is automatic but then she quickly realizes she is supposed to be speaking English. She thinks the attorney now understands her name at least and if the pronunciation is different, well, maybe that's the way it should be said in this country—even if it does sound funny. In the attorney's records she has just lost "Suero Sánchez de" as part of her full name. Since she does not realize that the attorney does not understand the complex formal structure of her complete last name, she will settle for Fernández in hopes of moving along and getting to the resolution of her problem.

The attorney thinks to himself: "Now, why didn't she say that in the first place?" As part of his legal training he has been taught to always maintain eye contact with the client and tries to do so now.

ATTORNEY: (Looking at her directly.) Okay, now, you want a divorce.

CLIENT: Yes. (Looks at hands on lap.)

Mrs. Fernández hears that painful word again—"divorce." She is the first in her family to even think of divorce. She is breaking a tradition and therefore believes that her action may reflect negatively upon her upbringing and upon her parents. She also wonders whether her son will understand. Although she "knows" that her family will eventually understand, right now it is very painful for everyone. How can she look directly at this person, this stranger, when it is difficult enough just to face her own situation? To the attorney, it just seems that she doesn't look too sure of herself.

ATTORNEY: Do you speak English?

CLIENT: Yes, a little.

The attorney wants to make sure that everything is fully understood and that everything he says won't have to be repeated several times. The client hears the question she has heard so often: "Do you speak English?" She's glad she can answer affirmatively. After all, she has already answered all the intake worker's questions.

ATTORNEY: Well, that's a help. (Continues to look at client directly. Client does not look up but tries to listen intently to each word. Attorney looks over the intake sheet, sits back, then stretches a bit. Talking to no one in particular:) This should be pretty cut and dried.

The attorney is relieved that she can speak English and, if this divorce case is like most he handles, no one will oppose it. Therefore, this should be a fairly routine matter.

The client is insulted that someone should behave so casually in front of her. Her presence here is the result of a great deal of effort and the divorce is something of tremendous importance to her. Why should he consider it so lightly? It's plain good manners not to stretch that way before anyone. It's true she can't pay for the divorce, but shouldn't she have, at least, a little respect? Shouldn't he, "una persona culta" show some courtesy?

CLIENT: I don't understand. "Cut?" . . . "Dried?"

The client thinks, "What is he talking about? 'Drying' something? What does that have to do with divorce?"

ATTORNEY: Oh . . . nothing. Just let me read this over a bit more.

The attorney realizes that he has used an idiomatic and colloquial form which perhaps the client doesn't understand, but he is very busy and doesn't have time to explain.

ATTORNEY: (Reads for a few more seconds then looks directly at client again.) Okay, please tell me specifically, in your own words, why you want a divorce What's the problem? What's up?

CLIENT: (Looks up briefly.) What you say? (Looks down again.)

The client feels more and more at a loss. She hears him say, "up," but it doesn't make any sense. She tried looking at him to see if she could get some visual hint of his meaning this time. Again, he's using words she knows but for which she can't figure out a meaning here. Confused, she forgets the usual English verb structure.

ATTORNEY: (Patiently) I don't mean to be rude or anything, but I've got a lot to take care of, Please answer the questions directly.

The attorney understands her answer as a defensive response, especially when she looks down. "Why," he wonders, "are these people always so touchy?' Perhaps if he speaks a little louder she will understand the words.

CLIENT: (She is trying very hard to understand.) Yes.

ATTORNEY: (His voice begins to get louder) You've got to do your part in order to help.

The client's attention catches on his last word: "help," because that is indeed the reason for her being here. She hopes he finally understands, even though she feels somewhat humiliated by what she considers his shouting at her.

CLIENT: (Looks up briefly, then down again.) Help? Yes, I want help.

Again she tries to gain some understanding from his facial expression and his mannerisms as to what his attitude and statements really mean. But at this point she is begining to realize that perhaps she doesn't understand English as well as she believed she did and she feels a bit embarrassed by this.

ATTORNEY: Great. I can see we're going to be here all day. (Sighs in attempted resignation.)

The attorney is begining to feel frustration but attempts to control himself in order to continue with the interview.

CLIENT: You no can help?

The client reads his reaction as impatience and rejection. She begins to feel anger as well as frustration. This causes her to slip into Spanish word structure. He can't help her either? The other person with whom she had spoken earlier (intake worker) apparently couldn't help her.

ATTORNEY: (Trying to "make the best of things.") Yeah, sure, I yes can help. (Laughs lightly, trying to be humorous, yet he shakes his head.) Let's see . . . Question number one (Reading from a questionnaire, louder.) "Where do you reside?"

The attorney does not mean to ridicule her. He merely finds humor in the sentence structure and believes she will too if he imitates it as a friendly joke. He is conscious of her discomfort and hopes that a bit of laughter will help improve the general atmosphere. Yet, as he speaks, he senses that the difference in sentence structure is in itself merely a symptom of the much greater differenece that has to be overcome if they are to communicate effectively. He instinctively speaks even louder to try to compensate for the lack of understanding.

The client hears the attorney laugh and thinks he is laughing at her. Is it so ridiculous for her to want a divorce? Many in her family think so. Does he also? Does she look ridiculous? Is it her speech? Why does he want to make fun of her? She is trying her best. She would like to run right out of the office, perhaps even strike out at him, but that would be unheard of. She wishes someone would understand.

CLIENT: (Having trouble pronouncing.) I just want a divorce. My husband leave. (Obviously upset.)

ATTORNEY: (Calmly) Well, I can see I'm not doing very well. (Calls out.) Ana. (Both wait a while in silence.)

The attorney decides to give up and ask for help. The client is supposed to know English but something's wrong. He feels that he has made a sincere effort but enough is enough.

INTERPRETER: (Ana enters.) Yes Lenny. What is it? (Smiles at client.)

The interpreter follows the informal office custom of calling everyone by his or her first name. The attorney assumes that Ana is a competent interpreter because she can speak and understand both Spanish and English.

ATTORNEY: This woman doesn't speak English.

CLIENT: (Raises her voice, visibly perturbed.) Yes, I speak English.

The attorney is aware that some women consider the term "lady" offensive so he employs the "liberated" form "woman" in order to let the client know that he is aware of her independence.

The client wonders why Ana has come in and what the relationship is between her and the attorney. She equates the words "this woman" with "esta mujer," a term which reflects disdain and which, she believes, culturally strips her of her respectability. She is incensed. She is a respectable woman, "una señora decente". "I may be asking for a divorce, but that doesn't make me an indecent woman," she thinks. Furthermore, she's able to make herself understood in the various stores where she shops. *They* understand her English, even if this man thinks she can't speak it.

ATTORNEY: (A bit louder still but in a conciliatory tone.) Yes, Mrs. Fernández, you speak English, but we need some help.

The attorney feels he has to get things under control. He has no idea why she is so angry.

INTERPRETER: (Addressing client.) Tienes que hacer lo que diga el abogado.

The interpreter is bilingual in the sense that she understands both languages and speaks them with no detectable accent. However, she has had no training in interpreting. She senses the common language and cultural bond between herself and the client and so, without thinking, she uses the familiar form of address. She feels that she is helping the client by advising her that she must follow whatever instructions the attorney might consider necessary. Also, she believes, again erroneously, that it is her duty to "be professional" in the sense of taking charge in this situation in which her services are indispensable. She can see that the client is upset so perhaps a firm hand is what is needed.

CLIENT: (Indignant and despairing.) Bueno, sea como sea, lo que yo quiero es mi divorcio. Hace más de una hora que estoy aquí esperando, y para qué ¿para que me digan que no hablo inglés?

The client practically explodes. She has been insulted and actually laughed at. Now in addition to this, some officious person comes in and tries to boss her around—this employee who talks to her as if she has known her all her life. The client hasn't indicated to the interpreter that she has given her permission to use the familiar form when addressing her. The client wonders "Why has she taken it upon herself to do so? Is she being condescending?"

INTERPRETER: No es para tanto. Cálmate.

The interpreter believes the client is merely upset because of her failure to understand English well and because of her legal problem. She is unaware that her use of the familiar "tú" form and her "take charge attitude" are contributing to the discomfort, frustration, and indignation of Mrs. Fernández.

ATTORNEY: Come on Ana, let's get going. Ask her where she lives.

INTERPRETER: Él quiere saber dónde vives.

CLIENT: ¿Él es abogado? Ya he hablado con otra. persona en esta oficina.

In spite of her anger, the client knows that now what she says will be understood by someone. So, disregarding the unfamiliar setting and apparently unfriendly atmosphere, she decides to ask a question herself. The first man asking questions might have been a paralegal, an attorney, or simply one more person for whom it was necessary to answer more questions before she could be helped with her legal problem. Is this person who speaks Spanish an attorney? She needs to know if at least one of them is the person who can help her.

INTERPRETER: Sí, y quiere saber dónde vives.

CLIENT: (Disheartened.) Ahí en la calle Grant.

The client can hardly believe that the Spanish-speaking person is continuing to use the familiar. A curt "sí" is all the explanation that she receives in answer to her question. She is disheartened because of the lack of understanding, but even more so by what she considers an affront to her personal dignity, her sensitivity, and her sense of self-respect. None of this has been taken into account. She does not want to provoke an argument over the interpreter's apparent discourtesy, yet it is painful and degrading for her to be addressed in this manner. If everyone whom she has met in that office is a representative of the American legal system, it seems to her that it is a harsh, inconsiderate and indifferent system which values expediency more than the people whom it is supposed to serve. However, she has no choice but to remain and make the best of the situation, answering each question as briefly and impersonally as possible.

INTERPRETER: ¿Qué número?

CLIENT: Quinientos sesenta.

INTERPRETER: She says she lives at 15-60 Grant.

ATTORNEY: Wait a minute. It says here 560...

INTERPRETER: Yeah, that's what I said.

ATTORNEY: (Disregards comment. Continues normal line of questioning until he reaches one of the final questions.) Ask her whether there is any possibility of reconciliation.

INTERPRETER: ¿Te vas a juntar con tu marido?

The interpreter gives a very free translation of the attorney's question which is absolutely shocking to Mrs. Fernández.

CLIENT: (Completely taken aback.) ¿Qué?... ¿Qué? (Thinks a moment and then replies almost in a whisper.) No. (Shakes her head dejectedly.) Mi esposo se fue hace tiempo y no me ha mandado ni un centavo.

She considers that the question can't possibly mean what the interpreter has asked her and she tries to figure out the possible intended meaning of the words. She tries to upgrade the characterization of her marital relationship by using "esposo" instead of "marido." Nonetheless, the poor choice of words used by the interpreter in this question addressed to the client is one more offense which the client feels that she has to endure in order to secure the assistance she has come for.

AS YOU COMPARED YOUR ANALYSIS WITH THIS ONE, THERE WERE UNDOUBTEDLY DIFFERENCES BETWEEN YOUR EXPLANATIONS OF THE VARIOUS PASSAGES OF THE DIALOGUE AND THE EXPLANATIONS OFFERED IN THE TEXT. THIS SERVES TO ILLUSTRATE THAT THERE ARE MANY DIFFERENT WAYS OF INTERPRETING THE MEANINGS OF WORDS AND GESTURES, SOME OF WHICH DO NOT SEEM OBVIOUS AT FIRST GLANCE. THIS IS ONE OF THE IMPORTANT REASONS FOR STRESSING THE NEED FOR LEGAL PERSONNEL TO AVOID ANY WORD OR GESTURE WHICH MAY PROVOKE NEGATIVE REACTIONS.

EXERCISE 2

Think about the role of each of the three persons involved in the dialogue. In the space below, try to summarize each participant's perspective of the situation. Consider words, actions, and reasoning. What is it about each one which contributes to the uncomfortable atmosphere which has been created? What suggestions can you make for improvement?

THE CLIENT:

As she is seeking help and because of her problem she is considerably nervous it is difficult to understand the questions after she had been asked the same questions already.

THE ATTORNEY:

He should be dressed in a formal suit. When a client enters his office he should greet him by standing up and possibly shake hands and smile. He should be courteous to the client and offer a seat and knowing that the clients comes because he has a problem, the attorney should prepare a confortable atmosphere towards the client.

THE INTERPRETER:

She should have better manners and be more courteous to a client -- in fact it is rude to speak to a client the way she did.

STEP THREE: DEVELOPING CULTURAL FLUENCY

All three persons in the interview situation wished to communicate with one another. Yet each was unconsciously contributing to the creation of barriers to open, candid communication. Such barriers may be caused by individual character traits, differences in the cultural backgrounds of the individuals involved, or they may be the product of the role each person plays in a given situation. In the interview described, an atmosphere of misunderstanding and resentment developed in spite of intentions to the contrary. By understanding each person's role in and view of the situation and comparing this with those of the others, we can increase our awareness of certain factors which may create problems in similar situations. By making use of this awareness, we develop Cultural Fluency.

AS YOU READ THE DESCRIPTIONS WHICH FOLLOW, COMPARE THEM TO THE SUMMARIES YOU WROTE IN THE LAST EXERCISE. SEE WHETHER YOU AGREE WITH THE SUGGESTIONS IN BOLD TYPE FOR ACHIEVING CULTURAL FLUENCY.

THE CLIENT'S ROLE AND PERSPECTIVE:

Mrs. Fernández is, like most clients, totally unfamiliar with the usual procedures of a legal aid office. This unfamiliarity is combined with cultural and linguistic differences to put her at a double disadvantage. Although she has some knowledge of the English language, she is unprepared for the type of informal speech she is hearing in what she would expect to be a formal setting. Nothing is said or done to make her feel comfortable. She has come to tell someone her problem and ask for help, but she finds herself immediately locked into a question-and-answer situation which may or may not permit her to tell all the facts that could be necessary for the attorney to best represent her.

Because of the interpretation of the "equivalent" word "mujer" for "woman," the client believes the attorney has intentionally insulted her. Being addressed in the familiar by the interpreter makes her feel that she is being considered unworthy of respect by her also. In addition, the incorrect and improper translation of the word "reconciliation" seems to her to degrade her whole marital relationship. By the time the interview has reached this point, she has become completely alienated from the events taking place.

Other factors which contribute to this alienation are that Mrs. Fernández is not a native of the United States, she does not have the financial resources to seek the services of a private attorney, she has difficulty with English, and she is morally unsure of her decision to seek a divorce. The totality of these individual circumstances must be considered in order to understand and deal with the client's particular problem.

Some basic principles and suggestions for improving this and similar legal situations are:

THE CLIENT MUST FEEL SOME FORM OF ACCEPTANCE FOR EFFECTIVE COMMUNICATION TO EXIST BETWEEN CLIENT AND ATTORNEY. THIS REQUIRES CULTURAL SENSITIVITY, THE CHIEF COMPONENT OF WHICH IS RESPECT. IT IS THE ROLE OF THE INTERPRETER TO FACILITATE VERBAL AND NONVERBAL COMMUNICATION. IT IS THE OBLIGATION OF THE LEGAL OFFICE PERSONNEL TO SERVE THE CLIENT IN THE MOST RESPECTFUL AND EFFICIENT MANNER POSSIBLE.

The reason that Mrs. Fernandez's comfort should be an important consideration at all times is that she is the client, the person to be served. Some people might fault Mrs. Fernández for not trying harder to understand the English language, the American legal system or the role of different staff members at the legal aid office. Perhaps, in some other context, some might say that she should try harder. Yet here, where she is the client, it is the personnel of the legal office who must do everything possible not to add to the problems which caused her to seek legal assistance in the first place and to help her to resolve her problem in as comfortable an atmosphere as possible.

THE ATTORNEY'S ROLE AND PERSPECTIVE:

Leonard Benson probably has a heavy case load and finds it necessary to work as quickly as possible. This would explain his desire to get other matters out of the way before attending the new client. However, it is not the type of behavior one would expect from, nor which one is likely to receive from, an attorney whose services are paid for. The contrast would seem obvious to a sensitive person.

The attorney might feel that his manner of dressing is in keeping with the general informality of some legal aid offices and that his "over-dressing" will make his clients uncomfortable. Yet, he should consider this from the client's point of view. If a significant number of the attorney's clients are of a cultural background different from that of the attorney, the attorney should make a special effort to familiariarize himself or herself with the client's culture. At the very least, the attorney should keep an open mind and a broad perspective.

Being able to speak the client's language is not the only aspect involved. Whether the attorney speaks the client's dominant language or not, a knowledge of the client's culture is of the utmost importance, since this knowledge may directly affect the handling of the legal problem. A familiarity with a client's culture, however, should not incline the attorney toward trying to fit the client into a cultural stereotype. Cultural consciousness should provide one with a wider perspective for understanding individual behavior, not a preconceived explanation for every individual word or action. A greater awareness of several possible reasons for behavior and attitudes as well as the circumstances when a particular one may be relevant, are part of developing Cultural Fluency.

Simple matters such as a knowledge of the use of two last names and which name is the "equivalent" of the "usual" last name used in the United States, could have prevented one of the barriers to understanding from being created in this situation between attorney and client.

> A SINCERE DESIRE TO HELP IS NOT SUFFICIENT TO ESTABLISH THE KIND OF COMMUNICATION ONE WOULD LIKE TO HAVE. CULTURAL AWARENESS IS AN IMPORTANT ELEMENT IN EXERCISING CULTURAL FLUENCY.

THE INTERPRETER'S ROLE AND PERSPECTIVE:

Ana Domínguez's lack of training as a professional interpreter is apparent. Courtesy gives way to an attitude of familiarity which is out of place here. She undoubtedly knows the difference between the familiar and polite forms of address, but she does not demostrate a sensitivity to the client's reaction when she uses the familiar form. She may be trying to make the client "feel at home" by using the familiar, but she should be aware that some clients find it very offensive. Certainly the *tú* form would be the one she would use with her friends, but its use with a client in almost every conceivable instance is absolutely improper.

The use of *usted* rather than *tú* will be discussed further in the next chapter, but here it should be noted that:

> IN A PROFESSIONAL SITUATION THE USE OF THE POLITE FORM OF ADDRESS IS MANDATORY.

The interpreter's translation of the term "reconciliation" which so shocked Mrs. Fernández is an example not only of incorrect interpreting but of the type of grave offense to the client which can be caused by a poor choice of words and by failing to consider the client's possible reaction to a translation.

An interpreter can be an invaluable asset to those who are not as knowledgeable in the two languages and in their cultural bases. She or he, perhaps more than anyone else, can help the client feel at ease through competence and a positive manner. A bond of a language in common is established from the first words of greeting. From this, it is possible for the interpreter to create an atmosphere in which a friendly and accurate interchange of information and ideas can take place. Officiousness interferes with this goal. The client is immediately put on the defensive. The proper role of the interpreter is to assist the client, regardless of the client's ability to pay, and to assist the attorney or other person requiring language assistance, by facilitating accurate communication between the parties.

ALONG WITH ACCURACY OF INTERPRETING, COURTESY IS ONE OF THE INTERPRETER'S PRIMARY OBLIGATIONS.

EXERCISE 3

Apply the comments and suggestions of the preceding step to the roles and the perspectives of each of the three participants in the interview situation. Include other suggestions which you could make, with regard to the behavior of the three persons discussed, which would help to improve communication. List these in the space provided.

WITH REGARD TO THE CLIENT:

....

....

....

....

WITH REGARD TO THE ATTORNEY:

....

....

....

....

WITH REGARD TO INTERPRETER:

....

....

....

....

IN GENERAL:

....

....

....

....

Compare your answers to the dialogue and comments in the next section.

EXERCISE 4

Before reading the following section, go back to the chart on page 9 which you filled in during your second reading of the initial dialogue situation.

In that chart you listed line numbers, characteristics, and possible explanations. Now, in the light of your analysis of the dialogue (steps 2 and 3), write a suggestion for improving communication for each item which inhibited Cultural Fluency.

LINE NUMBER(S)	SUGGESTED IMPROVEMENT

LINE NUMBER(S)	SUGGESTED IMPROVEMENT

Compare your answers with the dialogue and comments in the next section.

STEP FOUR: EXERCISING CULTURAL FLUENCY

The following is only one of perhaps several possible alternative solutions to the problems presented in the initial legal interview situation. Nonetheless, it incorporates the basic requirements of effective communication across cultures: sensitivity, courtesy, respect, and seeing the person as an individual.

AS YOU READ THE DIALOGUE, COMPARE THE NOTES MADE AT THE END OF THE LAST SECTION WITH THE CHANGES IMPLEMENTED IN THIS ONE. PAY ATTENTION TO THE NONVERBAL AS WELL AS THE VERBAL MEANS OF COMMUNICATION. EXPLAIN WHY THIS VERSION IS SHORTER THAN THE INITIAL ONE.

(Attorney at desk, working. He is neatly dressed without a jacket, but wears a tie and dress shirt with a vest or sweater. A Hispanic woman client is led into the office by another agency staff member, the intake worker. The attorney stands up.)

INTAKE WORKER: Mrs. Fernández, this is Mr. Benson, the attorney who will handle your case. I'm leaving with him the form we've just filled out together. (To attorney.) Mrs. Fernández understands English but may feel more comfortable speaking Spanish. (He has learned that from the intake session. He gives the attorney the folder containing Mrs. Fernández's intake sheet.)

ATTORNEY: Thank you. (Notices that Mrs. Fernández is ill at ease. He smiles as he stretches his hand to shake hers and says:) Buenos días. (Mrs. Fernández smiles immediately and responds by extending her hand and saying, "Buenos días". (The attorney still smiling, quickly adds:) That's about the extent of my Spanish. Won't you sit down. (Intake worker leaves. Attorney does not sit down until Mrs. Fernández is seated.) *Would* you find it easier to explain your problem to me in Spanish? We have a very good interpreter.

CLIENT: (Aware of the possible difficulty she may have in explaining some aspects of her problem which may require some subtlety, and favorably impressed with the attorney's concern for understanding her problem, she answers in heavily accented English:) Yes, I speak English but I can explain better in Spanish.

ATTORNEY: Very good. I'll call in Ms. Domínguez. (He makes a special effort to pronounce the name correctly. The client smiles.) Excuse me a moment. (He calls for the interpreter on the intercom or steps out to call her.)

(Interpreter enters. She is neatly dressed and attentive. Her demeanor is one of respect and competence.)

ATTORNEY: Señora Fernández, this is Ms. Domínguez, our interpreter.

CLIENT and INTERPRETER: Mucho gusto. (All sit down. Attorney and interpreter sit so that they may observe the client without being overbearing.)

ATTORNEY: All right, with your permission. I'll just read this information briefly first.

INTERPRETER: Muy bien, con su permiso, primero leeré brevemente estos datos.

ATTORNEY: Okay, Sra. Fernández, would you please explain your problem in your own words. Then we can clarify any specific points if necessary.

INTERPRETER: Bien, Sra. Fernández, ¿me hace el favor de explicar su problema en sus propias palabras? Luego podemos aclarar cualquier pormenor específico si es necesario.

(The interview continues to its conclusion in a like manner. The question whose form in Spanish so shocked the client would be translated directly:)

ATTORNEY: Is there any possibility of reconciliation?

INTERPRETER: ¿Hay alguna posibilidad de reconciliación?

It will be noted that courtesy has played a major part in facilitating communication between the persons involved. Without it, the interpreter's knowledge of the client's native language and English would have been insufficient to make Mrs. Fernández feel more at ease and more likely to express as openly as possible all the relevant details of her problem.

From the beginning the intake worker, who knew Spanish, noticed the client's possible need for language assistance. He was able to alert the attorney to this fact without making Mrs. Fernández feel uncomfortable. He also knew which "last name" to use thereby avoiding confusion. He showed respect not only by identifying the attorney and letting the client know that he was giving him the form they had just completed, but by using the correct form of introducing a woman to a man (presenting him to her and emphasizing this by stating her name first.)

The attorney contributed to the atmosphere of welcome by standing as soon as Mrs. Fernández entered the room and then by smiling and greeting her in her own language. His attempt in this way to make her feel a bit more at home in obviously unfamiliar surroundings predisposed her to cooperate and to feel more comfortable.

The interpreter's competence was preceded by her friendliness. Her respect was apparent even though no more than the words "mucho gusto" were addressed directly to Mrs. Fernández.

The atmosphere created here permits an interchange of information on an equal personal level, even though the roles of the individuals are quite different. If either the intake worker or the attorney had not been as well prepared for a client who had difficulty with English, it would have been the interpreter's responsibility to give the necessary explanations and to make the client feel at ease by acting as a cultural intermediary as well as a language assistant.

This version of the dialogue is much shorter because the barriers which existed in the first version are no longer present. A cordial atmosphere was established from the beginning. There are no words to confuse either the client or the attorney because the legal personnel have served the language needs of both.

Having completed the four steps in the process of developing Cultural Fluency by focusing upon and analyzing the cultural factors in a legal situation, suggesting changes, and reading a "recreation" of the initial dialogue, you should now be more conscious of the importance of cultural factors as well as the need to recognize them and to be selective in your words and actions especially with regard to the needs of the client.

The next chapter deals with specific cultural factors which are particularly important in an interview situation. In addition to a brief discussion of each factor, suggestions are given for improving one's awareness of their significance.

CHAPTER 2

THE ELEMENTS OF CULTURAL FLUENCY

An atmosphere which permits the client to feel as much at ease as possible is basic to any attempt to communicate effectively in a legal situation. Before Mrs. Fernández can deal directly with her divorce problem, an atmosphere must be established in which the client feels free to openly discuss his or her difficulty. Taking the time to create such an atmosphere will actually save time and permit the attorney to learn the necessary information with the least possible discomfort to the client who is often already upset by the very problem which must be discussed.

The following basics of Cultural Fluency are essential in any personal contact situation:

- WARMTH
- RESPECT
- COURTESY
- SEEING THE PERSON AS AN INDIVIDUAL

These factors, communicated through actions as well as words, are usually interdependent. In this chapter, for the sake of emphasis and analysis, each one will be discussed separately before the interrelationship between the factors is outlined and summarized.

A. Warmth: Making the Client Feel at Home

In the Introduction to this part of the text, you were asked to consider a hypothetical situation in which you are an English-speaking person seeking legal aid in a foreign country where little English is spoken. You would be in a parallel position to that of the non-English-speaking client who seeks legal services in the United States. Both of you might very well be skeptical about the nature of the law of a country which is foreign to you and the type of legal assistance you would be able to receive there. Negative experiences in the foreign country might lead each of you to expect less favorable attention than that which might be given others.

Friendliness —warmth— may be the one element which could begin to change an atmosphere of wariness and discomfort into one of cooperation. Greeting a client who is in a foreign country in his or her own language can easily be the first step. A phrase like "Buenos días" addressed to a Spanish-speaking client, for example, immediately brings about a positive response because the client is hearing "his" or "her" language spoken. Something very familiar has now been introduced into otherwise very unfamiliar surroundings. Even if the client is aware that the speaker knows only these words in Spanish, or perhaps especially because of this, the effort to communicate in the client's language is greatly appreciated. This greeting is a positive beginning. However, in order to sustain this initial attitude of warmth and welcome throughout the interview, the other factors which contribute to Cultural Fluency must also be kept in mind: Respect, Courtesy, and Seeing the Person as an Individual.

The following is a list of words and phrases which may be helpful in creating the desired atmosphere.

Suggested Words and Phrases to Help Create the Desired Atmosphere of Courtesy and Respect

Buenos días	Good morning
Buenas tardes	Good afternoon
Por favor	Please
Muchas gracias	Thank you very much
De nada, no hay de qué	You're welcome
¿Cómo está usted?	How are you?
Muy bien, gracias	Very well, thank you
Señor	Mr.
Señora	Mrs.
Señorita	Miss
Adiós	Good-bye
Siéntese Ud.	Be seated
Con su permiso	With your permission
Dispénseme	Excuse me
Me llamo	My name is
Soy	I am ....
(el abogado, la abogada)	(the attorney)
(el técnico o asistente legal, la técnica o asistente legal)	(the paralegal)
(el escribiente, el entrevistador, la persona que toma los datos iniciales)	(the intake worker)
(el recepcionista, la recepcionista)	(the receptionist)
(el secretario, la secretaria)	(the secretary)
Para servirle	In order to serve you
Espere Ud., por favor	Please wait

B. Respect: Regard for the Person and His or Her Concerns

Respect or the lack of it is perhaps the most easily reflected element in almost every word or action. It is indispensable to the maintenance of the type of atmosphere desired. Although its basis should be a sincere regard for the person and the person's concerns, this regard need not be dependent upon a thorough understanding of the cultural reasons for a person's behavior, beliefs or expectations. The client may be asking for assistance in a matter which may seem absurd to one not of the client's own background or for assistance in a matter in which no legal action is possible in this country. Nonetheless, it is the obligation of all office personnel to treat the individual with respect.

One of the most important ways of showing respect is the *use of the polite form of address, that is, the "usted" form.* It is always preferable to the familiar *tú* form because it avoids the possibility of given the impression of condescension on the part of the speaker. No Hispanic ever confuses the use of the familiar and polite forms of address. This, in a very real sense, is probably one of the basic elements of the sense of propriety that seems to underlie the Hispanic culture.

The familiar form is taught to be used for servants, employees, or for very personal friends and relatives. (Among some families, parents and older relatives are always addressed in the polite form.) To be addressed in the familiar form by a stranger can, therefore, be very offensive. Using the *tú* form with a young client gives the impression of an uncalled for paternalism on the part of the speaker. Knowing just when to use *tú* or *usted* requires more than a knowledge of the language. Using the familiar form in the belief that it is "friendlier" and therefore will make the client feel more at ease, is entirely incorrect unless the person knows the client extremely well or there exist other very special circumstances.

C. Courtesy: A Personal Initiative

Courtesy may be a simple formality or the result of a command of the various elements of Cultural Fluency, including genuine respect. Because courtesy is the most conspicuous of the principal elements comprising Cultural Fluency, it should be given special attention as part of the training of all law office personnel. The discussion of the five factors which follows should be a starting point, and indication of the type of knowledge or attention which may help the client to feel more welcome and an integral part of the process which will lead to the resolution of his or her problem. What matters more than knowledge about customs or expectations, however, is the personal initiative exercised by each member of the law office staff in contributing to a congenial atmosphere in which effective communication can take place. The five factors in this section are: Formality and Dress, Identification of Personnel, Personal Names, Importance of Taking as Much Time as Possible, and Professionalism.

1. Formality and Dress

The client who is in a foreign country or who is of a different cultural background often tends toward formality in the treatment of unknown persons. A handshake between men and women is a customary greeting and conclusion upon departure among Hispanics. Certainly it would be expected of the person who would most likely represent a client in court.

The client also expects a certain formality of dress and demeanor as an indication of courtesy and seriousness. Otherwise, the client might conclude that his or her case is not considered important by the very people who are supposed to help.

2. Identification of Personnel

Legal situations are generally unfamiliar to any lay person. To a foreign client or anyone who also may not know English, the particulars of the legal situation may be even more confusing. Not only does there exist a language barrier, but many of the procedures and functions of the legal system in the United States are also quite different from those of most non-English-speaking countries. Consequently, this client may not be aware of the distinctions between the roles of the different members of the office staff. Care should be taken to clearly identify the function of the intake worker, the paralegal, the attorney, and any other personnel whom the client may meet at the office. This is not only a courtesy but it lets the client know that there is a concern to clarify the roles of all personnel involved. It avoids needless repetition of data by the client since certain information is intended for specific personnel.

3. Personal Names

One of the first stumbling blocks for the non-Spanish-speaking person is the system of personal names used by many Hispanics. Though there is a tendency in some Hispanic countries to use only one last name, even in these countries, an initial is often added when writing the name of a person, to indicate the maternal last name. In a legal situation, the Hispanic client would usually, however, expect that the formal—therefore complete—legal name be given.

Hispanic names are usually composed of at least four distinct names: a first name, a middle name, and a compound last name. This last name is made up of the father's paternal last name plus the mother's paternal last name. "Y" is sometimes placed between the two: "Marta Isabel Suero y Sánchez" thus includes all four names.

A married woman often drops only her mother's paternal last name before adding "de" and her husband's paternal last name: Marta Isabel Suero de Fernández. She may occasionally shorten it further by dropping both parents' names: Sra. de Fernández. There is a tendency for a woman to omit the "de" in informal circumstances using only her husband's last name: Sra. Fernández, Marta Fernández. In documents, special announcements, formal signatures of any kind, or in other formal circumstances, however, an individual generally gives all four names; a married woman would add "de" plus her husband's paternal last name after all four.

One must also consider the existence of family surnames which are usually hyphenated. In the case of "José Alberto Valdés-Cruz y Martínez," the paternal family surname is "Valdés-Cruz" and he should be addressed as Mr. Valdés-Cruz.

It would be of some help to the client in certain circumstances to indicate, in the most courteous manner possible, which last name is the one customarily used in the United States.

4. Importance of Taking as Much Time as Possible

The client should always be allowed to explain his or her problem as fully as possible. Not only can one learn more pertinent facts about the case and gain the trust of the client which is necessary to work as the client's representative, but one is more likely to learn the truth of all relevant factors. This truth may not be obtainable by a question-answer interview exclusively one in which the client may feel him or herself already being questioned by an authority figure before whom personal actions must be justified.

5. Professionalism

When two persons of different cultures meet in a formal situation in which one is a foreign client, they are more likely to be conscious of gaining the respect and approval of each other than are two persons of the same national and cultural background who meet in a different country. For example, consider yourself as a non-Spanish-speaking client from St. Louis in an office in Argentina where you are being interviewed by an Argentinian. Now, compare this situation with one in which you are being interviewed in the same office but by someone who is also from St. Louis. In the second situation, the two of you are very likely to share a certain type of relationship which would be quite different from that of the first situation. The common language as well as the cultural and regional bonds between individuals can easily create a feeling of unity between a client and a professional. Yet this bond, whether it causes positive or possibly negative personal reactions, should never interfere with professionalism.

Consider a third situation: a person from Louisiana meeting a person from Vermont in a legal situation in Argentina. A bond and a barrier might both exist at the same time: a common bond because of a common language; a barrier because of dissimilar regional backgrounds, customs, and speech. In any of these situations the professional must emphasize that which is positive, avoiding or eliminating to the greatest degree possible any barrier to effective communication. Only in this way can the persons involved focus on the legal matter at hand while developing understanding and mutual respect.

Whether the individuals be English-speaking persons from the United States meeting in Latin America or Hispanics of the same national or regional group meeting in New York, in any legal situation, every means which can help solve the client's problem, especially common language and cultural awareness, must be used to advantage with the same care and professionalism as would be due any other client.

D. Seeing the Person as an Individual

Seeing the person as an individual should follow easily from the principle of respect. Yet in dealing with people who as a group speak a common language and have similar traditions, the temptation to generalize and therefore to oversimplify, often prevents barrier-free communication. The following four factors within the basic one of "seeing the person as an individual" should be conscientiously kept in mind: Overgeneralizations, Alienation, Language Variations, and Classifications.

1. Overgeneralizations

There are twenty-one Spanish-speaking countries, each with its own traditions, values, and language characterics. Familiarity with one or two of them should not interfere with the need to treat each client as an individual who has a unique set of personal as well as cultural characteristics.

For example, to consider the evasion of eye contact to be a sign of wariness or guilt may very well be to misinterpret what is intended by some Hispanic individuals to be a sign of respect for a person presumed to be in a position of authority.

Another example is to believe that what may be humorous to you will also be humorous to your listener. What may be humorous to some members of a group may be quite insulting to others.

2. Alienation

A client who is in a foreign country or who has difficulty with the language may appear more embarrassed because of a legal problem than someone else in similar circumstances because the client may feel that he or she will be judged not as an individual on the facts of the case alone, but as a representative of his or her ethnic group. The client may not be aware that the problem is a usual one affecting many people of various groups in many different areas. Not knowing this, however, may cause the client to appear either cynical about or disinterested in his or her own problem since an underlying feeling of alienation may already exist. The person who works with anyone in these circumstances must learn to look beyond the overt in order to deal more effectively with the client's needs. The professional should be aware of those factors which may cause the client's "apparent" attitude of indifference. The fact that the client has come to discuss the problem indicates an importance in and of itself worthy of serious consideration.

3. Language Variations

The Spanish spoken by any Hispanic group is understandable by all members of all the various national groups, just as the English spoken by any English-speaking group (Canadian, Australian, Scottish, Irish, etc.) is understandable by all members of all the national groups who speak English. Just as one would not expect an American to speak with an Oxford accent, it should not be expected that a Peruvian or an Argentinian should speak with a Castillian accent. The people of Andalucía, Spain, do not themselves speak with a Castillian accent, just as Texans do not speak like Bostonians. No national or regional form is more "valid" than another and each contributes to the total enrichment of the language.

Subsequent parts of this text will deal with the linguistic variations of Spanish in different national and regional groups, but here the aspects of language which may affect Cultural Fluency are briefly pointed out because they may well affect the tone of the entire interview. To take the attitude that Mexican-Americans, Cubans, etc. "don't speak real Spanish" is not only offensive to the individuals who make up these groups but is incorrect. To find it difficult to initially understand the speech of someone who speaks very fast, who does not pronounce all the syllables of words, or who uses many regionalisms, should not cause one to reject the content of the person's speech or the person him or herself. Understanding regional variations should be part of the training of a professional who wishes to work with individuals from another country or even from another region of the professional's own country.

4. Classifications

Although "classifying" someone may be completely unavoidable at times, it should generally be rejected since labels often prevent one from considering persons in individual terms and may create a defensive attitude.

For example, it may be offensive to a client to use the term "American" to refer exclusively to non-Hispanic Americans (as it is for some Hawaiians to hear someone refer only to the continental United States as "the" U.S) since the term is valid for the citizens of all the countries of the two continents. Many Spanish-speaking persons use the term "North American" to refer to a citizen of the United States. To call all Hispanics "Spanish" is an oversimplification which is often very offensive to many. Similarly, for some, the term "Hispanic" itself is unacceptable. In Latin America other cultures besides the Spanish —Indian, French, Italian— form part of the character, art, and philosophy of the members of individual countries. The classifications "Spanish" and "Hispanic" linguistically exclude these. Whenever possible, therefore, the classification which the client uses for him or herself should be the one employed if one is absolutely necessary.

THE FOLLOWING DIAGRAM SUMMARIZES THE FOUR BASIC GROUPINGS AND INDICATES THEIR RELATIONSHIP.

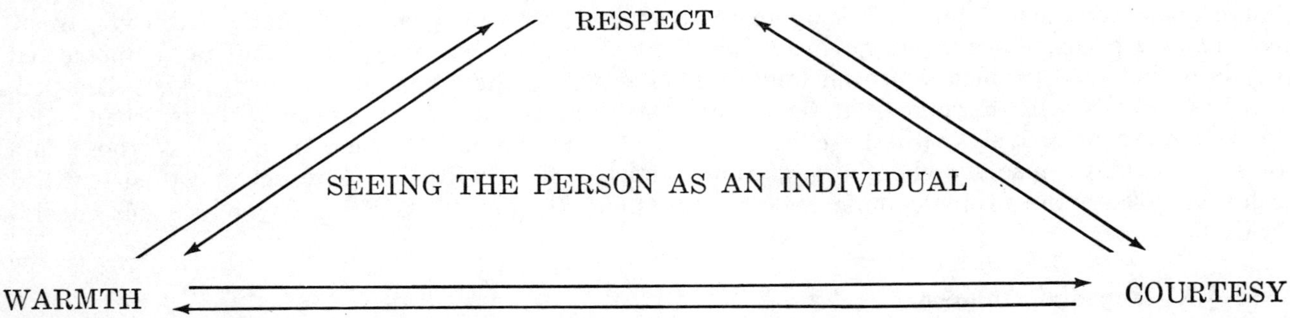

Each part, in fact, really sustains the others. Yet, central to the type of sensitivity necessary to exercise Cultural Fluency is "Seeing the person as an individual." This does not mean that the individual is or should be considered as isolated from a particular cultural background, but rather that the perception of certain cultural elements should help, not inhibit, one's understanding of another individual.

The following set of "Do's and Don't's" summarizes the various factors discussed in this chapter and should serve as a brief review.

Do's

1. Use the polite form of address (*usted*).
2. Ask whether the client would feel more comfortable with an interpreter —for all of the interview or just certain parts.

Don't's

1. Don't use the familiar form of address (*tú*).
2. Don't assume that a client understands English merely because he or she understands the words, "Do you understands English?"

Do's	Don't's
3. Learn language variations. Become familiar with as many forms of the vernacular as possible.	3. Don't take the attitude that you don't or can't understand someone else's Spanish.
4. If there is a need to classify the client, use the classification that the client applies to him or herself.	4. Don't classify a person as "Hispanic," "Spanish," etc., unless he or she applies this classification to him or herself.
5. Dress in a manner appropriate to a formal office setting.	5. Don't dress carelessl. or too informally.
6. Let the client know the name and function of each person with whom he or she comes in contact at the office.	6. Don't assume that the client knows or can guess the role or function of each member of the office staff.
7. Familiarize yourself with the personal name formula used by most Hispanics.	7. Don't ignore the use of more than one last name or assume that you can correctly guess which is the "equivalent" of that used generally in the United States.
8. Consider the client in individual terms as much as possible.	8. Don't prejudge the client based upon what you believe must be his or her cultural background.
9. Learn about the culture of the major groups with whom you work.	9. Do not assume that general cultural characteristics will be found in each individual.
10. Become familiar with the possible cultural meanings of gestures.	10. Don't ignore gestures in interpreting.
11. Give the client as much time as possible.	11. Don't rush.
12. Call the client by his or her last name always.	12. Don't assume that calling the client by his or her first name will make the client feel more at home.
13. Be professional. Maintain a friendly but serious attitude.	13. Don't assume that laughter or a facetious response to a question means that a client does not care.
14. Remember that you are there to serve the client.	14. Don't expect the client to make all the adaptations necessary to communicate with you.

EXERCISE 1

On the basis of the information contained in this chapter, answer the following questions in the space provided.

1. When asking Mrs. Fernández where she lives, should you say, *"¿Dónde vives?"* or *¿Dónde vive Ud?"*

   ....

   ....

2. What should your reaction be to the sincere request of a client that you take legal action on something which is beyond the scope of your office or something which seems absurd in this society?

   ....

   ....

   ....

3. Should you ask a client who says that he or she speaks English but who is obviously having some difficulty with the language, whether he or she would prefer that an interpreter be available in case there should be an idea which might be difficult to explain?

   ....

   ....

   ....

4. In addressing a client, what is wrong with saying, *"Pasa María, ahora te atienden."*

   ....

   ....

   ....

5. When addressing a married woman should you say, for example, *"Sra. Fernández," "Sra. de Fernández"* or *"Sra. Suero de Fernández."*

   ....

   ....

6. When addressing a young adult client, should you say, *"Pasa, joven"* or *"Pase Ud., Sr. Suero."*

   ....

   ....

7. If the client does not maintain eye contact, what could you possibly assume?

   ....

   ....

8. Should you be surprised or suspicious if the client and interpreter seem quite friendly even if they did not previously know each other?

   ....

   ....

EXERCISE 2

Each of the following "situations" is an example of the lack of Cultural Fluency. Identify the particular factor(s) which illustrate(s) this deficiency. Write you answer in the space provided after each situation.

Situation 1

Attorney to Client: Do you want custody of your child?
Interpreter: ¿Quieres custodia de tu hijo?

....

....

....

....

Situation 2

Client enters; attorney does not stand up to greet client. He (she) stretches over the desk to shake hands.

....

....

....

....

Situation 3

Intake Worker to Client: I'm sorry but you're going to have to use just one of these names. Which one would you like?

....

....

....

....

Situation 4

Attorney to Client: Mr. Franco, I'd prefer that you look at me when we talk. I need to have all the facts.

....

....

....

....

Situation 5

Interpreter to Client: Now, Mrs. Álvarez, you must understand you have to do things the way they're done here.

Situation 6

Receptionist to Client: Hello, how are you? We always enjoy seeing Hispanic clients. They're so courteous.

Situation 7

Paralegal to Client: Mucho gusto en conocerlo, Sr. Méndez . . . Mira, como todavía eres muy joven, te voy a tratar de "tú."

Situation 8

Interpreter: Would you please speak more slowly? I can't understand South American Spanish very well.

* * *

The next chapter deals with some of the more general elements of the cultural background of some groups of Hispanics. In reading about these, the diagram on page 32 should serve as a reminder that although a person may belong to a certain cultural group —Irish-American, Black, Asian, Scandinavian, etc.— the person must still be, first of all, considered in individual terms.

CHAPTER 3

BEYOND STEREOTYPES

In Chapter 1, stereotypes were identified with the kind of oversimplification which might interfere with an accurate perception of individuals and their circumstances at any given time. Nonetheless, it was noted that a knowledge of certain accepted practices by a particular group —that which is often considered a basis for stereotypes— might serve as background information to improve relationships with individual members of a group. A contradiction seems to exist: on the one hand, a person should be considered as an individual; on the other hand that same person may be included in a cultural group whose practices may be understood in general terms. Despite the apparent contradiction, this is in fact what is often required to understand a person and his or her concerns more fully since *an individual cannot be totally isolated from all cultural influences.* Generalizations may be useful in providing insights or possible explanations relevant in the case of a given individual. The important word of warning is never to apply generalizations *automatically* to a given individual.

Being aware of some explanations which may be different from those ordinarily assumed to be the "usual" or "expected" should help one be more sensitive to a different point of view. The explanations should help one to be more open to cultural cues which may indicate the type of response most likely to be appropriate in a particular situation and therefore most useful in helping the client feel more at ease.

As in the case of all generalizations, the ones here presented will apply to some individuals in some instances and not at all to others in similar circumstances. The term "Hispanic" is itself a generalization which is used throughout this text to indicate persons from Spain or Latin America or persons native to the United States who share Spanish as a common language and whose cultural heritage is primarily, but not necessarily exclusively, Spanish. Similarly, the term "American" is used to indicate the cultural mixture found in the United States which is not "Hispanic" nor specifically identified with any other ethnic group.

This chapter contains brief descriptions of concepts relating to what is generally considered the "Hispanic culture". "Hispanic culture" may be considered an amalgam of the practices and values common to most persons whose country of origin is Spain or any of the twenty Latin American countries where Spanish is the principal language. Although each of these countries has its own individual Hispanic culture, in this text we will limit consideration to Hispanic culture as a whole.

Persons newly arrived in the United States will usually adhere strongly to the values, views and practices of their native countries. The views and practices of persons who are members of a second or third generation living in the United States must of necessity differ from theirs. While second and later generations may continue to follow some of the traditions of their family members who first came to the United States and continue to find worth in their system of values, their own culture has undergone a transformation due to the influence of the culture of the United States in general. The degree to which any of the following concepts may be relevant to the individual or group must therefore be considered, along with other factors, with regard to place of birth, length of time living in a Hispanic country and length of time living in the United States. Familiarity with such concepts may serve to broaden the perspective of legal personnel serving the Hispanic community.

BEFORE YOU CONTINUE WITH THIS CHAPTER, READ THE FOLLOWING LIST. WHAT CONCEPT COMES TO MIND WHEN YOU READ EACH TERM? BRIEFLY SUMMARIZE THIS CONCEPT ON THE LINES WHICH FOLLOW.

FAMILY: ....

....

WOMAN: ....

....

DIVORCE: ....

....

LAST NAME: ....

....

MACHISMO: ....

....

DINNER TIME (With regard to usual set time): ....

....

PROXIMITY: ....

....

EYE CONTACT: ....

....

SHOWING AFFECTION: ....

....

HUMOR: ....

....

FORMALITY: ....

....

THE LAW: ....

....

KEEP THESE CONCEPTS IN MIND AS YOU READ THE FOLLOWING DESCRIPTIONS.

THE FAMILY

In general, the Hispanic family in the United States is still a close-knit group usually encompassing grandparents who live in the same home or nearby. It is nonetheless changing as is any other family unit in this country. Traditions and beliefs are being modified by greater mobility, education, and the gradual acceptance of divorce and remarriage at all levels of society even though there is still a less liberal attitude toward divorce among Hispanics than among the general population.

The fact that more and more women work, and for longer periods than did their ancestors, alters the old stereotypes of "*machismo*" and "femininity" formerly accepted as inviolable by most traditional families. This notwithstanding, a male-dominant Hispanic family —ostensibly at least— is still the rule as it is in most American families even though exceptions are numerous. The difference is in emphasis. In the Hispanic family, roles are more carefully followed and there is often no question as to who has the ultimate say in any matter concerning the family as a whole or any member of the household. The wife's role is supportive, and women and girls in general are made acutely aware of "proper" behavior and virtues: modesty, demureness, chastity. The practice of a woman living alone is still generally not accepted or common.

Legal personnel may observe the overt signs of this type of family organization and role acceptance, but they may also find that the self-assertiveness usually associated with *machismo* is at times observable in Hispanic women as well. Often the women who seem to demonstrate this characteristic are single parents or persons responsible for relatives unable to function as usual because of language or other problems. They may be persons who have simply chosen to live outside the family group. The last usually face the same problems as men who live alone, but the social pressures which the woman must confront are much more severe.

A person working in a legal office or agency should not expect a clear-cut profile of any stereotype but rather be prepared to deal with the many possible exceptions to any generalization.

One fairly valid general statement is that the term "family", for the Hispanic, in itself includes more members than the nuclear family. In some cases it may include god-parents and grand-uncles and aunts, but it will nearly always include grandparents.

CONVERSATION: CULTURAL CHARACTERISTICS

Conversation among some Hispanics as among some members of many other groups is often considered "too loud" by those having other habits. Interruptions and simultaneous talking may be frequent and it may appear that neither person conversing is paying attention to what the other is saying. Hand gestures seem to be an indispensable accompaniment to any word said. Yet, these as any other "cultural characteristics," are not universal throughout the group and are merely *a* way of doing something, neither right nor wrong because one group participates and another does not.

FORMAL VS. INFORMAL MANNER

Hispanics have, as has been pointed out, a formal and an informal manner of speech dictated by the forms of address which are considered appropriate for particular circumstances and individuals. Making constant distinctions as to when each is the better form to use perhaps contributes to a possible consciousness of other factors in personal relationships such as differences in dress, manner, demeanor, etc. Often, formality is associated with a desire to show respect just as in the use of the "*usted*" form of address.

Most persons of any cultural group expect a certain degree of formality in legally-related situations because legal problems are usually not taken lightly and it is expected that they will be dealt with in a serious manner. Hispanic clients, therefore, will most likely consider a visit to a legal office a formal rather than an informal situation in which appropiate formal speech and behavior should be observed. Consequently, even though office personnel may be aware of certain practices of Hispanics which indicate friendliness among members of their cultural group, the personnel should be equally aware that the Hispanic client may actually feel more at ease within the framework of a formal situation for which he may be better prepared from a cultural standpoint. This type of formality, however, does not in any way preclude warmth, respect, courtesy and a regard for the person as an individual.

EYE CONTACT: SEEING EYE-TO-EYE

American attorneys are often trained to maintain eye contact with their clients. While many Hispanics are also "trained" within their families to look directly at someone because this demonstrates self-confidence and helps one to better assess the other person, some Hispanics as some Americans find it offensive to be "stared at" especially at a time when they might be trying to explain a difficult legal problem. Some persons of almost any cultural background regard it as a sign of respect not to look directly at someone in a position of authority. As with other generalizations, the problem comes in trying to apply the same explanation to every case. However, being aware of another possible explanation for the avoidance of eye contact or someone's insistence upon it is important to the maintenance of a cooperative attitude between the parties.

DISPLAYING EMOTIONS

Hispanics are sometimes considered to be very affectionate and emotional, as are many Southern Europeans, because many of them seem not to hesitate to reveal their emotions. Nonetheless, many Hispanics are trained within their families *not* to demonstrate their personal feelings outside the immediate family group.

When one is discussing a legal problem, it is easier to appreciate restraint. Yet, whether or not it seems to the office personnel that the client is being more emotional than the circumstances warrant, this should not interfere with taking the client and the client's problem seriously.

A SENSE OF TIME

Americans and Hispanics alike often single out as unquestionable a difference in their "concept of time." An American appears to feel satisfaction in being on time and in having others be on time also. A Hispanic may at times be heard to say that he or she dislikes being "ruled by the clock" and that a life pattern which permits flexibility is preferable to a rigid one. Therefore, when an American and a Hispanic must meet for an appointment, the meeting time may not signify the same hour to each one.

Attention to time —punctuality as well as the length of time which an activity should involve— may be considered an absolute necessity by the American businessman, whereas these factors may seem to the Hispanic businessman to interfere with conducting business on the most amicable terms possible.

It may appear to some Americans that Hispanics have a tendency to treat time commitments casually, but this may in part be due to a difference in what "set time" means to each. The usual times for certain set activities such as meals and social activities are definitely later in all Hispanic countries than they customarily are in the United States. For example, dinner time in Hispanic countries is often at ten in the evening.

Adapting to a new time pattern in a different country is difficult and the old pattern is likely to persist, especially when the individual maintains the old pattern within his family and social group. Yet, it should not surprise office personnel to find some Hispanic clients waiting ten minutes before the agreed upon appointment time.

A SENSE OF SPACE

Hispanics, like most Southern Europeans, maintain as a rule a closer conversational space limit between the conversing parties than do most Americans. An attempt to preserve one's habitual personal distance may inhibit communication. Discomfort must be weighed in terms of one's objectives. Perhaps merely understanding that another distance is perfectly acceptable and actually necessary for the other person to discuss a concern or express an opinion will help each to try to be more accommodating.

Because the "use of space" becomes intuitive for most persons within their culture, persons of the same culture share an understanding which persons from other cultures may not comprehend or be sensitive to. For this reason, in the case of "space," which of course is related to other types of nonverbal communication, it is not uncommon for the Hispanic client to get closer to the interpreter who speaks his or her language and communicates through the same nonverbal system. This may, if not corrected, lead to a situation in which the client is almost completely ignoring the non-Hispanic, even though this person may be the attorney and therefore the only person who may ultimately be able to help. The reverse circumstance, equally detrimental to effective communication, exists when the non-Spanish-speaking attorney or other non-Spanish-speaking personnel talk almost exclusively to the interpreter and ignore the client if the client does not speak English. The objective of the interpreter is to facilitate communication between attorney or other agency personnel and the client, not to create an alternate channel of communication. The interpreter should take care to avoid this possibility, explaining if necessary his or her function and its limitations the persons involved.

A certain psychological distance must be maintained not only for the purpose of professionalism, but to prevent an association in which the client or a member of the legal staff is willing to confide certain information to the interpreter but does not wish it to be communicated to others. The dangers of this problem are discussed in the interpreting section of this text.

A SENSE OF TOUCH

For a Hispanic to greet another Hispanic friend whom he or she has not seen in a while with a sample handshake or verbal greeting would signify the end of that friendship. The *"abrazo"* or hug, is intuitive. Between men, the *"doble abrazo"* in which they embrace by placing their arms around each other's shoulders, would be expected. Also common between men is placing the left hand on each other's shoulder during a handshake. Among women, it is quite customary to embrace upon greeting and taking leave. During a conversation, touching one another's arm or shoulder is quite common. For friends of the same sex to walk arm in arm or with one holding an arm around the other's shouler, is a perfectly acceptable practice. Touch simply signifies acceptance and/or affection. This acceptance of touch itself is not extended, however, to the acceptance of couples kissing and embracing in public in a romantic or sexual way.

A SENSE OF HUMOR

Humor is often considered a regional or national quality because it requires instantaneous associations not likely to be made by a person unfamiliar with their basis. For this reason it is better to create a friendly atmosphere through respect and consideration without trying to make jokes or to be humorous in general. The humor of a situation or of a word or phrase may be abundantly clear to the speaker, but it can very easily be misinterpreted by others since the object of the humor may not be perceived or may be assumed to be a person or a situation totally unrelated to the intended one.

Similarly, for one to believe that he or she fully understands why someone is laughing or otherwise finding something humorous when that person is of a different cultural background, is to presume too much. Sometimes a client may seem to be laughing at a situation when in fact that client may simply be embarrassed or indeed ashamed of the circumstances at that time.

A sensitivity to this form of dissociation or "protective device" can prevent office personnel from making an already unpleasant condition worse.

THE LEGAL ENVIRONMENT*

Much greater than mere geographic distances are the differences separating the civil law code-based legal systems from the common law legal system of the United States. A Spanish-speaking resident of the United States is frequently faced with the need to adjust to a new environment whose characteristics are markedly different from those of Latin American countries. This compounds the problems caused by linguistic and cultural barriers.

For the sake of simplicity we speak here of "Latin American law." Obviously, there are variations in legal systems from country to country. Yet, the legal systems of the Spanish-speaking Latin American countries can be grouped together because they all retain the code-based heritage which they received from Spain. Based essentially on the Roman Code, some of them may reflect the Spanish Code, the French Code, or the Italian Code in a given instance, and in some countries codes of original inspiration have been developed, but the concept of the code, in Spanish *código,* is the key unifying factor. A code is the embodiment of the law in a specified area. A commercial code, for example, contains the essence of the law governing certain classes of transactions. A code is more than a mere collection of laws. It is a unified treatment of an area of the law, characterized by succinctly stated principles developed by learned scholars in a particular country. Codes give to the legal system a kind of uniformity and predictability which comes from having the law all written down. Principles of personal, family, property, and decedent estate laws will be found in the Civil Code and in Latin American countries are generally well known among the population at large.

In the legal system of the United States, there are two primary sources of law: case law and statutory law. A primay source of law is one which, if applicable to a given situation, can be relied upon as authoritative. All other sources of law, such as treatises, legal periodicals, annotations, etc., are called secondary sources. They are merely guides to authority, and are not authority in and of themselves.

We said that case law and statutory law are primary sources "if applicable." It must be appropriate to apply them to a given situation. If they are applicable they constitute mandatory authority. This means that they can be relied upon with great assurance, and will normally be binding. Cases and statutory materials not directly analogous as well as all secondary authority, may still be considered to be persuasive authority. That is to say, they may be influential, but not binding.

According to the principles of the common law legal system of the United States, a case decided between the two parties can, as primary authority, be influential or decisive in the resolution of similar controversies between other parties. This doctrine, called *stare decisis,* is fundamental to an understanding of the common law system. In contrast, in the code-based civil law countries of Latin America, the outcome of one case will only rarely —and not obligatorily— influence the outcome of future cases. Case law, called *jurisprudencia* in Spanish, is thus only a secondary source of law in Latin America.

Legislation, or statutory law, is important in both the common law and civil legal systems. Yet, the contrast in the role of legislation within the two types of legal systems reveals some marked differences between them. In the code-based civil law legal system, legislation is passed in ac-

---

*Materials for this section were provided by Professor Milton Schwartz of New York University School of Law, Member of the New York Bar, whose law practice involves extensive work with Latin American countries, and prepared by Dr. Marilyn Frankenthaler.

cordance with and as a supplement to the codes. In the United States, legislation shares with case law the position of primary sources of law. There is no code which can override or dictate where legislation must fit within an overall framework. This gives the American legal system greater freedom but less predictability.

Puerto Rico presents a unique mixture of the civil law code-based heritage from Spain and the common law system of the United States. The Spanish heritage has left many lasting imprints on the Puerto Rican legal system, for example, in the substantial body of notarial law. In the United States, the function of a notary is limited to such duties as attesting to a signature. In the civil law code-based legal systems, the notary is a lawyer with additional qualifications whose role is fundamental in the legalization of documents. Thus, the *notario público* of Latin America is a far cry from the American "notary public." The role of the notary will be discussed in further detail in Part III of these materials, "Translating for Legal Personnel."

Another difference between the civil law and common law legal systems is revealed by the importance of the writings of noted treatise writers, which are called *doctrina*. These writings are treated with a respect which is second only to the importance of the codes in Latin American countries. In contrast, in the United States, such treatises are at best persuasive secondary authority for a legal argument.

To summarize, the pillars of the Latin American code-based civil law systems are:

- THE CODE = *CÓDIGO*
- WRITINGS OF NOTED JURISTS = *DOCTRINA*
- CASE LAW = *JURISPRUDENCIA*
  (questionable as authority)

The common law legal system of the United States rests upon two pillars:

- CASE LAW (*stare decisis*)
- LEGISLATION (statutory law)

The approach of a Latin American to the law is influenced by the uniformity and importance of the written word, which is code-based. It is important to realize how markedly this outlook differs from that of a person raised within our common law legal system. The approach to the law fostered by a code-based legal system can influence perceptions of government, law, and the role of the individual within these institutions. Even if a particular individual is not especially educated in the legal area, the expectation of predictability in the law which comes from a code-based system should be understood by legal personnel in the United States. Without this knowledge and understanding, legal personnel may not be conscious of the fact that legal institutions may evoke completely unexpected associations and connotations in the minds of Latin American clients.

EXERCISE 1

Recall the terms you were asked to consider at the beginning of the chapter on page 38. Now, keeping in mind the material discussed in this chapter, indicate the differences between the "American" and "Hispanic" concepts. Refer to your answers on page 38. Have your ideas changed?

TERM	"Hispanic" Concept	"American" Concept
FAMILY		
WOMAN		
DIVORCE		
LAST NAME		
MACHISMO		
DINNER TIME		
PROXIMITY		
EYE CONTACT		
SHOWING AFFECTION		
HUMOR		
FORMALITY		
THE LAW		
Code Law		
Case Law		
Doctrina		
Stare Decisis		

EXERCISE 2

Assume that you are the interpreter in an interview situation. What would you do under each of the following circumstances? Write your answer in the space provided.

1. A Spanish-speaking client starts to converse exclusively with you as the bilingual employee ignoring the attorney or other English-speaking personnel for whom you are interpreting.

   ....

   ....

   ....

   ....

   ....

2. A young client comes in to a law office for assistance. Which form of address is appropriate?

   ....

   ....

   ....

   ....

   ....

3. You have asked a client a question regarding the run-down conditions of his/her rented apartment and he/she laughs lightly.

   ....

   ....

   ....

   ....

   ....

4. A client asks you to take legal action against a person because of a situation which seems absurd to you and about which nothing can be done legally.

   ....

   ....

   ....

   ....

   ....

5. Describe the best manner to greet a Hispanic client. (Handshake, stand, etc.)

   ....

   ....

   ....

   ....

   ....

6. A client refuses to look at you.

7. A client continues to stand so close to you when conversing that he/she makes you feel uncomfortable.

8. You're tempted to joke about a matter you're "pretty sure" the client will find funny.

9. Your client is half an hour late for his/her appointment.

10. A non-Spanish-speaking employee, for whom you are interpreting, ignores the client.

CHAPTER 4

ASSESSING PROGRESS IN CULTURAL FLUENCY

Throughout this part of the text the reader has been urged to pay careful attention to cultural factors which might encourage or inhibit effective communication. In order to assess the development of greater cultural awareness, a second legal situation is presented for analysis in this final chapter. To distinguish this second dialogue from the dialogue analyzed in Chapter 1, we will call this "Situation II" and refer to the dialogue presented in Chapter 1 as "Situation I."

The process of developing Cultural Fluency is again divided into four steps as it was for the divorce interview situation. (Situation I). The analysis found here will be much briefer than that of the first interview situation since the *student* is now asked to apply to this new situation many of the ideas already discussed in this part of the text.

Differences between the two interviews may be attributed in part to the contrasts between the participants and between the situations themselves. In the first situation the client, Marta Fernández, was a person seeking a divorce but unable to pay for legal services at the time. Here the client, Armando López Gil, is a businessman who wishes to conclude a business transaction in his native Colombia. He has conducted business in Latin America and in the United States in his professional capacity but this is his first visit to an American law office. The first situation takes place in a legal aid agency; here, in a private law office. In this situation the lawyer is an attorney in private practice, Ms. Thompson. She has not assisted a Hispanic client before and is unfamiliar with Hispanic culture. The receptionist in this law office is well trained for her job in the American legal environment but she, too, is unfamiliar with Hispanic names and customs. The bilingual paralegal, George Adams, is not a native speaker of Spanish but since he is fluent in both English and Spanish and has been trained as a paralegal, he is now being asked to serve as an interpreter.

STEP ONE: FOCUSING ON AN INTERVIEW SITUATION

SITUATION II: INTERVIEW IN PRIVATE LAW OFFICE CONCERNING A BUSINESS TRANSACTION

(The receptionist is working at her desk in the spacious waiting room of a private law firm. She looks up immediately as a well-dressed Hispanic client, Armando López Gil, enters and walks toward her desk. He has a self-assured manner and looks at her directly as he approaches.)

RECEPTIONIST: (Greeting client.) Good morning.

CLIENT: (Speech heavily accented.) Good morning.

RECEPTIONIST: (Since he does not give his name) Do you speak English? . . . Do you have an appointment?

CLIENT: Yes. I speak English and I have an appointment. My name is Armando López Gil. (He pronounces "Gil," "Hil" — the Spanish pronunciation.) A Ms. Thompson should be expecting me.

RECEPTIONIST: (Somewhat flustered when she hears the Spanish pronunciation.) Oh, . . . yes, I see your name here. (As she looks at the appointment book on her desk.) Won't you please sit down? I'll let Ms. Thompson know you're here.

(Mr. López sits down. The receptionist calls Ms. Thompson, the attorney, and in a few minutes she appears at the office door. Mr. López stands immediately.)

RECEPTIONIST: (Trying to imitate Mr. López's pronunciation.) Mr. López Gil, this is Ms. Thompson.

(As they exchange greetings, he walks forward extending his hand for a handshake but she doesn't seem to notice. When she does, it is too late. He tries to pretend he's doing something else. He gives her his business card.)

ATTORNEY: Won't you come in Mr. . . . (Looking at card.) López? (English pronunciation "Lo/péz".)

CLIENT: Yes, López. (Emphasizes Spanish pronunciation, "Ló/pez".)

ATTORNEY: (Continuing to look at card.) There's another letter here.

CLIENT: Yes.

(The attorney does not understand the significance of the initial "G" printed after the name "López" on the business card but neither says any more. After they are seated in her office she begins to ask him a few questions but soon becomes aware that the type of explanations required necessitate a freer form of expression than he is apparently capable of in English.)

ATTORNEY: I believe I understand your problem, but there are a few points I'm not clear on. Do you think it might help us both if we were to have an interpreter present to help us explain those few questions which seem difficult? We have a bilingual paralegal in this office.

CLIENT: All right. We can try.

(Ms. Thompson calls the paralegal. He enters. He is slightly uneasy because he has not been trained as an interpreter.)

PARALEGAL: (Nods at the attorney, then addresses the client, smiling.) Buenos días. ¿Cómo estás?

CLIENT: (Who has gotten up to shake hands, withdraws his hand as he frowns and states in a matter-of-fact manner.) Un momento. Creo que no nos conocemos.

PARALEGAL: (Taken aback but immediately aware of his blunder.) Dispénseme Ud. Me llamo George Adams.

CLIENT: (Still annoyed.) Buenos días, señor.

(The attorney, judging from the expressions on the men's faces and the tones of their voices senses something is wrong but doesn't understand what. All sit down.)

ATTORNEY: Mr. López, as I understand it, you want to conclude a transaction you initiated in Colombia. Is that correct?

CLIENT: (Looking from the attorney to the paralegal and back.) Yes, but . . . (Then addresses the paralegal and speaks very rapidly.) Dígale por favor que esto es precisamente lo que quiero pero que entiendo que habrá cierta dificultad en que no deseo regresar a Colombia para hacerme cargo personalmente de los trámites.

PARALEGAL: (Realizes that he has missed a word or two but doesn't know what to do. Translating the client's words.) This is just what I want to do, but I don't want to return to Colombia.

(The client shakes his head a bit but apparently decides that the loss of meaning is not worth speaking out about at this time.)

ATTORNEY: (Speaking slowly and deliberately for the benefit of the paralegal.) I see. Our correspondent attorney in Colombia . . .

PARALEGAL: (To attorney) Excuse me. What was the last term?

ATTORNEY: (To paralegal.) "Correspondent attorney," the attorney in Colombia who would represent our case there. (To Mr. López.) Would you wait just a moment while I look up the name of our correspondent attorney?

PARALEGAL: (Translating only the last part to Mr. López.) Espérese . . .

CLIENT: (Interrupting the paralegal and speaking directly to him. Creo que me pedía permiso . . .

(The interview continues in like manner to its conclusion.)

EXERCISE 1

Reread the dialogue. As you do so, list in the chart which follows, according to the number of the line of the dialogue (column A), the cultural characteristic(s) and apparent cause of misunderstanding(s) which affect communication between client and the agency personnel (column B), and the possible explanations for these (column C).

A LINE NUMBER	B CULTURAL CHARACTERISTIC OR CAUSE OF MISUNDERSTANDING	C POSSIBLE EXPLANATION

EXERCISE 2

Now that you have completed Exercise 1, compare the second legal situation with the first (pages 5 through 8). In the chart that follows, identify the situations, persons, and personal actions or opinions by indicating the situation (I or II) and the corresponding line number(s) of the dialogues (column A) where the difference can be noted (column B) and give a reason (or reasons) for the difference (column C).

A SITUATION AND LINE NUMBER	B DIFFERENCE	C REASONS

STEP TWO: ANALYZING THE DIALOGUE

AS YOU READ THIS SECTION, COMPARE YOUR OBSERVATIONS WITH THE DIALOGUE ANALYSIS WHICH FOLLOWS. FOR REFERENCE, THE LINE NUMBERS AND TEXT OF THE SITUATION OF THE ORIGINAL DIALOGUE ARE INCLUDED HERE.

(The receptionist is working at her desk in the spacious waiting room of a private law firm. She looks up immediately as a well-dressed Hispanic client, Armando López Gil, enters and walks toward her desk. He has a self-assured manner and looks at her directly as he approaches.)

RECEPTIONIST: (Greeting client.) Good morning.

CLIENT: (Speech heavily accented.) Good morning.

The client is familiar with business settings and therefore is confident he can manage well in this one. He responds to the greeting but his pronunciation causes the receptionist to question his ability to speak English a bit sooner perhaps than she ordinarily would have.

RECEPTIONIST: (Since he does not give his name.) Do you speak English?... Do you have an appointment?

CLIENT: Yes. I speak English and I have an appointment. My name is Armando López Gil. He pronounces "Gil," "Hil" — the Spanish pronunciation.) A Ms. Thompson should be expecting me.

The client is somewhat surprised by the question. He answered her greeting in English, did he not? And, what would he be doing here if he didn't have an appointment? He gives his complete last name for complete identification, especially since "López" is a very common last name.

RECEPTIONIST: (Somewhat flustered when she hears the Spanish pronunciation.) Oh, I see. Yes, I see your name here. (As she looks at the appointment book on her desk.) Won't you please sit down? I'll let Ms. Thompson know you're here.

The receptionist may have written the name phonetically when she first took it down, but at least she's able to identify it.

(Mr. López sits down. The receptionist calls Ms. Thompson, the attorney, and in a few minutes she appears at the office door. Mr. López stands immediately.)

RECEPTIONIST: (Trying to imitate Mr. López's pronunciation.) Mr. López Gil, this is Ms. Thompson.

(As they exchange greetings, he walks forward extending his hand for a handshake but she doesn't seem to notice. When she does, it is too late. He tries to pretend he's doing something else. He gives her his business card.)

ATTORNEY: Won't you come in Mr. . . . (Looking at card.) Lopez? (English pronunciation "Lo/péz".)

Mr. López, according to training, stands as soon as a woman appears. He feels that a handshake is doubly appropriate as a social gesture as well as a formal one in that this is the person who will be representing him legally. Ms. Thompson, according to business custom in the United States, realizes that in a business situation a handshake is often expected of a woman as well as of a man but in considering whether her client would think it appropriate, she does not do so immediately. She's glad that the client is able to gracefully convert his action of offering his hand into one of giving her his card. She is glad to have it as a distraction from this embarrassing moment.

CLIENT: Yes, López (Emphasizes Spanish pronunciation, "Ló/pez".)

ATTORNEY: (Continuing to look at card.) There's another letter here.

CLIENT: Yes.

(The attorney does not understand the significance of the initial "G" printed after the name "López" on the business card but neither says any more.)

Mr. López prefers the Spanish pronunciation of his name and would like to have this known. The attorney is unfamiliar with the practice in some countries of abbreviating the second last name on business cards. Mr. López does not want to bother with a long explanation so he answers curtly. He wants to get on with his legal problem.

(After they are seated in her office she begins to ask him a few questions, but soon becomes aware that the type of explanations required necessitate a freer form of expression than he is apparently capable of in English.)

ATTORNEY: I believe I understand your problem, but there are a few points I'm not clear on. Do you think it might help us both if we were to have an interpreter present to help us explain those few questions which seem difficult? We have a bilingual paralegal in this office.

CLIENT: All right. We can try.

Ms. Thompson understands that Mr. López doesn't care to discuss the matter further and therefore regards it as being of little consequence since at any rate she knows he acknowledges "López" as his name. She wishes to be as tactful as possible in saying that they need language assistance and perhaps Mr. López has become aware of this also.

(Ms. Thompson calls the paralegal. He enters. He is slightly uneasy because he has not been trained as an interpreter.)

PARALEGAL: (Nods at the attorney and then addresses the client, smiling.) Buenos días. ¿Cómo estás?

CLIENT: (Who has gotten up to shake hands, withdraws his hand as he frown and states in a matter of fact manner.) Un momento creo que no nos conocemos.

PARALEGAL: (Taken aback but immediately aware of his blunder.) Dispénseme Ud. Me llamo George Adams.

The paralegal's conversational training in Spanish has included the familiar form of address almost exclusively. He wishes to be friendly so he automatically uses the familiar. Mr. López is insulted and immediately lets Adams know the basis of his displeasure.

CLIENT: (Still annoyed.) Buenos días, señor.

Mr. López intends to let the paralegal know that he is upset by merely saying "señor" instead of adding Adam's last name which would indicate some acceptance or deference. Using "señor" alone indicates distance, a separation.

(The attorney, judging from the expressions on the men's faces and the tones of their voices senses something is wrong but doesn't understand what. All sit down.)

ATTORNEY: Mr. López, as I understand it, you want to conclude a transaction you initiated in Colombia. Is that correct?

CLIENT: (Looking from the attorney to the paralegal and back.) Yes, but . . . (Then addresses the paralegal and speaks very rapidly.) Dígale, por favor, que esto es precisamente lo que quiero pero que entiendo que habrá cierta dificultad en que no deseo regresar a Colombia para hacerme cargo personalmente de los trámites.

The paralegal does not begin interpreting immediately, giving the client the impression that he should try to answer. Uncertain, Mr. López starts to answer in English but then changes to Spanish.

Mr. López has apparently never worked with an interpreter before and believes that since the interpreter knows Spanish, he should be able to interpret whatever the client says at his usual rate of speech which here may be just a bit faster than usual since he has been offended and is therefore upset.

The paralegal has not been professionally trained as an interpreter. An interpreter should interpret the words of the speaker verbatim, signaling the speaker, usually by raising a hand, if he or she speaks too rapidly for the interpreter to follow. These and other interpreting skills will be fully discussed in Part II of this text.

PARALEGAL: (Realizes that he has missed a word or two but doesn't know what to do. Translating the client's words.) This is just what I want to do, but I don't want to return to Colombia.

(The client shakes his head a bit but apparently decides that the loss of meaning is not worth speaking out about at this time.)

The paralegal summarizes instead of interpreting verbatim. See Chapter 1 of Part II of this text for a description of the different modes of interpreting. Mr. López knows enough English to be aware of what has been omitted. Most importantly, he would prefer not to leave the impression that he doesn't want to return to his native country. He merely doesn't want to return there at this time for this particular business matter.

ATTORNEY: (Speaking slowly and deliberately for the benefit of the paralegal.) I see. Our correspondent attorney in Colombia...

PARALEGAL: (To attorney.) Excuse me. What was the last term?

ATTORNEY: (To paralegal.) "Correspondent attorney" the attorney in Colombia who would represent our case there. (To Mr. López.) Would you wait just a moment while I look up the name of our correspondent attorney?

The attorney has become aware of the need to slow down in speaking but expects the interpreter to be able to interpret any term because he knows both English and Spanish and is unaware that interpreting requires specialized training. She is somewhat surprised by his interruption and gives as brief a response as possible before once again directing herself to the client.

PARALEGAL: (Translating only the last part to Mr. López.) Espérese...

CLIENT: (Interrupting the paralegal and speaking directly to him.) Creo que me pedía permiso...

The paralegal uses the formal (Ud.) form of the verb "espere," but adds the pronoun which converts it from a request into a command form that connotes great familiarity or condescension.

Mr. López is highly offended and counters by pointing out that he was being *requested* to do something, not commanded.

In spite of the differences —in the clients involved, business experience, problems and matters, as well as in the setting and manner of the office personnel— between this dialogue and the one in Chapter 1, in both, the client is being made to feel very uncomfortable and effective communication is being seriously hampered.

AS YOU COMPARED YOUR ANALYSIS WITH THIS ONE, UNDOUBTEDLY THERE WERE DIFFERENCES BETWEEN YOUR EXPLANATIONS OF THE VARIOUS PASSAGES OF THE DIALOGUE AND THE EXPLANATIONS OFFERED IN THE TEXT. IF MORE SITUATIONS WERE TO BE GIVEN, MORE DIFFERENCES WOULD SURELY RESULT. NONETHELESS YOU NOW HAVE A STARTING POINT FROM WHICH TO BEGIN YOUR ANALYSIS OF REAL SITUATIONS.

EXERCISE 3

Think about the role of each of the three persons involved in the dialogue. In the spaces below, try to summarize each participant's perspective of the situation. What is it about each one which contributes to the uncomfortable atmosphere which is being created? What suggestions can you make for improvement?

THE CLIENT: ....

THE ATTORNEY: ....

THE PARALEGAL: ....

STEP THREE: DEVELOPING CULTURAL FLUENCY

AS YOU READ THE FOLLOWING DESCRIPTIONS AND SUGGESTIONS FOR IMPROVING COMMUNICATION, COMPARE THEM TO THE SUMMARIES AND SUGGESTIONS YOU WROTE IN THE LAST EXERCISE.

THE CLIENT:

Mr. López expects to receive the attention and respect he is entitled to as a person and as a client able to pay for any services rendered him. His command of English does not prove to be as thorough as he might have hoped, but a competent interpreter could have taken care of this problem without any difficulty. He is not at all reticent in letting the interpreter know that he has been offended perhaps because he expects the interpreter to be fully acquainted with certain cultural practices since he is familiar with the Spanish language. He is made uncomfortable by the attorney's not offering her hand for a handshake but is somewhat more willing to overlook this lack of social amenity in someone whom he might consider totally unfamiliar with Hispanic social practices. He is probably proud of the fact that he is Colombian and is annoyed by the paralegal's statement that he does not want to return to his native country. Even if this were so, the inaccuracy of the translation is upsetting to the client. Being told "Espérese" might well have been enough to cause him to leave the office, so one can only surmise that his need to take care of his legal problem was urgent or that perhaps he felt he might not receive better service in any other law office.

OFFICE PERSONNEL SHOULD TRY TO FAMILIARIZE THEMSELVES WITH COMMON SOCIAL PRACTICES. THEY SHOULD BE AWARE THAT LANGUAGE REFLECTS RESPECT OR LACK OF IT WHETHER THE SPEAKER'S INTENTIONS CORRESPOND WITH CERTAIN FORMS OR NOT. THE INTERPRETER SHOULD ALWAYS BE AWARE THAT ACCURACY OF INTERPRETING HAS SOCIAL AS WELL AS LANGUAGE IMPLICATIONS.

THE ATTORNEY:

The attorney was probably confident of her professional ability but was not aware of the need for a handshake nor of common practice of abbreviating the second last name. Both seemingly unimportant factors exposed her unfamiliarity with the Hispanic culture and probably contributed to the client's feeling of alienation, of a separation rather than a meeting of two cultures. This feeling had been initiated by the receptionist's questions, "Do you speak English?" "Do you have an appointment?", as if he were in the wrong place or had arrived at the wrong time. The attorney was quite tactful in suggesting an interpreter help *them*, but she assumed that someone who was a bilingual paralegal would automatically be qualified to serve as an interpreter. Had the attorney briefly explained to Mr. López the usual procedure for interpreting, or better, shown him by her example, other problems could have been avoided.

ATTENTION TO ALL POSSIBLE FACTORS WHICH REFLECT COURTESY AND RESPECT IS VERY IMPORTANT. INTERPRETING PROCEDURES SHOULD BE WELL UNDERSTOOD BY ALL PERSONNEL. EVERY MEMBER OF THE STAFF SHOULD CONTRIBUTE TO MAKING THE CLIENT FEEL WELCOME.

THE PARALEGAL:

The paralegal was trained in paralegal work, not as an interpreter. He wished to be friendly, but did not realize that warmth does not preclude the use of the polite form of address. Aside from the faults in interpreting, he should have been aware of the possible implications of saying something categorical like, "I don't want to return to Colombia" unless he were absolutely sure that that was what the speaker had said. Proper training would have made him aware of the possible negative effect of "espérese" and prevent its use.

PROPER TRAINING AS AN INTERPRETER SHOULD INCLUDE CULTURAL AWARENESS. FRIENDLINESS MUST BE ACCOMPANIED BY PROPER SPEECH AND ACTIONS.

EXERCISE 4

Apply the comments and suggestions of the preceding step to the roles and perspectives of each of the three participants in the interview. Include other suggestions which you would make, with regard to the behavior of the three persons discussed, which would help to improve communication. List these in the space provided which follows.

WITH REGARD TO CLIENT: ....

....

....

....

....

....

....

WITH REGARD TO ATTORNEY: ....

....

....

....

....

....

....

WITH REGARD TO INTERPRETER: ....

....

....

....

....

....

....

IN GENERAL: ....

....

....

....

....

....

....

STEP FOUR: EXERCISING CULTURAL FLUENCY

REREAD THE DIALOGUE IN STEP ONE OF THIS CHAPTER. WHAT CHANGES WOULD YOU MAKE TO IMPROVE THE ATMOSPHERE AND COMMUNICATION? COMPARE YOUR IDEAS FOR IMPROVEMENT WITH THOSE INCORPORATED IN THE FOLLOWING VERSION OF THE DIALOGUE.

(The client enters the waiting room of the law office and directs himself to the receptionist's desk.)

RECEPTIONIST: (Greeting the client as he approaches her desk.) Good morning.

CLIENT: (Speech heavily accented.) Good morning.

RECEPTIONIST: (Since he does not give his name.) How are you? May I please have your name?

CLIENT: Armando López Gil. (He pronounces "Gil," "Hil" — the Spanish pronunciation.)

RECEPTIONIST: One moment please, sir. (She uses "Sir" since she may not have known which name to call him but could recognize a name which began with "López" on her appointment book.) Ms. Thompson is expecting you. I'll let her know you're here. Won't you please sit down?

(Mr. López sits down. The receptionist calls Ms. Thompson, the attorney, and in a few minutes she appears at her office door. Mr. López stands immediately as Ms. Thompson comes forward to greet him.)

RECEPTIONIST: (Smiling at client and making a gesture of presentation toward Ms. Thompson.) This is Ms. Thompson.

(As Ms. Thompson and Mr. López approach one another, he extends his hand for a handshake. She immediately notices and extends hers.)

ATTORNEY: I'm glad to meet you.

CLIENT: How do you do? This is my card.

ATTORNEY: Thank you. Won't you come in Mr. López. (After a brief look at the card. She pronounces "López" carefully, trying to give it her best Spanish pronunciation). Client smiles.

(After they are seated in her office she begins to ask him a few questions but soon becomes aware that the type of explanations required necessitate a greater command of English than Mr. López now has.)

ATTORNEY: Mr. López, I believe I understand your problem, but there are a few points I'm not clear on. Would you mind if I asked an interpreter to come in, just to make sure I don't miss any detail which might be important to your case. We have a bilingual paralegal in this office.

CLIENT: All right.

(Ms. Thompson calls for the paralegal. He enters. George Adams, the paralegal has been trained not only as a paralegal but as an interpreter as well.)

PARALEGAL: (Smiles as he comes in.) Buenos días. (As he stretches his hand to shake Mr. López's. Mr. López stands and offers his hand.) (Addressing Mr. López.) Muchísimo gusto, señor. Me llamo George Adams.

CLIENT: Mucho gusto.

ATTORNEY: Mr. López, this is our bilingual paralegal.

CLIENT: Very good.

(All sit down — attorney facing client, paralegal to one side.)

ATTORNEY: (Speaking distinctly and at a slightly slower rate than her usual.) Mr. López, as I understand it, you want to conclude a transaction you initiated in Colombia. Is that correct?

PARALEGAL: Sr. López, tengo entendido que Ud. quiere concluir un negocio que inició en Colombia. ¿Correcto?

CLIENT: Precisamente. Mi problema es éste: no deseo regresar a Colombia por el momento para hacerme cargo personalmente de los trámites...

PARALEGAL: (Smiles and holds up hand indicating a need for a pause. Mr. López smiles in understanding.) Precisely, My problem is this: I don't want to return to Colombia at the moment to take personal charge of the transaction.

ATTORNEY: I see. Our correspondent attorney in Colombia...

PARALEGAL: (Holds up his hand as he first looks at the attorney and then at the client to indicate the necessary pause. To the client.) Dispénseme un momento, es necesario aclarar un término. (To the attorney.) Excuse me, I've just told the client that a certain term needs to be clarified. What was the last term you used, "correspondent attorney"?

ATTORNEY: Yes, that's right. "Correspondent attorney," the Colombian attorney who would represent our client and us in Colombia.

PARALEGAL: (To attorney), Thank you. I'll explain this to Mr. López before we continue.

(The paralegal does so and the interview continues to its conclusion.) The line which was poorly translated would be better translated as follows:

ATTORNEY: (To client.) Would you please wait just a moment while I look up the name of our correspondent attorney in Colombia?

PARALEGAL: ¿No me hiciera Ud. el favor de esperar un momento mientras busco el nombre de nuestro abogado correspondiente?

In this revised version of the dialogue, care was taken to ensure that Mr. López felt as much at ease as possible in that courtesy and respect were always present. The client was seen as an individual, which does not mean he was seen as not belonging to a certain cultural group.

The receptionist did not automatically assume that the client did not have a command of the English language because he had a heavy accent. She proceeded to ask his name and made an extra effort to cope with the problem of trying to understand a name which was probably unfamiliar to her. Her concern was the client. She wished to avoid any possible embarrassment to the client.

The attorney may not have known that it is a custom in Latin America for men and women to shake hands but since her attention was on the client, she was able to notice his offer and respond at once. Since Mr. López was speaking English despite a heavy accent, it might well have seemed discourteous to him to immediately call in an interpreter, indicating in this manner her lack of confidence in his language ability. Although it is preferable to ask the client from the start whether an interpreter might not be desirable for at least part of the interview, in this case the attorney was able to obtain most of the necessary information and pinpoint those areas where both she and the client became aware that greater clarity was necessary.

Although the paralegal's language problems remained insofar as his mastery of speed of interpreting and terminology, he was nonetheless able to take the necessary steps to clarify an unfamiliar term while at the same time letting the persons for whom he was interpreting know his reason for interrupting. He kept in mind the best choice of words to make the client feel assured of respect as a person and attention to his legal concerns.

CONCLUSION

The process of developing Cultural Fluency requires constant attention to the many and varied factors which may come into play in a given situation. Perceptiveness, care, and a consciousness of one's objective must always be present. With practice and experience, the thought processes involved in the various steps toward the exercise of Cultural Fluency become more and more a part of the individual's personal response to a situation. Misunderstandings cannot be totally eliminated but the probability of their occurence and the severity of their effects can be minimized.

Remember the factors discussed in Chapter 2:

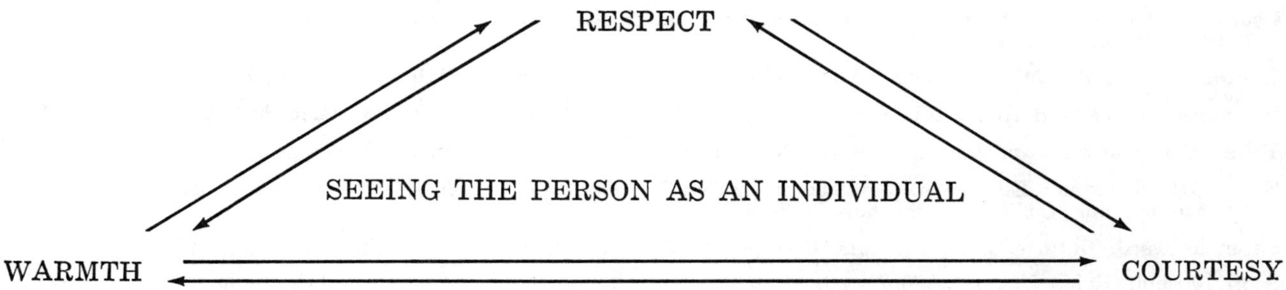

These factors are important to the creation of an atmosphere in which individuals can communicate on an equal personal level, confident that they can express themselves freely and that what they say will be seriously considered.

The value of Cultural Fluency is apparent in the greater ease of communication possible and in the avoidance of offending someone. The presentation and analysis of cultural factors in this text is a starting point. Only by observing and analyzing cultural elements of a situation and then integrating the information derived into one's own awareness can Cultural Fluency be exercised to improve communication across cultures.

REFERENCE MATERIALS

Barker, Marie E. *Español para el bilingüe.* Chicago: National Textbook Company, 1973.

Castells, Matilde O. and Harold E. Lionetti. *La lengua española: gramática y cultura.* New York: Charles Scribner's Sons, 1974.

Hall, Edward T. *Beyond Culture.* New York: Anchor Press/Doubleday, 1976.

———. *The Silent Language.* Greenwich: Fawcett Publications, Inc., 1959.

Hauberg, Clifford A. *Puerto Rico and the Puerto Ricans.* New York: Twayne Publishers, Inc., 1974.

Holtzman, Wayne. *Personality Development in Two Cultures.* Austin: University of Texas Press, 1975.

Kany, Charles E. *American-Spanish Syntax.* Chicago: The University of Chicago Press, 1945.

Leonard, Olen E., Editor. *Readings in Latin American Social Organizations and Institutions.* Michigan State College Press, 1953.

LeVine, Robert A. *Culture, Behavior and Personality.* Chicago: Aldine-Atherton, Inc., 1972.

Narganes, Joseph and Richard I. Javert. *Hispanic Culture Capsules.* New York: Gessler Publishing Co., Inc., 1976.

Poyatos, Fernando. *Man Beyond Words.* New Brunswick: Rutgers University Press, 1976.

Saitz, Robert L. and Edward J. Cervenka. *Handbook of Gestures: Colombia and the United States.* The Hague: Mouton and Co. N.V. Publishers, 1972.

Sapir, Edward. *Culture, Language and Personality.* Berkeley: University of California Press, 1966.

Scott, Joseph Reid. *Understanding Spanish-Speaking Cultures.* Hayward, California: Alameda County School Department, 1972.

Siegman, Aron and Stanley Feldstein. *Noverbal Behavior and Communication.* Hillsdale, New Jersey: Lawrence Erlbaum Associates, Publishers, 1978.

Snyder, Barbara. *Encuentros culturales.* Skokie, Illinois: National Textbook Co., 1976.

Wagenheim, Karl. *Puerto Rico: A Profile.* New York: Prager Publishers, 1975.

PART II

INTERPRETING FOR LEGAL PERSONNEL

John Zahner

INTRODUCTION

The purpose of the materials presented in this part of the text is to provide bilingual personnel with the basic skills necessary to serve effectively as interpreters in a variety of situations where Spanish-speaking persons have contact with a legal system similar to that of the United States. The interpreter is an individual who is completely fluent in the two languages involved — here Spanish and English. The interpreter's primary function is to take words in context as originally expressed in one language, which we may call the "source language", and to communicate their precise meaning in another language, which we may call the "target language".

The initial chapters of this part of the text deal with essential considerations which are applicable in general to interpreting situations such as: the differences between translating and interpreting, the theory of the interpreting process, ethical considerations, and regional differences.

As will be evident in the pages that follow, interpreting situations may be said to fall into two groups: formal and informal interpreting situations. Each calls for a distinct approach on the part of the interpreter.

Court interpreting may be termed a "formal interpreting situation". Similarly, in a deposition, the situation approximates the formality of the courtroom, although the sworn testimony is taken outside of court. The duty of the interpreter in formal situations is to facilitate communication among all concerned, while dealing with the legal system in a formalized manner.

Telephone conversations and client interviews may be termed "informal interpreting situations". Since the client is seeking help or advice in these situations, a more personal, though no less objective approach than in the formal court interpreting situation may be required.

Bilingual legal personnel whose role is generally that of paralegal, legal secretary, attorney, or administrator, may at times be called upon in the role of interpreter, simply because they are bilingual speakers. Yet, the skills involved in interpreter training cannot be assumed to be a natural result of the ability to speak the two languages involved.

These materials are designed as an introduction to and a training guide for the specialized skills which must be acquired by a bilingual person acting as interpreter. Before interpreter training can begin, the bilingual speaker must become conscious of the need to develop specialized skills in order to function effectively as an interpreter. Once this consciousness is developed, then the materials which follow can serve as a basic training guide.

* * * *

I would like to acknowledge the contribution of the C.E.T.A., staff of the Montclair State College Hispanic Community Program Internship in Law who, under the direction of Dr. Marilyn Frankenthaler, prepared the Divorce and Tenancy Client Interview Questionaires which are found in Chapter 5, for Essex-Newark Legal Services of New Jersey.

CHAPTER 1

THE ESSENCE OF INTERPRETING

INTERPRETING VERSUS TRANSLATING

The terms translating and interpreting are often used interchangeably or as synonyms. However, they in fact represent two distinct, though related, skills or professions.

The role of the translator is to render the content and meaning of a written document into its equivalent in another language, in the form of another written document. The translator must read the entire document many times, in order to choose the words which will best express the precise ideas to be translated.

While the translator deals with the written word, the interpreter is concerned with the spoken language. The interpreter works with a speaker and a listener. It is the interpreter's duty to facilitate communication and understanding between persons who are unable to communicate directly because of a language barrier. Immediate responses are required and there is no time for the interpreter to pause and ponder over the choice of words.

At times, the skills of interpreting and translating are combined. For example, when a Spanish-speaking client is interviewed by a bilingual paralegal, the client will necessarily give information to the paralegal in Spanish. The paralegal must write this information down in English, so that non-Spanish-speaking personnel can understand what the client has communicated. This combination of interpreting and translating skills will be discussed more fully in the section dealing with informal interpreting situations.

The skills of interpreting, in all instances, require precision and accuracy on the part of the person who facilitates oral communication between speakers of different languages.

EXERCISE 1

Distinguish between the characteristics of translating and interpreting in the following chart:

TRANSLATING	INTERPRETING
....	....
....	....
....	....
....	....
....	....
....	....
....	....

Compare the characterististics which you have noted with those described in the preceding section of the text.

THEORETICAL CONSIDERATIONS

Having distinguished between the fields of translating and interpreting, it is essential to understand exactly what is involved in the process of interpreting. Basically, interpreting is a skill which makes communication possible despite language barriers. Through the interpreter, the original message of the speaker is made intelligible to the listener. Language is the medium which enables two or more persons to reach the goal of understanding and communicating with each other. Words, therefore, serve as the "tools of the trade".

The actual process of interpreting can be broken down into three phases:

1. The interpreter *hears the message* as communicated by the speaker.

2. Upon hearing the words, the interpreter *comprehends the meaning* behind them. In grasping the meaning of what the speaker wishes to communicate, the interpreter goes beyond the literal meaning of the speaker's words, retaining only the underlying meaning which the words convey in context.

3. In the final step of the process, the interpreter *formulates the accurate message and expresses it in the language of the listener.* Complex legal terminology, sophisticated vocabulary, regionalisms, slang, or profanity must all be communicated. The precise meaning of the original message must be preserved conveying tone, expression and choice of words to the listener.

To exemplify the three steps in the interpreting process, let us consider the case of a client who is told by his or her attorney that the opposing party refuses to settle the case without a court hearing. The client, desirous of having a "day in court", remarks: *"Me importa un comino."* This seemingly simple four-word message must first of all be heard and understood by the interpreter. The direct literal meaning of the message in English would be: "A cumin seed is important to me." This of course makes no sense whatsoever to the listener. The interpreter must then proceed to the second step of the process, going beyond the literal meaning of the speaker's words. The interpreter thus retains only the basic underlying meaning of the words in context. In the third step, the interpeter formulates the accurate message of "I could care less" and expresses it in English, the language of the listener. The interpreter has thereby conveyed the true meaning of the original message to the listener.

Usually, differences between the literal meanings of expressions in two languages are not nearly so great as in the preceding example. For instance, the process involved in interpreting the sentence *"El dueño no compró aceite"* is much less intricate. The interpreter hears the message. In the second step, the interpreter does not have to go far to understand the meaning of the words in context. The final step of formulating and conveying the message of "The landord didn't buy oil" is much closer to the structure and literal meaning of the speaker's original expression in Spanish than in the previous example. Yet, even where the literal meanings are close, the interpreter must still choose the words which convey the tone, expression, and choice of vocabulary of the original speaker. In the present example, *"dueño"* can mean landlord, owner, or proprietor. *"Aceite"* can refer to heating oil or olive oil. Thus, no matter how close the meanings of the overall message may be, the final choice of words to express that meaning is of the utmost importance.

EXERCISE 2

Describe in detail the three steps involved in the interpreting process.

FIRST STEP:

....

....

....

....

....

....

SECOND STEP:

....

....

....

....

....

....

THIRD STEP:

....

....

....

....

....

....

Compare your answers with the descriptions found in the preceding section.

ROLES OF THE INTERPRETER: INFORMAL INTERPRETING SITUATIONS

In any office where legal services are rendered —be it a private law office, a legal aid office, or an administrative agency— the duty of legal personnel is to aid the client in an objective manner. Once a non-Spanish-speaking professional or paraprofessional discovers that the client can better express ideas in Spanish, an interpreter should immediately be called. The role of the interpreter is to facilitate communication between client and legal personnel by accurately conveying information as soon as it is spoken.

The informal interpreting situation may be a face-to-face interpersonal contact situation, such as a client interview. It may be a telephone conversation, where the interpreter is relaying information over the telephone between non-Spanish-speaking legal personnel and a Spanish-speaking client. The following diagrams illustrate two variants of the informal interpreting situation, as exemplified by an attorney interviewing a client:

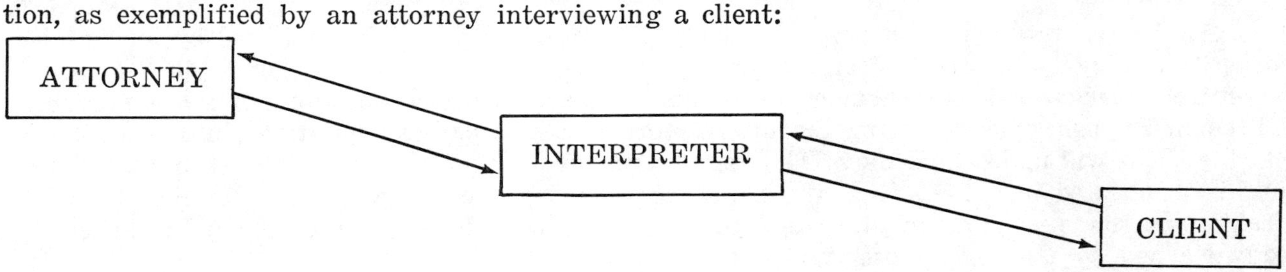

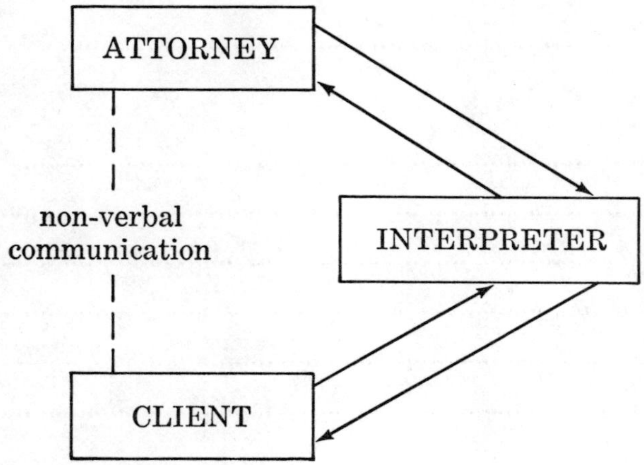

What distinguishes the first diagram from the second? In both diagrams, attorney and client alternate in the roles of speaker and listener. In the first diagram, attorney and client both use the interpreter as the focal point for their dialogue. The interpreter, rather than the client, becomes the central figure in the conversation. While the *role* of the interpreter is fundamental, the position of the interpreter should facilitate as much *direct* contact as possible between client and attorney. The second diagram illustrates this improved relationship. Client and attorney converse directly, and the focus is where it properly belongs: centered upon the client's legal problem.

THE HYBRID INFORMAL INTERPRETING SITUATION

What we call the hybrid informal interpreting situation refers to an interaction between *two* persons, one of whom is the interpreter. Here the interpreter converses directly with the client, in a face-to-face interview or over the telephone, without immediately relaying what is being said to a non-Spanish-speaking listener. In the hybrid situation, both written and oral language skills come into play.

A client may, for example, converse directly with a bilingual receptionist in making an appointment to visit an attorney. The receptionist is not usually required to convey this information immediately. Nor is there the necessity of the usual word-for-word and idea-for-idea accuracy which is crucial to the traditional interpreting situation. Here, the receptionist may simply write down the information in English or else orally inform the attorney.

Similarly, we have the example of the initial interview which is conducted by an "intake worker" at a legal aid office or an administrative agency. If the intake worker is bilingual, then the entire interview will be conducted in Spanish. Nevertheless, the questionnaires are probably written in English, thus requiring the intake worker to translate all questions into Spanish so that the client will understand them. The answers to the questions, given in Spanish by the client, must be translated into English in the notes taken during the interview, so that non-Spanish-speaking personnel who later interview the client will be able to refer to the information already learned by the initial interviewer.

The following diagram illustrates this hybrid interpreting situation:

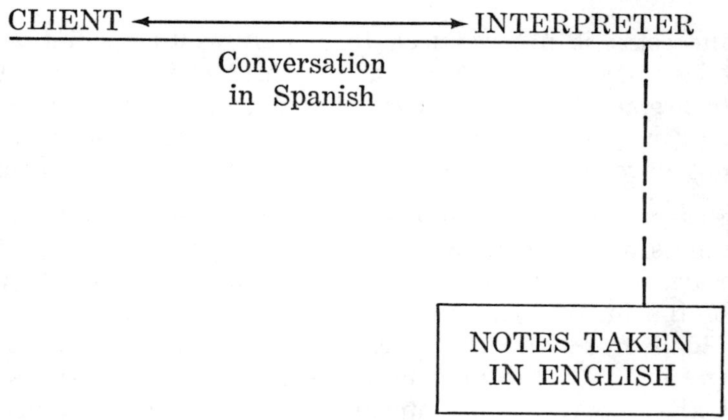

Thus, the skills utilized by bilingual legal personnel in this type of informal situation combine the oral and the written, both translating and interpreting.

ROLES OF THE INTERPRETER: FORMAL INTERPRETING SITUATIONS

Informal interpreting situations are distinguished from formal interpreting situations by the setting where the interpreter applies his or her skills. A formal judicial proceeding may be a courtroom trial, an administrative hearing, or a deposition. In contrast to the informal office interview or telephone conversation, there are set rules governing the conduct of formal judicial proceedings.

COURT INTERPRETERS: MANDATORY VERSUS DISCRETIONARY APPOINTMENT

One major difference between formal and informal interpreting situations is that in this latter case an interpreter *may* be required by law. Historically, in the United States, the legal right to an interpreter was only recognized in a very small number of criminal cases, where it was determined that a defendant could not comprehend anything that was going on in the courtroom. In those rare cases when the right to an interpreter was recognized, it was viewed as a part of the defendant's Sixth Amendment right of confrontation. A court might, in other cases, permit an interpreter upon the request of a party, but that party would have to pay all costs involved.

In 1978, President Carter signed into law the Federal Bilingual Court Interpreters Act. This landmark legislation provides for the right to an interpreter in civil or criminal cases in the Federal district courts. However, these positive features of the act are severely limited by the restriction that the United States must be plaintiff in order for court interpreters to be required.

Some states, such as California, Arkansas, and Kentucky, have enacted court interpreter legislation which is broader in scope than the Federal Bilingual Court Interpreters Act. In most states, however, the decision as to whether or not a court interpreter will be required rests solely within the discretion of the judge —if it is a court case— or with the hearing officer —if it is an administrative hearing.

WHAT IS A "COURT INTERPRETER"?

An interpreter who is appointed by a court to interpret is a formally-appointed "court interpreter". The term "court interpreter" is also used in a much more general sense to mean any person interpreting in court.

In many cases where the court is not required to or refuses to appoint an interpreter, bilingual legal personnel may be called upon to serve as interpreters in formal judicial proceedings. The requirement of interpreter objectivity never changes, even where the bilingual legal personnel serving as interpreters may be employees of one of the attorneys involved in a case; however, the interpreter cannot have any direct personal interest in the case being heard.

Frequently, a non-English-speaking person may bring a friend or relative to serve as interpreter. The lack of awareness and formal interpreter training of these inexperienced interpreters may result in inaccuracies or injustice. It is therefore indispensable that bilingual legal personnel be conscious of the importance of precise, accurate interpreting, so that they may be prepared to interpret in lieu of untrained friends and relatives. In matters relating to the legal system, where a single error on the part of an interpreter may very well affect the entire future of an individual, the importance of interpreter training and excellence cannot be overstressed.

Since these materials deal with the role and function of the interpreter, we shall use the term "court interpreter" to refer to the person performing interpretive services in a formal courtroom situation, without regard to whether the interpreter is appointed by the court or provided by one of the attorneys.

EXERCISE 3

In the spaces next to each term listed below, write a definition for the term. Check your definitions by reviewing the preceding section.

Court Interpreter: ....

....

Mandatory Appointment of Court Interpreters: ....

....

Legal Right to a Court Interpreter: ....

....

Discretionary Appointment of Court Interpreters: ....

....

INTERPRETERS FOR PARTIES VERSUS INTERPRETERS FOR WITNESSES

In a formal judicial proceeding, the term "party" refers to the plaintiff or the defendant. The plaintiff is the party who initiates the suit through the filing of a complaint. In a civil matter, the plaintiff may be a private individual, a corporation, or a governmental agency. In a criminal matter, the complaining party is the state, represented by the prosecutor or district attorney. The defendant is the party against whom the suit is being brought. In a criminal matter, the defendant is also frequently called "the accused".

A non-English-speaking party may require an interpreter in order to understand the proceedings and assist the attorney in his or her case. The interpreter for a party who is not on the witness stand is called a "party interpreter". Since courts are rarely obliged to appoint party interpreters, bilingual legal personnel are frequently called upon to serve as interpreters for a party at counsel table.

The term "witness" refers to a person who gives testimony under oath in a courtroom or other formal judicial proceeding. The interpreter for a witness on the witness stand is called a "witness interpreter". The witness interpreter facilitates the conduct of judicial proceedings by making it possible for the non-English-speaking witness to understand questions as they are posed and for all who are present to understand what the witness is saying.

Just as a witness is under oath, so the interpreter for the witness is also under oath. It is the interpreter's words in rendering the testimony into English, *not* the original testimony of the witness in Spanish, which become a part of the official court record. Thus, the interpreter's words are said to be "on the record". Because the court depends upon the expertise of the interpreter, the interpreter must qualify as, and is considered to be, an expert witness. The role of the interpreter as an expert witness may be likened to that of a physician who may be called upon to testify as an expert regarding medical questions with which he or she is familiar. Similarly, the witness interpreter is an expert witness, whose testimony consists of a precise rendering of the non-English-speaking witness's testimony into English for the official court record.

The party interpreter, in contrast to the witness interpreter, is *not* under oath and is speaking off the record in relaying information to the non-English-speaking party and from the party to the party's attorney. While interpreting for a party at counsel table, the interpreter should speak in a low voice, in order to be heard only by the party and his or her attorney.

To illustrate the differences between party and witness interpreters, let us take the example of Mr. Rodríguez, who is the plaintiff in a suit against Mr. Smithson. Mr. Rodríguez has repaired the roof of Mr. Smithson's house, and Mr. Smithson has refused to pay for the work done because he finds it unsatisfactory. Spanish is the primary language spoken by the plaintiff, Mr. Rodríguez. The plaintiff's attorney does not speak Spanish. In a civil suit such as this one, it is unlikely that the court would appoint an interpreter for the non-English-speaking party, especially in the case of a party who can afford the services of a private attorney. In this case, the plaintiff's attorney has asked a bilingual paralegal trained in interpreting skills to serve as an interpreter. When Mr. Rodríguez is not testifying, the interpreter acts as a party interpreter, relaying information between Mr. Rodríguez and his attorney as well as providing the English translation of the testimony of the other witnesses for Mr. Rodríguez. While the plaintiff is testifying, the interpreter functions as a witness interpreter, translating all questions into Spanish for the witness and providing the English rendering of everything that the witness says.

THE DOUBLE STANDARD

In the preceding example, Mr. Rodríguez was fortunate in having the services of a competently trained bilingual person to serve as interpreter.

Let us take another example, which will point out the double standard which courts tend to follow in the appointment of interpreters. Marta Triana has been accused of shoplifting. She cannot afford the services of a private defense attorney and so a public defender is appointed for her. The public defender does not have any bilingual personnel in his employ who can serve as interpreters. At the beginning of the trial, the judge asks the defendant if she understands English. From her response, the judge determines that she understands a little English, but that she cannot express herself very well in English. The judge appoints a witness interpreter in order to facilitate the conduct of the judicial proceeding by making it possible for all who are present to understand what the accused is saying.

It is far less likely that the judge will appoint an interpreter for a party who is not on the witness stand. While the party is on the witness stand, the judge is conscious of the need to provide interpretive services in order to facilitate the conduct of the trial. All too often the court may provide an interpreter to elicit testimony from a non-English-speaking party when that party is on the witness stand, only to leave the party without the aid of an interpreter at counsel table throughout the rest of the proceedings, when direct testimony by that party is not involved. If the party has some knowledge of English, the judge may feel that the party is nervous on the witness stand but will not need the assistance of an interpreter to understand the remainder of the proceedings.

It must be noted that the party interpreter and the witness interpreter may be the same person. The distinguishing factor is the *role*, that is to say, whether the interpreter provides services for a witness or for a party at counsel table.

The double standard, whereby courts appoint witness interpreters with much greater frequency than party interpreters, is one of the reasons for the importance of interpreter training for all bilingual personnel working in the legal environment. The function of bilingual legal personnel is vital here, since courts rarely appoint such party interpreters.

EXERCISE 3A

In the following list, a series of attributes for witness interpreters are noted in the left-hand column. Compare these with the attributes of party interpreters by filling in the corresponding attributes in the right-hand column of the chart below.

WITNESS INTERPRETER	PARTY INTERPRETER
• Expert Witness	•
• Under oath	•
• On the record	•
• Goal: to facilitate the conduct of judicial proceedings	•
• Appointed more frequently than party interpreters because they assist in the conduct of the court's business.	•

Check your answers against the material in the preceding section.

EXERCISE 3B

Using the characteristics noted in the list in the preceding exercise, describe the role of the interpreter in each of the following situations.

1. Julia Hernández is the interpreter for Mr. Ramírez, defendant in a negligence suit. Mr. Ramírez is not testifying.

2. Ana Romero is the interpreter appointed by the court to provide interpretive services while Julio Valdés testifies during a criminal trial.

METHODS OF INTERPRETING

The objective of all interpreting is the communication of information from the language in which it is originally expressed into another language. The interpreter's role is to convey an accurate version of what is said into the target language, in a complete and comprehensible manner. Yet, the *method* employed by the interpreter can be an important factor in the realization of this goal.

There are three distinct methods of interpreting which may be employed: simultaneous verbatim, consecutive verbatim, and summary interpreting. In certain situations, the use of one form may be more appropriate, or may even be required by court rules. It is therefore important that the interpreter be familiar with all three modes of interpreting.

(A) SIMULTANEOUS VERBATIM

In this method of interpreting, a message is conveyed from the speaker to the listener as soon as the interpreter is able to make the transformation from the source language into the target language. The source language is the language of the original speaker; the target language is the language of the listener, the language into which the interpreter is communicating the meaning of the words spoken.

The term "simultaneous" is not quite an accurate description of this method, since the interpreter cannot be speaking at precisely the same instant as he or she is hearing the message of the speaker. The time lag, and the consequent communication gap should however be minimal, perhaps only a few seconds.

Simultaneous interpreting requires intense concentration on the part of the interpreter, since the speaker and the interpreter are both talking at the same time. The interpreter lags behind the speaker by only a phrase or a word group. For example:

SOURCE LANGUAGE	TARGET LANGUAGE
Speaker 1:	
Are you	¿Es Ud.
a member	miembro
of a	de una
tenant organization?	organización de inquilinos?
Speaker 2:	
No,	No,
no señor,	no sir,
nunca lo he sido.	I have never been one.

In the preceding example, note the immediacy of the interpreter's response. The question is posed in the source language of English. The interpreter must render it simultaneously into Spanish. Speaker 2 responds in Spanish. With the same speed and accuracy, the interpreter must verbalize the response into English. Despite the rapidity of the response time, the interpreter must still preserve the style, tone, and choice of words of the original speaker. Simultaneous *verbatim* means the rendering of every word and every idea using the simultaneous method.

A very high degree of training is required for an interpreter to be skilled in simultaneous verbatim. This type of interpreting is used, for example, in sophisticated settings such as the United Nations. Interpreters in the judicial setting will rarely use this method because of the degree of expertise required. Courts will very rarely recommend or mandate this method of interpreting because of the costliness of the proceedings.

(A-2) SIMULTANEOUS BUT NOT VERBATIM

Another simultaneous form of interpreting is sometimes used by party interpreters at counsel table during court proceedings. This form resembles simultaneous verbatim in that the interpreter interprets at the same time as the speaker is speaking, but the result is not a verbatim rendering. Rather, it more closely resembles a running narrative, a contemporaneous and continuous explanation of the proceedings. This "thought by thought" rendering is much more feasible for certain aspects of the average courtroom proceeding than the simultaneous verbatim method.

One drawback of any simultaneous method is that it may cause confusion, due to the concurrent communication which is inherent in the process.

(B) CONSECUTIVE VERBATIM

The word "consecutive" means "following in order without gaps". Thus, consecutive interpreting is a method by which the interpreter relays a message in the target language in a sequential manner *after* the speaker has completed a thought. The speaker may pause at the end of a sentence or a question, or pause before the end of a statement if the ideas involved are complicated. Often it will be the interpreter, rather than the speaker who requires a pause, since the interpreter may not be able to retain and accurately interpret very long or complex messages.

Like simultaneous verbatim, consecutive verbatim means the precise rendering of everything which is said by the speaker. Approximations, summaries, or running narrations will not suffice. With consecutive verbatim, the length of the communication gap will depend upon the length of the statement of the original speaker, which may of course vary from several seconds to several minutes. Since the interpreter utilizing this mode must render *all* that is said, the length of the interpreter's rendering will not be shorter than the time required for the original statement.

The following example illustrates consecutive verbatim interpreting. Contrast this example with the previous one relating to simultaneous verbatim interpreting:

SOURCE LANGUAGE	**TARGET LANGUAGE**
Are you a member of a tenant organization? →	
	¿Es Ud. miembro de una organización de inquilinos?
No, no señor, nunca lo he sido. →	
	No, no sir, I have never been one.

Whenever consecutive interpreting is used, the interpreter and all speakers should clearly establish hand signals. These should be used by the interpreter to indicate to the speaker the need for a pause. If communication is to proceed smoothly, these signals must be clearly understood by all persons involved. The most frequently used hand signals are the following:

> A raising of the hand by the interpreter indicates that the speaker should pause.
>
> An affirmative nod of the head by the interpreter indicates that the speaker may continue.

Consecutive verbatim is the type of interpreting most frequently used for witnesses and for client interviews. It is, however, more time consuming than the simultaneous method since all who are present must wait for each question or statement to be interpreted before the dialogue can continue. There is a necessary loss of spontaneity with the consecutive method, since normal dialogue is so frequently interrupted. This effect can be minimized if all persons are familiar with the need to pause and with the interpreter's use of signals.

SUMMARY INTERPRETING

Both simultaneous and consecutive interpreting are verbatim methods which necessitate the precise rendering of everything that is said into the target language.

In contrast, summary interpreting is a non-verbatim method. Here the interpreter summarizes the words of the speaker, by paraphrasing and condensing the original message. This method differs from the running narrative form of simultaneous non-verbatim interpreting in that there is no requirement of a continuous stream of words flowing. The interpreter may listen for a time and then relay a much condensed version of what has been said.

In the summary method, in contrast to the simultaneous and consecutive verbatim methods, the intervals at which the interpreter speaks cannot be described with precision. The interpreter may choose to summarize at frequent intervals, or may wait until the end of a part of the proceeding.

There are very limited circumstances where summary interpreting is the preferred method. In court proceedings, if a party does not speak English, the summary method may be valid at counsel table for interpreting certain procedural matters discussed by the judge and the attorneys involved. Sometimes, the intricacies of complex or lengthly scientific or technical testimony may be meaningless to the person requiring interpretive services because of the specialized expertise required to understand the testimony. Here again, the summary method may be appropriate.

There are grave dangers inherent in the use of summary interpreting. By the very nature of the method, the interpreter is forced to omit information. Since the omissions must be made at the interpreter's discretion, statements which may seem unimportant to the interpreter —which the interpreter consequently omits— may very well be of prime concern to the party requiring interpretive services. Because the non-English-speaking party is wholly dependent upon the version furnished by the interpreter, such deletions by the interpreter can have disastrous results.

The potential harm which can be done by abuse of the summary method is revealed by the following example:

> Mrs. Franco is asking her attorney to get some action in order to remedy the lack of heat in her apartment on various occasions over the past few months. She says: "El 5 de febrero no había calefacción. El 7 de febrero tampoco. El 9 de febrero tampoco." The interpreter summarizes all of this by saying: "She didn't have heat on lots of days."

Precision is a *sine qua non* in the legal environment. In the preceding example, the precise dates may have great importance in proving Mrs. Franco's case. It is not the role of the interpreter to judge the significance of such statements.

Given the dangers inherent in the summary method of interpreting, this method should be utilized rarely, and then only with the informed consent of all persons involved.

EXERCISE 4

Distinguish between the three methods of interpreting in the following chart:

METHOD	DEFINITION	CHARACTERISTICS (INCLUDE SITUATIONS WHERE METHOD IS USED)	ADVANTAGES AND DISADVANTAGES
SIMULTANEOUS			
CONSECUTIVE			
SUMMARY			

Compare your answers with the preceding section of the text.

CHAPTER 2

ETHICAL CONSIDERATIONS

CONFIDENTIALITY

When we say that a client has a confidential relationship with legal personnel, we mean that the client has a right to expect that legal personnel will not disclose any information obtained from the client to persons who are not directly involved in the case. The requirement of confidentiality, or non-disclosure, extends to paralegals, secretaries, interpreters, and any other parties who are involved with the confidential subject matter which the client reveals to the attorney. Just as in the relationship between physician and patient, between husband and wire, or between priest and penitent, communications between attorney and client are generally considered "privileged", meaning that there is a duty not to discuss such communications with third parties.

The interpreter has the obligation to keep confidential all matters interpreted as well as anything which has been overheard between attorney and client. This applies equally to informal and formal interpreting situations. The interpreter is a necessary third party who is present to make communication possible between attorney and client. Thus, the interpreter is a part of the privileged confidential relationship between attorney and client. The interpreter should not and must not discuss with any third parties what has transpired between attorney and client.

The interpreter should never disclose any information regarding a case to the opposing parties, to the media, or to anyone not directly associated with the case. The interpreter may only discuss information of public record such as the time and place of a court hearing.

The interpreter should at no time divulge a personal opinion to any branch of the mass media referring to or related to any legal matter in which the interpreter has rendered service.

PROFESSIONAL RELATIONSHIPS

Perhaps one of the most difficult problems with which the interpreter must deal involves the interpreter's professional relationship to the client in need of assistance. Because interpreter and client speak the same language, intangible bonds may grow between them. The interpreter may feel empathy, pity, and frustration upon hearing the client's story. The client, speaking in Spanish, may disclose certain pieces of information to the interpreter, not realizing that it is the interpreter's duty to disclose to the attorney *all* information revealed by the client.

It is the interpreter's duty to maintain objective detached relationships. Personal displays of emotion or subjective involvement in a case are to be avoided.

The interpreter and client should not address each other on a first-name basis. This includes, of necessity the avoidance of the use of the familiar *"tú"* form in Spanish. While the relationship between client and interpreter must be formal and objective, this does not preclude the presence of compassion and understanding as part of the basis of the professional relationship.

THE GIVING OF LEGAL ADVICE BY THE INTERPRETER

The interpreter should at no time offer or give any type of legal advice to the non-English-speaking individual. Rather, the individual should be referred to an attorney. When an individual who does not have an attorney asks an interpreter for legal advice, the interpreter should refer the individual to an Attorney Referral Service for a private attorney or to Legal Aid if the individual cannot afford the services of a private attorney. The interpreter should not function as a referral service for specific attorneys.

If an interpreter gives any legal advice to a person for whom he or she is interpreting, then the interpreter is violating the objectivity which is vital to his or her role. This problem is particularly acute when a Spanish-speaking person, who sees the interpreter as a kind of ally, asks the interpreter a question such as: "Should I tell the lawyer this?" *The interpreter must inform the Spanish-speaking person that everything which is said must be translated.* The interpreter should refer the client to his or her attorney regarding any legal questions.

In informal interpreting situations such as client interviews, a problem frequently arises for bilingual legal personnel serving as interpreters when the attorney leaves the room for a short period of time. The client may frequenty feel that this is the perfect opportunity to ask the interpreter for legal advice or to inquire as to whether the interpreter feels that the client should disclose certain information to the attorney. Since the interpreter should not talk to the client when the attorney is not present, there are several possible ways for the interpreter to deal with this situation:

—Interpreter remains in the room but does not talk to client.
—If conversation cannot be avoided, the interpreter relays everything to the attorney upon his/her return.
—Interpreter leaves the room.

In formal interpreting situations such as a courtroom, the interpreter should never engage in conversation with any person for whom he or she is interpreting. Similarly, in hallways, outside the courtroom, the interpreter should never engage in social conversation with any person for whom interpretive services may be rendered in court.

CONFLICT OF INTEREST

A conflict of interest is said to exist for an interpreter when the interpreter's personal situation, needs, or desires could possibly cause the interpreter to violate his or her professional duty. A conflict of interest may possibly exist when any condition or circumstances arises which may have an effect on the objectivity of the interpreter. Such a condition may be said to exist in the following circumstances:

—If the interpreter was previously acquainted with any of the parties involved in the case.
—If the interpreter has a personal interest of any kind in the outcome of the proceedings.
—If the interpreter is not entirely independent of the opposing parties or agencies.
—If the interpreter has been previously acquainted with any of the witnesses involved.

The potential for bias or conflict of interest leading to less than accurate interpreting is clearly present when a Spanish-speaking person brings a friend or relative to serve as interpreter.

If a conflict exists for the interpreter or if there is even a remote possibility that a conflict may exist, the interpreter has the duty to inform all concerned of the problem. All parties, attorneys, and judicial officers involved in a case must *knowingly* agree that the interpreter is to continue despite an actual or potential conflict of interest.

INTERPRETER COMPETENCE

It is assumed that an interpreter has a complete mastery of standard Spanish and English. At times, however, the Spanish-speaking person who requires interpretive services may employ dialectical or regional forms. If the interpreter cannot render a precise equivalent for the meaning of such expressions, then it is his or her duty to explain the difficulty to the person for whom the interpreting is being carried out. In the informal situation, it must be explained to the attorney or other non-Spanish-speaking professional. In the formal interpreting situation, it should be explained to the presiding judicial officer. If an interpreter is otherwise competent, he or she has nothing to fear from a difficulty with dialectical or regional forms. Quite the contrary, *if the interpreter does not explain to all persons involved that he or she does not understand a term or expression, then the interpreter is doing an injustice to all concerned.*

Once the interpreter has explained that there exists a problem in rendering the precise equivalent for an expression, the problem can frequently be rectified if the interpreter is permitted to ask the non-English-speaker to re-state the expression using different words. Sometimes the interpreter must question the Spanish-speaking individual in order to clarify the expression. The cause for and the meaning of this dialogue between the interpreter and the non-English-speaking individual must be made *explicitly* clear to non-Spanish-speaking persons who are present, lest they think that some impermissible conversation is taking place in Spanish between the interpreter and the non-English-speaking individual.

This same problem arises in the converse situation, when the non-Spanish-speaking party asks a question or makes a comment using a phrase which the interpreter does not understand or for which the interpreter cannot find a precise Spanish equivalent. As in the prior instance, the interpreter should immediately inform all concerned, so that the question can be re-phrased or a synonym found.

A more serious problem is presented when the interpreter encounters technical terminology with which he or she is unfamiliar, vocabulary which a lay person would not understand in either English or Spanish. If the interpreter knows that a given case may involve specialized terminology, then it is the interpreter's duty to become familiar with such vocabulary in advance. For example, there is a specialized vocabulary which is used by those dealing with narcotics. In a trial where this vocabulary may be encountered, the interpreter must be aware of these special meanings, lest a vital word be misconstrued. Additionally, in order to maintain and enhance competence and ability, an interpreter should continue to study in related areas such as grammar, syntax, commercial and technical aspects of the languages involved, and legal terminology.

If the interpreter feels unable to master the material at hand, then the interpreter must withdraw. *An incompetent interpreter who remains on a case can be more dangerous than no interpreter at all.*

In many cases, the interpreter is the only bilingual person who is present. Thus, many errors or words not understood would go undetected if the interpreter were not to call attention to the problem. Calling attention to such problems is an integral part of interpreter competence and is based upon the most fundamental ethical considerations. *It is absolutely necessary that all errors and shortcomings be promptly admitted by the interpreter.* It is vital that the interpreter recall that the primary duty is to *accuracy.*

In some states, agencies, and judicial bodies, codes of ethics embodying standards of performance have been set out to guide the interpreter. Individually, all interpreters are responsible for the elevation of the standards of performance of the profession.

QUESTIONS

Based upon the preceding chapter, answer all of the following questions. Check your answers by again reading "Ethical Considerations".

1. During a client interview, the interpreter learns that a wife is seeking to divorce her spouse because the husband had beaten her every night. What obligations does the interpreter have regarding the confidentiality of what was interpreted?

2. What may a court interpreter say to the newspapers, radio, or television regarding the proceedings where he or she has served as interpreter?

3. What should an interpreter do if he or she is asked for the name of a good lawyer?

4. If asked for legal advice, what should the interpreter do?

5. Under what circumstances may there be said to exist a conflict of interest for an interpreter serving in a particular case?

6. What actions are possible and permissible for an interpreter who does not feel competent to interpret material in a certain case? Compare the case of the interpreter who does not understand several phrases to the case of the interpreter who knows nothing of drug terminology in a narcotics case.

CHAPTER 3

REGIONAL LANGUAGE DIFFERENCES

The role of the interpreter is to present a totally objective rendering of what is said during an interview, a telephone conversation, or a formal judicial proceeding, without interjecting personal perceptions of the "correctness" or "incorrectness" of the language used by the speaker.

It should not be forgotten that, while the cultured *written* language is relatively uniform in the Spanish-speaking world, the Spanish generally *spoken* throughout Spain differs from that spoken in the Americas, although there does not exist complete uniformity among all Spanish-speaking countries. In addition, standard oral language is confined, even in Spain, to the most educated groups. The Spanish which is spoken in many regions or countries may vary in both pronunciation and grammatical structure from certain facets of what, for the sake of simplicity, we shall call "standard Spanish".

At the time of the discovery of the Americas, the state of the language in Spain was unstable and all this instability was inherited by the new Spanish-speaking world. Furthermore, the character and places of origin of the first settlers were different in each populated region. The different indigenous civilizations encountered by the Spaniards each had a predominant native language which also influenced the Spanish spoken in a given region. Objects that were indigenous to the Americas and therefore unfamiliar to the settlers were either given a new word by association, (i.e., *piña* for pineapple, from the similarity in appearance that this fruit bears with *pino* or cones from the pine tree) or adapted phonetically from the native language into Spanish. For expediency, the different indigenous languages and dialects can be divided into five main linguistic zones:

1. Caribbean region — *arahuaco*, *caribe*
2. Mexico and Central America — *nahuatl*, *maya-quiché*
3. Andean region — *quichua (quétchua)*, *aimará*
4. Río de la Plata región* — *tupi-guaraní*
5. Chile — *mapuche*

*This region is comprised of Argentina, Uruguay and Paraguay.

Later on, the Spanish language was further altered by the arrival of various groups of immigrants: black slaves to the Caribbean and Atlantic coastal regions, Italians to Argentina, English, Germans, French throughout, etc. In summary, it can be said that the spoken language of each country has been molded by the prevailing conditions in each region, namely, the geography, the socio-economic necessities, and the psychological composition of the groups of people populating each linguistic zone.

A study of some of the major variations in pronunciation, grammatical structure, and vocabulary of the Spanish which is spoken in different areas of the Hispanic world is neccesary so that the interpreter may be aware of some regional language differences.

PRONUNCIATION

A phenomenon common in many Spanish-speaking regions is the omission of the letter "d" between two vowels. This is especially common in the pronunciation of past participles.

Estoy cans**ao**.
Estoy cansado.
I am tired.

Hemos trabaj**ao** mucho.
Hemos trabajado mucho.
We have worked a great deal.

Trabajé t**oa** la mañana.
Trabajé toda la mañana.
I worked the whole morning.

Another extremely common usage, especially in Caribbean Spanish, as well as in many coastal regions of South America and Southern Spain, is what is termed the aspiration of the final "s". This does not only occur at the end of a word but also between a vowel and a consonant. This aspiration is somewhat similar to the English "h" sound in the word "him".

El e**h**cribano de la corte bu**h**có la información en su**h** regi**h**tro**h**.
El escribano de la corte buscó la información en sus registros.
The court clerk looked for the information in his files.

El me**h** pas**ao** apunté cinco queja**h** contra e**h**te dueño.
El mes pasado apunté cinco quejas contra este dueño.
Last month I recorded five complaints against this landlord.

At times, the final "s" is not merely aspirated but rather is eliminated completely. This may be heard from second-generation children of Spanish-speaking parents who are living in the United States.

Lo cost**o** y honorari**o** son muy elev**ao**.
Los costos y honorarios son muy elevados.
The costs and attorneys fees are very high.

Another less common though important practice is the aspiration of the letter "h", a letter which is not usually pronounced. The sound given to the "h" is that of the "j".

Es **j**embra.
Es hembra.
She is female.

Son la**h** **j**ocho.
Son las ocho.
It's eight.

The interchanging of the vowel sounds "e" and "i" or "o" and "u" is a frequent occurrence.

revulución	=	revolución	=	revolution
josticia	=	justicia	=	justice
dispués	=	después	=	afterward
pior	=	peor	=	worse, worst
medecina	=	medicina	=	medicine
escuro	=	obscuro	=	dark
mesmo	=	mismo	=	same
semos	=	somos	=	we are

In most regions of the Hispanic world, the standard pronunciation of the double "r" sound occurs in the following circumstances:

(a) Wherever there is a written double "r" as in *perro* or *carro.*
(b) When a single "r" comes at the beginning of a word as in *Rosa* or *rico.*
(c) When the single "r" is preceded by either the letter "n" or the letter "s" as in *Enrique* or *Israel.*

In certain parts of Puerto Rico the sound given to the double "r" is similar to the pronunciation which the majority of Spanish-speaking individuals give to the "j" in words like *José* or *jamás.* This pronunciation is not found in all parts of Puerto Rico, but, when used, it may pose a problem for the interpreter not fully familiar with its use.

Josa	=	Rosa	=	Rose
pejo	=	perro	=	dog

The substitution of the consonants "r" and "l" for each other in Spanish is another quite common practice, mainly in Puerto Rico.

Er hombre fue carvo y goldo.
El hombre fue calvo y gordo.
The man was bald and fat.

un pedazo de calne
un pedazo de carne
a piece of meat

The term metathesis refers to the transposition of letters, syllables, or sounds in a word and is a fairly common practice by certain Hispanics. Its use at times poses an obstacle to comprehension.

estógamo	=	estómago	=	stomach
naide	=	nadie	=	no one
miraglo	=	milagro	=	miracle
murciégalo	=	murciélago	=	bat

SYNTAX

The gender of certain nouns will at times vary from standard usages.

la-el sartén	=	frying pan
la-el costumbre	=	custom
la-el idioma	=	language
la-el calor	=	heat

The formation of the plural of certain nouns may also at times be at variance with what is generally used:

mamáses	=	mamás	=	mothers
papáses	=	papás	=	fathers, parents
rubíses, rubís	=	rubíes	=	rubies

Certain prefixes are commonly used to express the superlative form. The following examples all employ the same basic word, "bueno", which in English would signify very good, very very good, etc.

rebueno, retebueno, requetebueno,
murrebueno, querrebueno, tarredebueno

Forms more common in the past are also retained by some speakers:

truje	=	traje	from traer	=	to bring
haiga	=	haya	from haber	=	to have (auxiliary verb)
vide	=	vi	from ver	=	to see

Verb forms may offer a problem to the interpreter, due to the wide variety of forms employed which vary from standard Spanish. For example, in the verb stem, at times a diphthong is heard where it is not expected:

tueso for toso from toser = to cough
cueso for coso from coser = to sew

The opposite tendency is also prevalent:

fr**a**go for friego from fregar = to scrub
f**o**rzo for fuerzo from forzar = to force

In an attempt to regularize certain irregular verb forms, new forms are created:

ca**y**a	=	caiga	from caer	=	to fall
tra**y**o	=	traigo	from traer	=	to bring
vai**g**a	=	vaya	from ir	=	to go
tradu**ci**	=	traduje	from traducir	=	to translate
ande	=	anduve	from andar	=	to walk
and**o**	=	anduvo	from andar	=	to walk

The *vos* verb form, or *voseo,* is found quite frequently in various Spanish-speaking countries. It is derived from the *vosotros* form, the second person familiar plural of the verb which is in use today in certain regions of Spain.

Although the *vos* form is originally derived from the plural *vosotros* form, the two must not be confused, since the *vos* form is used only in the singular. This form is used in place of the familiar *tú* form, with the pronoun *vos* replacing the pronoun *tú.*

Regional variations are found within the *vos* form. The most commonly encountered form is derived from the *vosotros* form by the omission of a vowel or a consonant.

Present	**vosotros**	**vos**
Indicative	amáis	amás
	tenéis	tenés
Imperative	amad	amá
	tened	tené

The actual spelling and pronunciation of the individual *vos* forms vary from country to country or from region to region. For example, in some areas, the pronoun *tú* is used with the verb form based on the *voseo.*

tu tomás	tú comés

In other areas, we find the opposite phenomenon; the pronoun *vos* is combined with the verb based upon the *tú* form.

vos tomas	vos comes

When the *voseo* is used in the verb form, stem-changing verbs do not suffer a change in the root from *e* to *ie* and from *o* to *ue.*

No te **sentés** ahí.	**Volvé** temprano.
No te sientes ahí.	Vuelve temprano.

The vos form has been extended, in one or another of its varieties, to the following geographic areas:

Argentina
Bolivia
Colombia
Chile (in conflict with **tú**)
Ecuador (the major part)
Panamá (the interior)
Paraguay (certain parts)
Perú (in the North, near Ecuador; in the South, near Chile)
Uruguay
Venezuela
Costa Rica (the major part)
El Salvador
Guatemala
Honduras
Nicaragua
Mexico (the states of Chaipas and Tabasco)

ANGLICISMS

Since the main purpose of language is communication, when a person moves to a different region or country it is necessary to learn to communicate through the use of the language of the new region or country. The difference in language may be slight, involving only the addition of a small number of new words or phrases to the individual's original language. This may occur, for example, when someone moves from one region to another within the same country. In other cases, it may entail the learning of an entirely new language. The latter may occur in the case of native speakers of Spanish who come to the United States.

As the process of learning a new language begins, an individual will naturally find it necessary to learn common, frequently used words before mastering more intricate vocabulary. For example, someone who has always used the word "centavo" when speaking of money will now constantly hear the English word "penny" and will thus learn the English word "penny" for "centavo". Examples of this process of word substitution are endless.

The process becomes much more complex, however, as the native speaker of Spanish hears English words with increasing frequency. As that person begins to learn more and more English in adapting to an English-speaking country and culture, he or she is hearing less Spanish and will tend to rely less and less upon Spanish. To this extent, English vocabulary will tend to increase at the expense of Spanish vocabulary. Decreased use of Spanish will increase the tendency to forget that language.

One possible consequence of hearing and using more and more English is that the native speaker of Spanish may begin to substitute English words for Spanish while speaking in Spanish. At times the person has forgotten the original Spanish form. At other times, the original Spanish form has not been forgotten but the individual may feel more at home with English, as he or she uses words more frequently in English than in Spanish.

A related phenomenon occurs when an individual is bilingual, for example, a Hispanic person who is born in the United States and whose family may speak Spanish or a combination of Spanish and English at home. The language interference in this instance may be more complex, since both languages, English and Spanish, are constantly present as in the case of new anglicized verb infinitives.

The interpreter cannot afford to ignore the new words or "anglicisms" which are a product of the influence of English upon the Spanish language. If a person speaking in Spanish employs such anglicisms, the interpreter must be able to recognize them. Although they are not "standard Spanish", anglicisms are a means to the desired end — that of understanding and communication.

Due to the wide variety of nationalities and regional groups among Hispanics living in the United States, it is nearly impossible to give a complete list of the anglicisms used by all groups. Thus, the list of anglicisms which follows cannot cover all of the usages which are familiar to all Hispanics. In the list of anglicisms, all verbs are in the infinitive form. Phonetic spelling is used for all anglicisms on the list.

ANGLICISMS

ANGLICISM	STANDARD SPANISH	ENGLISH TRANSLATION
armi	ejército	army
baquiar	retroceder	to go back
beisman	sótano	basement
bil	cuenta	bill
bloque	cuadra	city block
bonche*	manojo	bunch, handful
bondo	fardo, montón	bundle
bo	jefe, patrón	boss
caliente	calefacción	heating
carpeta	alfombra	carpet
clínica	hospital	clinic
colectar	recibir	collect
corte	tribunal, juzgado	court
craquiar	cuartear, quebrar	to crack
chainear	dar lustre, brillo	to shine
champeón, champión	campeón	champion
chance	oportunidad	chance
choque	tiza	chalk
chusar, chusiar	escoger	to choose
daime	diez centavos	dime
dilatarse	demorarse, retrasarse	to be delayed
dipo	estación	station depot
escuela alta	escuela secundaria, escuela superior	high school
espeletear, espeliar	deletrear	to spell
estimado	presupuesto	estimate
estraiquiar	pegar, ponchar	to strike, to strike out
factoría	fábrica	factory
frigidaire	refrigerador	frigidaire, freezer
frizar	congelar	to freeze
furnitura	muebles	furniture
gasetería	gasolinera	gas station
gasolín	gasolina	gasoline
greve, greivi	salsa	gravy
guachimán	sereno	watchman
huachar, guachar	mirar, ver	to watch, look, see
inspectar	inspeccionar	to inspect
janguear	pasear, frecuentar un sitio	to hang out (in a place)
liquear	gotear	to leak

*The word "bonche" or "bonchinche" is also a synonym of "relajo" meaning joking and kidding. This usage is frequent in Cuba.

ANGLICISM	STANDARD SPANISH	ENGLISH TRANSLATION
lonchar	almorzar	to have lunch
lonche	almuerzo	lunch
llamar para atrás	volver a llamar	to call back
machar, machear	emparejar, combinar	to match
magasín	revista	magazine
mecha	cerillo, fósforo	match
mistear	perder, faltar	to miss, to lose
mitin	reunión	meeting
nicle	cinco centavos	nickel
parquear	estacionar	to park
peni	centavo	penny, cent
pichar	tirar	to pitch
pompa	bomba	pump
populación	población	population
puchar, puchear	empujar	to push
pul	billar	pool, billiards
pul	influencia	influence
quechar, cachear	coger, agarrar	to catch
rai	vuelta	ride
reinear	llover	to rain
rentar	alquiler	to rent
rufo	techo	roof
sainear	firmar	to sign
signatura	firma	signature
taipiar, taipear	escribir a máquina, mecanografiar	to type
telefón	teléfono	telephone
tratar	probar	to try (on a garment or to try to do something)
unión	sindicato	union, sindicate
violación	infracción	building violation

ADDITIONAL ANGLICISMS

Add to the preceding list by noting all of the anglicisms which you encounter.

ANGLICISM	STANDARD SPANISH	ENGLISH TRANSLATION

CHAPTER 4

INFORMAL INTERPRETING SITUATIONS
TELEPHONE CONVERSATIONS

THE INITIAL TELEPHONE CONVERSATION

The initial contact between a client and a private attorney or between a client and a legal aid office is frequently a telephone conversation. The impressions formed by the client during this nnitial contact may help to solidify good future relations or, on the other hand, may create an atmosphere of mistrust and misunderstanding that cannot be easily improved at future meetings.

In the case of Spanish-speaking adults seeking legal assistance, it is not unusual that they ask their bilingual friends, relatives, or children to serve as interpreters during telephone conversations. Since these friends or relatives are rarely trained in the specialized skills required for accurate interpreting, there exists a very real danger that certain information of prime importance may be omitted or abbreviated, either because the friend or relative —especially if the person interpreting is a child— fails to see the importance of certain facts, or simply because the person interpreting does not possess the requisite linguistic skills to serve as a competent interpreter.

Since telephone conversations leave no possibility for non-verbal communication between client and legal personnel, an interpreter is undoubtedly necessary if a Spanish-speaking person is to be able to ask questions and obtain information from English-speaking legal personnel. There must, obviously, be a common language spoken by the person seeking assistance and the legal personnel furnishing the information. Since the quality of the interpreting carried out by well-intentioned friends and relatives cannot be regulated, the solution is to have competent, trained bilingual legal personnel who can deal effectively and efficiently with telephone inquiries by Spanish-speaking persons. This ensures a positive first impression for the client.

The impressions made by legal personnel during this initial contact may very well determine whether or not the client feels that it is worth his or her time and effort to seek further assistance. A disjointed, confusing, or discourteous initial contact may very well discourage an individual from pursuing the matter. Bilingual legal personnel should be particularly prepared for unclear or excited explanations of legal problems by clients. A person with a pressing problem is often desperate for assistance. Additionally, bilingual legal personnel must be prepared to frequently hear regionalisms and dialectical variations (as discussed in Chapter 3 of this part of the text). It is the legal personnel *not* the potential client with a legal problem who must make every effort to understand, especially over the telephone, where it is so easy to misconstrue what is said.

There exists, to begin with, a language barrier between the Spanish-speaking client or potential client and the English language legal system of the United States. Since a telephone conversation is a contact situation that relies completely upon speech and language for the communication of ideas, a negative impression may cause the potential client to feel that he or she really has no hope of having access to the English language legal system.

TELEPHONE CONVERSATIONS: NON-LINGUISTIC CONSIDERATIONS

After "Hello", perhaps the most frequently encountered phrase during telephone conversations is "Please hold". This is generally followed by a click and a wait of anywhere from several seconds to several minutes. In all likelihood, the office staff worker answering the telephone has not yet discovered that the person at the other end of the line speaks only Spanish. If the call has been placed from a public telephone, the potential client finds that he or she has been put "on hold" for several minutes and, before being able to speak to anyone about anything, is asked by a recorded voice to deposit more money or else the call will be interrupted.

The first solution to the problems described in the preceding paragraph is to have a telephone receptionist who speaks both English and Spanish. If that is not possible, then the receptionist should ascertain whether the caller speaks only Spanish *before* putting the caller on hold, so that the staff person who picks up the call will be able to converse directly with the caller.

If someone must be placed on hold, every attempt should be made to get back to the caller as soon as possible. If the telephone receptionist knows that the caller will have a wait of several minutes, then the caller should be informed of this fact immediately and given the option of waiting on hold or calling back at another time. Another possibility is for the receptionist to take down the caller's telephone number, letting the caller know how long it will be before the call can be returned. It is best to allow leeway and to over-estimate the time for the return of the telephone call so that the call can definitely be returned within the time limit indicated to the caller. Legal personnel who inform a potential client that a call will be returned in five minutes, and who then return the call two hours later, are not creating an atmosphere of trust and confidence for the client.

Such considerations as those described above should apply to *all* clients or potential clients who call a law office or legal aid agency. They are an integral part of the agency's responsibility to encourage clients to utilize the services offered. For Spanish-speaking clients, since communication has already been impeded because of the language barrier, an extra measure of courtesy and thoughtfulness can go a long way toward overriding such initial difficulties.

DYNAMICS OF TELEPHONE INTERPRETING SITUATIONS

Recall the different types of interpreting situations described in Chapter 1 of this part of the text. A telephone conversation will generally fall into one of two categories: the "Informal Interpreting Situation" or the "Hybrid Informal Interpreting Situation".

An initial telephone conversation will probably be a "Hybrid Informal Interpreting Situation." This term refers to a direct contact between the Spanish-speaking person and bilingual legal personnel, where the conversation is carried out completely in Spanish. A caller may, for example, converse with a bilingual receptionist in order to schedule an appointment with an attorney. A caller may inquire of a bilingual paralegal whether a given agency is the proper place to seek recourse in the case of a particular problem. The bilingual receptionist or paralegal does not directly communicate the information obtained to another individual. Generally, some notes will be taken for later use —either the recording of an appointment or some information regarding the nature of the problem discussed over the telephone. A verbatim record is generally not called for. Both written translating and oral interpreting skills may be involved in this type of hybrid informal interpreting situation.

Some telephone conversations may be termed the "Informal Interpreting Situations". The role of the interpreter during such a telephone conversation will be to relay information between the Spanish-speaking client and non-Spanish-speaking legal personnel. If the attorney, for example, does not speak Spanish, the interpreter may be relaying the words spoken by the client to the attorney and vice versa.

In contrast to a face-to-face interview situation, there is no possibility of direct contact between non-Spanish-speaking attorney and Spanish-speaking client. Here the interpreter will generally speak in the third person, referring to the non-Spanish-speaking attorney as "he" or "she". This situation is in marked contrast to the in-person interview or formal interpreting situation, where the interpreter generally speaks in the first person, acting as the mirror image of the person who is speaking. While the use of the first person "I" will make an interview seem as if it were truly a direct dialogue between the Spanish-speaking client and the non-Spanish-speaking legal personnel, in a telephone conversation the use of the third person is the only logical and practical solution.

INITIAL TELEPHONE CONVERSATION: AN EXAMPLE

In the following telephone conversation, many of the skills involved require a combination of linguistic expertise, cultural fluency, and human understanding. These should be integrated with the interpreting skills discussed in Chapter 5 (Informal Interpreting Situations: The Interview) and Chapter 6 (Formal Interpreting Situations).

READ THE FOLLOWING DIALOGUE ONCE. AT THE END OF THE DIALOGUE YOU WILL FIND DIRECTIONS INDICATING WHICH ASPECTS OF THE DIALOGUE YOU SHOULD PAY SPECIAL ATTENTION TO WHEN YOU READ THE DIALOGUE FOR A SECOND TIME.

(Mrs. Osuna, who speaks only Spanish, is calling an attorney's office for advice. She has asked her friend, Mrs. Moreno, to speak for her, since she does not know whether the law office has any bilingual personnel. Miss Brook, the telephone receptionist at the law office, does not speak Spanish. However, Miss Suárez, a bilingual paralegal working at the law office, is fluent in Spanish and trained in interpreting skills.)

(Telephone rings. Miss Brook anwers.)

Miss Brook: Hello, please hold for a moment. (Several minutes of silence while Mrs. Moreno and Mrs. Osuna are on hold.) Yes, may I help you?

Mrs. Moreno: Is there anyone there who speaks Spanish? My friend who is here has a problem that she wants to discuss, but she does not speak English.

Miss Brook: Well, hang on a minute, and I'll see if I can find someone. (Muffling the receiver, she says in the background.) Where did Ana go? There's someone on the phone who wants to speak in Spanish. Could somebody please look for her?

Mrs. Moreno to Mrs. Osuna: Parece que están buscando a alguien que hable español, pero no entiendo del todo lo que dicen.

Miss Suárez: Aló.

Mrs. Moreno: ¿Ud. habla español?

Miss Suárez: Sí, señora. ¿En qué puedo servirle?

Mrs. Moreno: Espere un momento, por favor. Hay una señora aquí que tiene un problema y que quiere hablar con Ud.

Mrs. Osuna: Aló.

Miss Suárez: Diga. ¿En qué puedo servirle?

Mrs. Osuna: Es que acabo de averiguar que mi hermano me ha dejado una herencia bastante grande y quiero averiguar cómo se inician los trámites para que yo la pueda recibir aquí en los Estados Unidos. Me han dicho que su oficina tiene mucho trato con el Uruguay, y me gustaría que Uds. me representaran en este asunto.

Miss Suárez: Bueno, señora. Lo que Ud. dice es cierto. En nuestra oficina se trabaja muy a menudo con abogados y agentes del Uruguay. Sin embargo, no podemos dar consejos legales por teléfono, y, en todo caso, como no soy abogada, no soy yo la que da los consejos. ¿Desea Ud. concertar una cita con uno de nuestros abogados?

Mrs. Osuna: Sí, pero quisiera concertarla para cuando Ud. esté allí, porque no vale nada que yo acuda a una cita, si no hay nadie que me entienda.

Miss Suárez: Por supuesto. Le arreglaré su visita. Espere un momento mientras yo averigüo cuando uno de los abogados dispone de una hora para la entrevista.

Miss Suárez to Miss Brook: (While Mrs. Osuna waits on the telephone.) This lady would like to see one of the attorneys. When is the next opening for an interview with a new client?

Miss Brook to Miss Suárez: Next Wednesday at 3 P.M.

Miss Suárez: (Once again speaking to Mrs. Osuna over the telephone.) ¿Le convendría venir el miércoles que viene a las dos de la tarde? La cita con el abogado será a las tres, pero necesitamos una hora antes para tomar los datos esenciales.

Mrs. Osuna: Muy bien. La hora me es muy conveniente.

(The telephone conversation concludes as Miss Suárez asks Mrs. Osuna for her address and telephone number.)

EXERCISE 1

Reread the telephone conversation carefully. As you read, note those elements which encourage and discourage a Spanish-speaking client such as Mrs. Osuna. List your answers in the chart which follows, according to the number of the line of dialogue (column A); the element which helps or hinders (column B); possible explanations for these (column C). Compare your analysis with the following section of this chapter.

(A) LINE NUMBER	(B) ENCOURAGING OR DISCOURAGING ELEMENT	(C) POSSIBLE EXPLANATION

INITIAL TELEPHONE CONVERSATION: ANALYSIS

In this section of the text, the lines of the preceding dialogue are repeated before the analysis of the various parts of the dialogue. In this way, the reader can easily compare the analysis carried out in the preceding exercise with the one which follows.

(Telephone rings. Miss Brook answers.)

Miss Brook: Hello, please hold for a moment. (Several minutes of silence while Mrs. Moreno and Mrs. Suárez are on hold.) Yes, may I help you?

The receptionist did not bother to find out anything before asking the caller to wait. If she had reversed her two statements, asking "May I help you?" before putting the client on hold, she would have been able to ascertain the caller's needs much more effectively. Every attempt should be made *not* to put a caller on hold at the very start of the conversation.

Mrs. Moreno: Is there anyone there who speaks Spanish? My friend who is here has a problem that she wants to discuss, but she does not speak English.

If the receptionist were bilingual, then she could have spoken directly with the client in Spanish. Even if the person answering the telephone at an office is not bilingual, a consistent and efficient office system should be established, as part of the regular office routine, so that bilingual personnel can be called to the telephone as soon as it is determined that there is a need for their services. A non-Spanish-speaking receptionist can also learn a few words of Spanish, in order to assist a Spanish-speaking client. The receptionist may say, for example: "No hablo español. Un momento, por favor." In Chapter 2 of the first part of the text, *Cultural Fluency*, there is a list of expressions which help to create a warm atmosphere for a Spanish-speaking client. Even a non-Spanish-speaking receptionist can learn expressions such as these, and telephone conversations with Spanish-speaking clients will become much more positive experiences for all concerned.

Miss Brook: Well, hang on a minute, and I'll see if I can find someone. (Muffling the receiver, she says in the background.) Where did Ana go? There's someone on the phone who wants to speak in Spanish. Could somebody please look for her?

The receptionist used the American idiom "hang on a minute". It should not be presumed that a bilingual caller will understand such colloquial expressions, especially if the caller's dominant language is not English. The combination of the phrase about "hanging on" and the muffled comments in the background leave Mrs. Moreno unsure as to what is going on.

Mrs. Moreno to Mrs. Osuna: Parece que están buscando a alguien que hable español, pero no entiendo del todo lo que dicen.

This doubt is transmitted to the potential client, Mrs. Osuna. A clearer initial explanation of the delay in locating the Spanish-speaking employee, coupled with a better system for handling phone calls from Spanish-speaking clients, would have avoided this kind of problem. If the receptionist was unable to locate the bilingual employee immediately, a good solution might have been for the receptionist to take note of the caller's name and telephone number. The bilingual employee could then return the telephone call as soon as possible.

Miss Suárez: Aló.

Mrs. Moreno: ¿Ud. habla español?

Miss Suárez: Sí, señora. ¿En qué puedo servirle?

Mrs. Moreno: Espere un momento, por favor. Hay una señora aquí que tiene un problema y que quiere hablar con Ud.

Mrs. Osuna: Aló.

Miss Suárez: Diga. ¿En qué puedo servirle?

Here, right from the start, Miss Suárez, the bilingual paralegal, is making an attempt to see what the caller's needs are. The potential client is treated with proper respect, and is addressed using the *Ud.* form of the verb.

Mrs. Osuna: Es que acabo de averiguar que mi hermano me ha dejado una herencia bastante grande y quiero averiguar cómo se inician los trámites para que yo la pueda recibir aquí en los Estados Unidos. Me han dicho que su oficina tiene mucho trato con el Uruguay, y me gustaría que Uds. me representaran en este asunto.

Mrs. Osuna, anxious for assistance, begins to describe her legal problem in detail.

Miss Suárez: Bueno, señora. Lo que Ud. dice es cierto. En nuestra oficina se trabaja muy a menudo con abogados y agentes del Uruguay. Sin embargo, no podemos dar consejos legales por teléfono, y, en todo caso, como no soy abogada, no soy yo la que da los consejos. ¿Desea Ud. concertar una cita con uno de nuestros abogados?

Miss Suárez's answer contains three important elements:

(1) A confirmation that the law office does indeed deal frequently with attorneys and agents in Uruguay. Mrs. Osuna can feel confident that she has come to the right place.

(2) A clarification that legal advice is not given over the telephone. If this is stated tactfully, a caller who is not yet a client of the law office should realize that the proper place for a full discussion of legal problems is during an interview at the office, and *not* over the telephone.

(3) An affirmation that the attorney, and not the interpreter is the proper person to render legal advice. This kind of initial statement may avoid the all-too-frequent problem of clients who incorrectly ask legal questions or attempt to confide in an interpreter regarding matters which are really the province of the attorney. The limitations of the role of the interpreter have been clearly and properly established at an early point in the relationship.

Mrs. Osuna: Sí, pero quisiera concertarla para cuando Ud. esté allí, porque no vale nada que yo acuda a una cita, si no hay nadie que me entienda.

The interpreter could have anticipated this question by initially telling Mrs. Osuna that her interview would be arranged when a interpreter could be present.

Miss Suárez: Por supuesto. Le arreglaré su visita. Espere un momento mientras yo averigüo cuando uno de los abogados dispone de una hora para la entrevista.

Miss Suárez to Miss Brook: (While Mrs. Osuna waits on the telephone.) This lady would like to see one of the attorneys. When is the next opening for an interview with a new client?

Miss Brooks to Miss Suárez: Next Wednesday at 3 P.M.

In contrast to the receptionist at the beginning of the conversation, the interpreter Miss Suárez has clearly explained to Mrs. Osuna why she has to wait on the phone during the arrangement of her appointment.

Miss Suárez: (Once again speaking to Mrs. Osuna over the telephone.) ¿Le convendría venir el miércoles que viene a las dos de la tarde? La cita con el abogado será a las tres, pero necesitamos una hora antes para tomar los datos esenciales.

Mrs. Osuna: Muy bien. La hora me es muy conveniente.

The client understands, from the very beginning, that she will not see the attorney until 3 P.M., although she is being asked to arrive at 2 P.M. in order to provide necessary information. It is this kind of clear and precise explanation which fosters client trust and confidence, thereby overcoming initial language barriers.

It should be noted that *no* verbatim interpreting took place in the prior telephone conversation. The use of the third person and summary interpreting will be found much more frequently in a telephone conversation than during an in-person interview.

THE FOLLOW-UP TELEPHONE CALL

The follow-up telephone call is an important type of phone conversation. In a follow-up telephone conversation, further information may be conveyed to or requested from the client. In the initial telephone conversation, where the parties did not know each other, it would not be proper to discuss or render legal advice. In contrast, the follow-up telephone conversation frequently involves the discussion of subjects pertaining to legal advice. Still, the rule remains that *no one other than the attorney may give legal advice.* There is also more likelihood that three persons will participate in this type of telephone conversation: a non-Spanish-speaking attorney, a Spanish-speaking client, and an interpreter.

The following example illustrates a follow-up telephone conversation in which the non-Spanish-speaking attorney, Anne Greer, is seeking further information from her Spanish-speaking client, Isabel Vallejo, regarding Mrs. Vallejo's pending divorce action. Julio Alegría, a bilingual paralegal employed by the law office, serves as interpreter during the telephone conversation. The set-up of the conversation will look something like the following diagram:

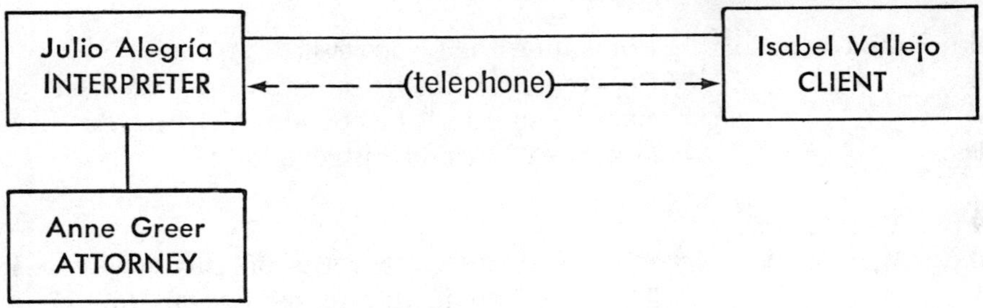

Julio Alegría: (Speaking on the telephone with Mrs. Isabel Vallejo.) Buenos días, señora Vallejo. Llamo de parte de su abogada, Anne Greer. La señora Greer desea hacerle algunas preguntas más con respecto a su divorcio. Puesto que, como Ud. sabe, ella no habla español, ella me comunicará las preguntas, y yo se las voy a traducir al español.

Isabel Vallejo: Muy bien. ¿Qué es lo que desea preguntarme?

(Julio nods to Anne Greer indicating that Mrs. Vallejo is ready for the first question.)

Anne Greer to Julio Alegría: Ask Mrs. Vallejo if she knows where her husband is living at the present time.

Julio Alegría: La señora Greer quiere saber si Ud. tiene idea de dónde vive su esposo actualmente.

Isabel Vallejo: Bueno, mi hermano dice que un amigo de Alfredo dice que vive en la calle Hamilton, número 56, en el segundo piso.

Julio Alegría to Anne Greer: She said: "Well, my brother says that a friend of Alfred's says that he lives at 56 Hamilton Street, second floor."

Anne Greer to Julio Alegría: Is he living alone or with someone else?

Julio Alegría: ¿Él vive solo o con alguien?

Isabel Vallejo: Vive con una muchacha que él conoció en el trabajo. Ella está divorciada y tiene dos hijos.

Julio Alegría to Anne Greer: He is living with a girl he met at work. She is divorced and has two children.

Anne Greer to Julio Alegría: Is he working now?

Julio Alegría: ¿Está trabajando ahora?

Isabel Vallejo: No, le dieron el "lay off" hace dos meses, pero yo creo que está cobrando.

Julio Alegría to Anne Greer: No, he was laid off two months ago but he's collecting. Anne, I think that she means he's collecting unemployment. I'll ask her for a clarification.

Julio Alegría: Cuando Ud. dice que su esposo "está cobrando", ¿se está refiriendo a los derechos de desempleo?

Isabel Vallejo: Sí, sí, eso mismo.

(The conversation proceeds in a like manner as the attorney, Anne Greer, elicits further information through the interpreter.)

Anne Greer to Julio Alegría: O.K. That's all I need right now. I'll get back to her sometime early next week.

Julio Alegría: Bueno, eso es todo por hoy. La señora Greer se pondrá en contacto con Ud. al comienzo de la semana que viene. Adiós, hasta luego.

Isabel Vallejo: Adiós, y muchas gracias.

While the initial telephone conversation, discussed earlier in this chapter, represents a "Hybrid Informal Interpreting Situation", the telephone conversation presented above describes a typical "Informal Interpreting Situation". It was the interpreter's role to convey everything that was said by both client and attorney.

As in an in-person interview situation, the interpreter was careful to explain to the attorney why he needed a clarification of the word "cobrando". This prevented the attorney from thinking that some sort of cross-conversation was going on between the client and the interpreter. Such a thought certainly seems logical if we bear in mind that the client and the interpreter are speaking in Spanish, a language which the attorney does not understand. Similarly, discussion between the attorney and the interpreter in English should be explained to the Spanish-speaking client, lest she believe that they are talking about her in English and do not want her to know what they are saying.

Note that, when speaking to Mrs. Vallejo, the interpreter used the third person ("she") in referring to Anne Greer. It would have been confusing and counter-productive for the interpreter to try to use the first person over the telephone. The concept of the interpreter as the mirror image of the speaker simply does not apply to telephone conversations. Note also that, when relaying information to Anne Greer, the interpreter at times repeated verbatim what Mrs. Vallejo had said, preceding the statement with the phrase "she said". This kind of introductory statement is rarely necessary to clarify statements during an in-person interview. In fact, it detracts from the image of the interpreter as the mirror image of the speaker. The interpreting skills particularly relevant to in-person interviews are presented in the following chapter.

EXERCISE 2

Indicate whether each of the topics listed in the left-hand column is a proper subject for an initial and/or a follow-up telephone conversation.

	INITIAL CONVERSATION	FOLLOW-UP CONVERSATION
1. INFORMATION REGARDING A SPOUSE IN A DIVORCE ACTION		
2. WHETHER THE AGENCY CALLED IS THE CORRECT ONE TO DEAL WITH A CERTAIN PROBLEM		
3. NAME AND ADDRESS OF CALLER		
4. INFORMATION REGARDING AN INJURY IN A WORKER'S COMPENSATION ACTION		
5. ADVICE ON WHETHER TO SUE SOMEONE		

CHAPTER 5

INFORMAL INTERPRETING SITUATIONS
THE INTERVIEW

THE INITIAL INTERVIEW

While the initial contact with clients is often made through a telephone conversation, with some vital information recorded at that time, it is during the actual face-to-face interview process that the client is given the opportunity to fully explain the problem at hand. The client must understand and be able to be understood, in order to be able to explain the problem which caused the need for legal assistance.

Just as in the case of telephone conversations, legal personnel in the in-person interview situation must make every effort to create an atmosphere which fosters trust and confidence.

Frequently a client brings along a friend, a relative, or a child to serve as interpreter. It may be felt that a friend or family member will be better acquainted with the problem at hand, and thus more capable of serving as interpreter. It is not possible for the client who cannot understand both English and Spanish to objectively judge the interpreting skills of a sympathetic friend or family member. Accurate interpreting may be affected by the very fact that the interpreter *is* a sympathetic friend or family member. If the interpreter brought along by the client is a child, there is another possible problem. While a child may possess bilingual ability to cope with everyday matters, a client's particular problem may be of a complex nature which is beyond the child's interpreting competency. IT IS UP TO THE BILINGUAL PERSONNEL AT A PARTICULAR OFFICE OR AGENCY TO DEMOSTRATE TO THE CLIENT THAT HE OR SHE CAN HAVE CONFIDENCE IN THE AGENCY AND ITS STAFF. This includes confidence in the ability of bilingual legal personnel to accurately facilitate communication between the Spanish-speaking client and non-Spanish-speaking legal personnel.

It is often helpful to explain to the client the importance of accurate, impartial interpreting. The staff should explain that, in order for the attorney to properly assess the client's problem, it would be best for the client to explain his or her problem *directly* to the bilingual legal personnel at the agency. While friends or relatives certainly have the best of intentions, they may, in their desire to help, unintentionally add or delete information that may have a bearing upon the case at a later date. Since the client cannot speak both Spanish and English, these additions or deletions of information may be very difficult to correct subsequently. The client will be more receptive to these explanations if bilingual legal personnel have made every effort to give the client a positive impression from the very begining of his or her visit to the law office or legal aid agency.

A related difficulty may be termed the "some English" problem. A client may give the impression of knowing more English than he or she actually comprehends or can verbalize. The client should be asked, as tactfully as possible, if he or she feels that it would be easier to express certain thoughts with the assistance of an interpreter. Wherever possible, bilingual legal personnel should be present to assess the extent of the client's language difficulties. Non-Spanish-speaking personnel should be made aware that the fact that a client understands the question

"Do you understand English?" means that the client understands just those four words. This should *not* be mistaken for a more generalized knowledge of English. In some instances, the interpreter may serve a supplemental role, assisting the client only when the client has difficulty in expressing certain concepts in English.

If the attorney or other professional who is interviewing a Spanish-speaking client knows "some Spanish", the interpreter may have to render similar assistance in supplementing that person's knowledge of Spanish. As was mentioned in the chapter dealing with telephone conversations, non-Spanish-speaking professionals should be encouraged to learn as much Spanish as possible, in order to make a Spanish-speaking client feel at home. However, like the client who may overestimate his or her own knowledge of English, the attorney may overestimate his or her own knowledge of Spanish. The interpreter must tactfully and diplomatically aid other legal personnel when there are gaps in their knowledge of Spanish.

THE INTERVIEW: NON-LINGUISTIC CONSIDERATIONS

A technical problem, not strictly within the scope of the interpreter's duties is the scheduling of client appointments. Optimally, when a client has been given an appointment for a scheduled time, the client should be seen at that time. In the legal environment, last minute unscheduled court appearances by the attorney, emergency client problems, clients who come for an initial visit perhaps without making an appointment, and many other unforeseen occurrences all contribute to delays. Therefore, realistically, clients will frequently not be seen on time. When a delay does occur, the client should be informed *as soon as possible* of the length of the delay and, where possible and appropriate, given a brief explanation of why there has been a longer wait than anticipated.

A client may, for example, have other business commitments, and the fact that an appointment cannot be kept for the hour originally indicated may necessitate changing the appointment to another date. It is unfair to keep a client waiting without an explanation. A client with young children at home, may have had to schedule babysitters, and a delay may cause inconvenience and also additional expense.

A client who is left waiting may begin to feel that he or she is really not receiving first-rate service from a given office or agency. There may even be a suspicion, however irrational or unjustified, that there is some prejudice because the client does not speak English. Recall from the dialogue in Chapter 4, Telephone Conversations, how the bilingual employee explained to the potential client, over the telephone, that her appointment with the attorney was scheduled for 3 P.M., but that she should come at 2 P.M. so that necessary information could be written down. A brief explanation such as this one goes a long way toward cultivating a feeling of trust and confidence on the part of the client.

In learning the skills of Cultural Fluency, it was emphasized that stereotypes and preconceived cultural notions should never be allowed to interfere with a perception of the unique situation of an actual client. For example, *"machismo"* may be important in the typical Hispanic family, and may or may not apply to the family of the client. In either case, it may not be relevant to the problem at hand. While such cultural generalizations should be kept in mind for purposes of general cultural background, each client must be viewed *as an individual.* Similarly, it should be borne in mind that among the twenty-one Spanish-speaking countries, there are differences in traditions, values, cultures, and linguistic characteristics. Sense of humor, sense of time, etc., differ from culture to culture as well as from individual to individual.

Many external elements which affect the interview process are definitely beyond the control of legal personnel. Heavy case loads, insufficient staff —in particular insufficient bilingual staff— or budgetary considerations often create less than optimal conditions. Because bilingual legal personnel may not have it within their ability or power to improve such conditions, it becomes all the more important to strive constantly to improve the human relationships which are within their power to improve. Bilingual legal personnel are of extreme importance because they are often the only practical link betwen the legal system and a client who does not speak English.

Gaining the confidence of the client and learning the pertinent facts of the case which are necessary for the law firm or legal aid agency to serve as the client's representatives are part of a slow and deliberate process. A client may be self-conscious of the need to explain his or her problem to a non-Hispanic attorney or other professional. The skills learned in the *Cultural Fluency* part of the text come into play here. There may be an instinctive feeling on the part of the client that someone is passing judgment on his or her actions. A client may have a generalized skepticism toward the legal system.

Interpreters may alleviate these concerns, but *the common language between client and interpreter should never interfere with the interpreter's professionalism.* The client must be made aware of the limitations of the interpreter's role, especially that the interpreter cannot give legal advice. Through a sincere, concerned, yet *always* objective attitude, the interpreter can do a great deal to improve the effectiveness and efficiency of the process of helping the client.

DYNAMICS OF IN-PERSON INTERVIEW INTERPRETING SITUATIONS

As in the case of telephone conversations, in-person interview siutations may be either "Informal Interpreting Situations" or "Hybrid Informal Interpreting Situations".

When a client first visits a law office or legal aid agency, the first interview is generally a "Hybrid Informal Interpreting Situation". When the client arrives, a bilingual intake worker, receptionist, or paralegal will generally take down basic information. The interviewer combines translating and interpreting skills, conducting the interview itself completely in Spanish, and usually writing down the basic imformation in English, so that non-Spanish-speaking personnel can understand what is written. Verbatim oral interpreting is not generally involved in this first interview.

Following this interview, there is usually a second interview with an attorney or other professional. If the professional is bilingual, then this interview will again be conducted in Spanish. As in the prior hybrid informal situation, the information will be recorded in English for the benefit of non-Spanish-speaking personnel.

If the attorney or other professional is not Spanish-speaking, then the dynamics of the second interview correspond to the "Informal Interpreting Situation". Three persons are present: the client, the interpreter, and the attorney. In contrast to telephone conversations, here it *is* appropriate for the interpreter to act as the mirror image of the speaker. Rather than to preface a sentence with "he said" or "she said", the interpreter *should* speak in the first person ("I"), acting as a conduit for the speaker's words and ideas. In this way, the dialogue despite the fact that attorney and client speak different languages.

Depending upon the information required, follow-up interviews will repeat the pattern of either the informal interpreting situation or the hybrid informal situation.

THE OTHER SIDE OF THE COIN:

TECHNIQUES FOR NON-SPANISH-SPEAKING PERSONNEL WHO WORK WITH INTERPRETERS

The interpreter can make his or her own job much easier by discussing with non-Spanish-speaking personnel some of the techniques for working with an interpreter. All personnel should, for example, be aware that the interpreter's function is to express what the speaker is saying through the use of the closest possible equivalents from one language to another. The interpreter transmits questions as posed. For example, if the attorney says "When did you begin to receive Social Security?", the interpreter should repeat the question in the second person "you". Non-Spanish-speaking personnel should pose questions as though speaking directly to the client. What should *not* be said is "Ask him when he started to receive Social Security". This converts the interpreter rather than the attorney and client into the focal point of the conversation. Similarly, if the client answers "Empecé a recibir el Seguro Social el año pasado", then the interpreter should say "I began to receive Social Security last year". The interpreter should *not* say "He said that he began to receive Social Security last year." The conversation thus remains, a direct dialogue between attorney and client.

Initially, the interpreter may have to become accustomed to the dialect, accent, and idiomatic expressions of the client. Non-Spanish-speaking personnel should be aware that, despite the presence of a common language, there is a great diversity of speech and language patterns among the many Spanish-speaking countries. Client and interpreter must become accustomed to each other's speech. In order to do so, they may, for example, exchange a few initial words, such as greetings. The interpreter may also explain the interview process to the client. These few initial sentences should not be understood by anyone as a license for interpreter and client to engage in idle conversation unrelated to the legal problem or to otherwise consult "aside" with the interpreter. In this regard, recall the advice to the interpreter to try to leave the room if the attorney does so, or, if the interpreter must stay, to inform the client that everything said must later be translated for the attorney.

Both client and attorney should be aware that *all* words will be translated. Thus, the client cannot ask a question of the interpreter and expect that it will not be translated, and the attorney should not say anything about the client which is not to be translated. There are no "off-the-record" comments.

Clients may use gestures to express thoughts. The interpreter should always attempt to communicate the meaning and importance of gestures to the non-Spanish-speaking professional. For example, if a Spanish-speaking person from certain countries brings the thumb to the lips it means "Por ésta, la cruz", the person, in other words, is swearing to the truth of what he or she is saying. The importance of such non-verbal communication must be emphasized. THE INTERPRETER SHOULD *EXPLAIN, NOT IMITATE, THESE GESTURES*, since they may have different meanings in different languages or cultures.

Non-Spanish-speaking personnel should be asked to try to avoid the use of idiomatic expressions when working with an interpreter. Such expressions cause unnecessary delays, since they usually have a nonsensical or inappropriate meaning when translated literally and extra time is required for the interpreter to find the corresponding expression in Spanish. As a rule of thumb, questions in the source language should be phrased in as simple and straightforward a manner as possible.

The non-Spanish-speaking professional should be aware that *all expressions* will be conveyed to the listener at a level and tone which correspond to that used by the speaker in the source language. Foul or vulgar language, pejorative remarks, etc., will all be translated as such. It is not the role of the interpreter to change the choice of vocabulary of the speaker.

Non-Spanish-speaking personnel should become familiar with the three modes of interpreting. The interpreter should explain that consecutive verbatim will be used under most circumstances. The attorney should be aware of the limited circumstances when summary interpreting may be used. It should be made clear that the interpreter's role is not to edit what *is* said by either the attorney or the client. It is up to the two parties conversing, not the interpreter to decide upon the relative importance of what is being said.

Hand signals should be arranged between the interpreter, client, and attorney. For example, the interpreter may want to signal a speaker to stop if a sentence is too long to be relayed at once. Also, the speaker should attempt to pause at the end of long clauses or thoughts, to give the interpreter the opportunity to convey the message. The interpreter should explain to the non-Spanish-speaking party that he or she is not conveying a word for word translation, but rather an idea by idea rendering, taking the words in context.

It takes practice for a non-Spanish-speaking person to learn the techniques of working with an interpreter. While some of the points mentioned here can be conveyed to a client, it is essentially the non-Spanish-speaking professional who should consciously develop these skills. Since a client already comes to the law office with one problem, a legal problem, the staff should do everything possible to alleviate the language problem. If attorney and interpreter can effectively work together, the best possible dialogue can be carried out with the client.

INTERVIEW SITUATIONS: SOME EXAMPLES

The remainder of this chapter is devoted to dealing with frequently-encountered types of situations in the legal environment, where interpreters may be called for: (A) Domestic Relations; (B) Landlord /Tenant; (C) Criminal Law; (D) Change of Name; (E) Welfare Assistance and (F) Immigration. Varied and different kinds of practice are provided for the student in the different situations: questionnaires, sample interviews and dialogues, exercises, etc.

SITUATION A: DOMESTIC RELATIONS — DIVORCE INTERVIEW

The Divorce Questionnaire Form utilized by Essex-Newark Legal Services of New Jersey is found, in English and Spanish, on the next four pages of the text. This questionnaire contains typical questions asked of an individual seeking a divorce. Bilingual legal personnel working at a law office or legal aid agency where separation or divorce cases are handled should become familiar with questions such as these.

The Divorce Waiver Form, in English and Spanish, follows the questionnaire. This is a form which all clients of Essex-Newark Legal Services must sign, once the case is accepted by Legal Services. Since the client may be giving up property rights by signing the form, it is important that the client *understand* the precise meaning of what he or she is signing. Similar forms are utilized by many law offices and legal aid agencies.

Following the sample forms, the divorce interview analyzed in the *Cultural Fluency* part of the text is reproduced. In an exercise, you are asked to analyze this interview for strong and weak points in interpreting skills, and then to compare your analysis with the commentary included after the exercise.

DIVORCE QUESTIONNAIRE FORM

BASIC INFORMATION

1. Date .... Interviewer's Full Name ....

2. Client's Full Name ....
(Print) Ask Client for Spelling!

3. Address ....Newark.................................
Number Street Apt. Zip Code

4. Phone (a) .... (b) .... (c) Ms. Mr. ....
home work neighbor or local relative

5. List client's addresses for past year with dates, current address first.

Full Address	**From**	**To**
....	....	....
....	....	....

6. Spouse's Full Name ....
(Print) Ask client for spelling!

7. Spouse's Present Address ....
Number Street Apt. City State Zip

8. Spouse's age ...., Height ...., Weight ...., ..., ...,
Skin color Hair color
Social Security Number (If known) ....
Present ( ) or last known ( ) occupation ....
Full name and address of employer ....
....

9. If client is not sure of spouse's present address, ask client for names and address of each of these: all spouse's relatives, friends, business associates, employers or employees who might know. (Use separate sheet).

10. Ask client for marriage certificate. Check here ( ) when you obtain it. If client does not have certificate, ask client for date .... and place ....
..................................of marriage.

Note: Ascertain from N.J. Lawyer's Diary (p. 178 of 1977 ed.) the Vital Statistics Source for certificate, and have client prepare check or money order for the amount and payable as indicated. Then you must obtain the certificate.

11. A. Has client been married before? .... To whom? ....
B. Has spouse ever been married before? .... To whom? ....
C. How was previous marriage terminated?
Divorce ( ) Annulment ( ) Death ( )
Ask client for the divorce judgment or death certificate. If client does not have same, follow same procedure as for marriage certificate.

CUESTIONARIO PARA DIVORCIO

INFORMACIÓN BÁSICA

1. Fecha .... Nombre completo del entrevistador ....
2. Nombre completo del cliente ....
(En letra de molde) ¡Pídale al cliente que lo deletree!
3. Dirección .... Newark ....
Número Calle Apto. Zip Code
4. Teléfono (a) .... (b) .... (c) ....
casa trabajo vecino o pariente
5. Anote las direcciones donde el cliente vivía durante el año pasado con fechas, la dirección actual primero.

Dirección completa	**Desde**	**Hasta**
....	....	....
....	....	....

6. Nombre completo de esposo(o)(a) ....
(En letra de molde) ¡Pídale al cliente que lo deletree!
7. Dirección actual ....
de espos(o)(a) Número Calle Apto. Ciudad Estado Zona Postal
8. Edad de espos(o)(a) ...., Estatura ...., Peso ....,
Color de la piel
....
Color del pelo

No. de Seguro Social (Si lo sabe) ....

Actual ( ) o última conocida ( ) ocupación ....

Nombre completo y dirección de la persona que lo emplea ....

....

9. Si el cliente no está seguro de la dirección actual de(l) (la) eposo(o)(a), pídale al cliente los nombres y las direcciones de cada uno de los siguientes: todos los parientes, amigos, asociados en negocios, y patrones o empleados de(l) (la) espos(o)(a) que sepan la dirección. (Use hoja separada).
10. Pídale al cliente el certificado de matrimonio. Indique aquí ( ) cuando lo obtenga. Si el cliente no tiene el certificado, pregúntele la fecha .... y ....el lugar del matrimonio.

Nota: Averigüe por medio del Diario del abogado de New Jersey (p. 178 de la ed. de 1977) la fuente de Estadísticas Vitales para el certificado y haga que el cliente prepare un cheque o giro bancario por la cantidad debida y pagadero como se indique. Después usted debe obtener el certificado de matrimonio.

11. A. ¿Ha estado casado anteriorment el cliente? .... ¿Con quién? ....

    B. ¿Ha estado casado anteriormente (el) (la) espos(o)(a)? .... ¿Con quién? ....

    C. ¿Cómo se terminó el matrimonio anterior?

    Divorcio ( ) Anulación del matrimonio ( ) Defunción ( )

    Pídale al cliente el certificado de divorcio o de defunción. Si el cliente no lo tiene, siga el mismo procedimiento utilizado para obtener el certificado de matrimonio.

12. Children born to the parties or adopted* by the parties;

Name	Date of Birth	Lives with whom?
....	....	....
....	....	....
....	....	....
....	....	....

* If any of the children were adopted either by both parties or by one spouse adopting the child of the other spouse, obtain the judgment of adoption.

13. Does client have any other children? .... If so get name of child, date of birth, and name of other parent. (Use separate sheet.)

14. Were there previous court actions between the parties? ....
If so, check nature of court action(s).

Support ( ) Divorce ( ) Annulment ( ) Separate maintenance ( )

Custody or visitation ( )

If so, list name of court, docket number, date of trial, judgment or decision. Obtain copies of any papers from previous action(s) which client may have.

....

....

....

GROUNDS FOR DIVORCE

SEPARATION

15. On what date did parties separate? ....

16. Since date of separation have parties resumed living together? ....
If so, when, for how long, and what were the reasons? (Use separate sheet.)

VENUE

If date of separation was later than March 13, 1970, answer question 17.
If it was earlier than March 13, 1970 answer question 18.

17. Where did parties live at the end of 18 months from the date of separation?

Client ....
Number Street City County State

Spouse ....
Number Street City County State

18. Where did parties live on September 13, 1971?

Client ....
Number Street City County State

Spouse ....
Number Street City County State

12. Hijos nacidos de, o adoptados* por los cónyugues:

Nombre	Fecha de nacimiento	¿Vive con quién?

* Si alguno de los hijos fue adoptado por ambos cónyugues o si uno de los cónyugues adoptó al hijo del otro cónyugue, obtenga la decisión de adopción.

13. ¿Tiene otros hijos el cliente? ....Si los tiene, pídale el nombre, la fecha de nacimiento y el nombre del otro padre. (Use una hoja separada.)

14. ¿Hubo acciones jurídicas anteriores entre los cónyugues?........................... Si las hubo indique la clase de acción(es) jurídica(s).

Mantenimiento ( ) Divorcio ( ) Anulación ( ) Manutención aparte ( )

Custodia o derecho de visita ( )

Si hubo alguna acción, anote el nombre del tribunal, número del caso, fecha del juicio, sentencia o decisión. Obtenga copias de cualquier papel de la(s) acción(es) previa(s) que el cliente pueda poseer.

....

....

....

CAUSAS DEL DIVORCIO

SEPARACIÓN

15. ¿En qué fecha se separaron los cónyuges? ....

16. Desde la fecha de separación ¿han vuelto a convivir los cónyugues? .... Si así fuera, ¿cuándo, por cuánto tiempo, y cuáles fueron las razones? (Use una hoja separada.)

JURISDICCIÓN

Si la fecha de separación fue después del 13 de marzo de 1970, conteste la pregunta 17. Si fue antes del 13 de marzo de 1970, conteste la pregunta 18 de su separación?

17. ¿Dónde vivieron los cónyuges al cabo de 18 meses a partir de la fecha de su separación?

Cliente ....

Número Calle Ciudad Condado Estado

Cónyugue ....

Número Calle Ciudad Condado Estado

18. ¿Dónde vivían los cónyugues el 13 de septiembre de 1971?

Cliente ....

Número Calle Ciudad Condado Estado

Cónyugue ....

Número Calle Ciudad Condado Estado

DIVORCE WAIVER FORM

I, , hereby state:

I have retained the attorneys of Essex-Newark Legal Services to file a law suit or counter-law suit to try to obtain a divorce for me. I understand that a court may award me any or even all of the five additional items listed below if I ask for such item(s) in my law suit and if I can prove in court that I have a legal right to such item(s). In addition to a divorce I authorize my attorney to seek each of the checked items below and understand that any items *not* checked will *not* be asked for from the court.

I understand that by *not* asking for certain of the items I am waiving my rights and that this might prevent me from getting the items *not* checked in the future as well as the present.

( ) Alimony (money from my spouse for my own suport)

( ) Child Support (money from my spouse for our children's support)

( ) Custody and/or Visitation (the right to have my children live with me or the right to have them visit me)

( ) Equitable Distribution (having the Court divide the property owned by myself and my spouse between us)

( ) Resumption of former name (the right to use the name I had before I got married)

DATED: ....

FORMA DE RENUNCIA (de ciertos derechos) EN EL DIVORCIO

Yo, , por la presente declaro:

He contratado a los abogados de Servicios Legales de Essex-Newark para entablar una demanda o contrademanda para que traten de obtener mi divorcio. Entiendo que el tribunal me puede adjudicar cualquiera y hasta todas de las cinco opciones mencionadas abajo, si solicito dicha(s) opción(es), y si puedo demostrar ante el tribunal que tengo el derecho legal a dicha(s) opción(es). Además del divorcio, autorizo a mi abogado para que solicite cada una de las opciones indicadas abajo y entiendo que cualquier opción *no* indicada, *no* se le solicitará al tribunal.

Entiendo que, al *no* solicitar alguna opción, renuncio mis derechos y que esto me impediría conseguir las opciones *no* indicadas tanto en el futuro como en el presente.

( ) Pensión alimenticia (dinero de mi esposo(o)(a) para mi propio sostén)

( ) Mantenimiento de hijos (dinero de mi espos(o)(a) para el sostén de nuestros hijos)

( ) Custodia y/o visitas (el derecho a que mis hijos vivan conmigo o el derecho a que me visiten)

( ) Distribución equitativa (que el tribunal divida entre nosotros los bienes poseídos por mi espos(o)(a) y por mí)

( ) Reasunción del apellido anterior (el derecho a usar el apellido que tenía antes de casarme)

FECHADA: ....

DIVORCE INTERVIEW

(Attorney Leonard Benson is seated at his desk, working. He is casually dressed in slacks and a plaid shirt — no tie or jacket. A Hispanic woman client, Marta Fernández, is led into the room by the intake worker, another member of the staff. This intake worker has already asked many questions of the client, and has noted much basic information on an "Intake Sheet" in order to determine that the client is in fact eligible for legal services. The attorney looks up briefly, smiles, but does not further acknowledge the presence of the client when she comes in.)

INTAKE WORKER: (Addressing the client as he indicates the attorney.) This is the person who takes care of divorce cases. (He puts the folder containing the Intake Sheet on the desk and leaves.)

ATTORNEY: Thanks, Frank. (Not looking up.) Be with you in a minute. (Keeps working. Finally looks up. Speaks courteously.) Just a few more things to get out of the way . . . Okay Mrs. . . . (Looking at Intake Sheet in folder. Baffled, he ask:) *What* is your last name?

CLIENT: (Speech is heavily accented.) My last name is Suero Sánchez de Fernández.

ATTORNEY: Sorry, but I can't make head or tail of this. Your *real* last name.

CLIENT: (Looking at him quizzically.) My last name is Suero Sánchez de Fernández.

ATTORNEY: Well, it must be Fernández. (Pronounces name with English accent.)

CLIENT: Sí . . . yes. (Her tone indicating that she is willing to agree to this pronunciation to get on with the matter. Imitating English accent:) Fernández.

ATTORNEY: (Looking at her directly). Okay, now, you want a divorce.

CLIENT: Yes. (Looks at hands on lap.)

ATTORNEY: Do you speak English?

CLIENT: Yes, a little.

ATTORNEY: Well, that's a help. (Continues to look at client directly. Client does not look up but tries to listen intently to each word. Attorney looks over the Intake Sheet, sits back, then stretches a bit. Talking to no one in particular:) This should be pretty cut and dried.

CLIENT: I don't understand. "Cut?" . . . "Dried?"

ATTORNEY: Oh . . . nothing. Just let me read this over a bit more. (Reads for a few more seconds then looks directly at client again.) Okay, please tell me specifically, in your own words, why you want a divorce. What's the problem? What's up?

CLIENT: (Looks up briefly). What you say? (Looks down again.)

ATTORNEY: (Patiently) I don't mean to be rude or anything, but I've got a lot to take care of. Please answer the questions directly.

CLIENT: (She is trying very hard to understand.) Yes.

ATTORNEY: (His voice begins to get louder) You've got to do your part in order to help.

CLIENT: (Looks up briefly, then down again.) Help? Yes. I want help.

ATTORNEY: Great. I can see we're going to be here all day. (Sighs in attempted resignation.)

CLIENT: You no can help?

ATTORNEY: (Trying to "make the best of things") Yeah, sure, I yes can help. (Laughs lightly, trying to be humorous, yet he shakes his head.) Let's see . . . Question number one (Reading from a questionnaire, louder.) "Where do you reside?"

CLIENT: (Having trouble pronouncing.) I just want a divorce. My husband leave. (Obviously upset.)

ATTORNEY: (Calmly) Well, I can see I'm not doing very well. (Calls out.) Ana. (Both wait a while in silence.)

INTERPRETER: (Ana enters.) Yes Lenny. What is it? (Smiles at client.)

ATTORNEY: This woman doesn't speak English.

CLIENT: (Raises her voice, visibly perturbed.) Yes, I speak English.

ATTORNEY: (A bit louder still but in a conciliatory tone.) Yes, Mrs. Fernández, you speak English, but we need some help.

INTERPRETER: (Addressing client.) Tienes que hacer lo que diga el abogado.

CLIENT: (Indignant and despairing.) Bueno, sea como sea, lo que yo quiero es mi divorcio. Hace más de una hora que estoy aquí esperando, y ¿para qué? ¿para que me digan que no hablo inglés?

INTERPRETER: No es para tanto. Cálmate.

ATTORNEY: Come on Ana, let's get going. Ask her where she lives.

INTERPRETER: El quiere saber dónde vives.

CLIENT: ¿Él es el abogado? Ya he hablado con otra persona en esta oficina.

INTERPRETER: Sí, y quiere saber dónde vives.

CLIENT: (Disheartened) Ahí en la calle Grant.

INTERPRETER: ¿Qué número?

CLIENT: Quinientos sesenta.

INTERPRETER: She says she lives at 15-60 Grant.

ATTORNEY: Wait a minute. It says here 560 . . .

INTERPRETER: Yeah, that's what I said.

ATTORNEY: (Disregards comment. Continues normal line of questioning until he reaches one of the final questions.) Ask her whether there is any possibility of reconciliation.

INTERPRETER: ¿Te vas a juntar con tu marido?

CLIENT: (Completely taken aback.) ¿Qué? . . . ¿Qué? (Thinks a moment and then replies almost in a whisper.) No. (Shakes her head dejectedly) Mi esposo se fue hace tiempo y no me ha mandado ni un centavo.

(The interpreter continues to interpret the attorney's questions in the same manner until the interview is completed.)

EXERCISE A

Reread the preceding dialogue carefully. As you read, note the presence and/or absence of the interpreting skills which have been studied. List your observations in the chart which follows, according to the line number of the dialogue (Column A); the skill which is present or absent (Column B); possible explanations (Column C). Compare your analysis with the commentary which follows.

(A) LINE NUMBER	(B) INTERPRETING SKILL (PRESENCE OR ABSENCE)	(C) POSSIBLE EXPLANATION

COMMENTARY

Line 9 — From the very begining of the interview, it would be helpful for the intake worker to determine whether the client speaks and/or understands English. In the case of "some English", it should be determined how much interpreter assistance the client is going to need. If the extent of interpretive needs is established early in the interview process, the client will most probably be more at ease for the entire interview. In this case, the fact that the intake worker has already interviewed Mrs. Fernández should make it much easier to establish interpretive needs before the client is sent to talk with Mr. Benson, the attorney.

Line 21 — The problem arising from the confusion over the client's last name is both a cultural and a language difficulty. The problem will become more serious as the divorce proceedings progress, since the client's and spouse's last names must be precisely established. This is an example of a misunderstanding which an interpreter, who is also aware of cultural differences, can help to resolve at the very beginning of the case.

Lines 31-69 — This entire part of the dialogue could have been avoided through the use of trained bilingual personnel from the start of the interview. A bilingual employee trained in interpreting could quickly assess the client's knowledge of English, and thus save the attorney valuable time by rendering appropriate assistance.

Line 46 — The words "cut" and "dried" illustrate the kind of idiomatic expressions which should be avoided in phrasing questions for a non-native speaker. These make no sense literally. It also requires time for the interpreter to explain and find equivalents in the target language, even if a trained interpreter is present. Here, the client's limited English obviously does not include a knowledge of such expressions.

Lines 60 and 61 — Here we see an illustration of another linguistic misunderstanding. This time, it is the word "help". The attorney asks the client to help —presumably by trying to understand him better— and the client assumes that he has finally recognized that what she wants is help.

Lines 85-86 — The interpreter, here, has incorrectly used *"tú"* rather than *"usted"* when addressing the client. The relationship between the attorney and client is a formal one. Since the interpreter's role is to serve as a conduit for the attorney's words, it would be incorrect for her to use the familiar *"tú"* when addressing the client.

Lines 90-92 — At no time during the interview should the interpreter and the client engage in conversation. This encourages the client to feel that he or she can confide in the interpreter in a manner which is impermissible.

Lines 102-103 — The confusion resulting from the incorrect translation of the client's address demonstrates the dangers which may arise from the careless interpreting of a seemingly innocuous phrase from one language to another. *Precision* is the key.

Lines 109-112 — Here the interpreter has improperly translated the attorney's question, using a phrase which horrifies the client. Remember that the tone, level, and choice of vocabulary of the speaker must all be preserved by the interpreter. In this case, the interpreter has failed on all counts.

Another important element to watch for is the tense. The interpreter must use the *tense* of the verb which corresponds to that used by the speaker. If Mrs. Fernández says of her husband: "Me golpeaba todos los días", the interpreter must be sure to translate this as "He used to hit me every day" or "He would hit me every day". *Past or present, imperfect or preterite, all tenses must be carefully and correctly translated.*

SITUATION B: LANDLORD/TENANT LAW — TENANT INTERVIEW

The Tenant Questionnaire Form utilized by Essex-Newark Legal Services of New Jersey is found, in English and Spanish, on the following pages of the text. This questionnaire includes questions relating to typical landlord/tenant problems. Following the questionnaire is found a Housing Repair List, in English and Spanish. This problem checklist, utilized by Essex-Newark Legal Services, contains specialized vocabulary which is very useful in conducting interviews on this subject. Bilingual legal personnel working at agencies or law offices where landlord/tenant cases are handled should become familiar with these questions and terminology.

Following the sample forms is found an example of a tenant interview at a private law office. In an exercise at the end of the interview you are asked to analyze the interview for strong and weak points in interpreting skills, and then to compare your analysis with the commentary included after the exercise.

TENANT QUESTIONNAIRE FORM

1. DATE .... Interviewer's *Full* Name ....

2. CLIENT'S FULL NAME ....
(PRINT) Ask client for spelling *even* if you know it!

.... Newark ....
Address Apt. # Zip Code

\# of rooms in apt. .... Floor .... PHONES (a) .... (b) ....
home work

When did client move in? ....
Does client wish to move? ....
Has client arranged to move? .... Ms. Mr. (c) ....
Neighbor or local relative
When and where ? ....
Who lives with you? ....

3. ...., ...
LANDLORD'S NAME Address

....................PHONES (a) .... (b) ....
City State Zip home work

4. BUILDINGS TYPE (A) House .... (B) Multi Apt. .... (C) Cooperative ....
\# of apts. # of apts.

(D) Condominium .... (E) Rooming/Boarding House ....(F) Hotel ....
Call Newark License Division (733-63000) to confirm (E) or (F).

5. SUPERINTENDENT .... Lives on Premises? ....
Name Phone

6. LEASE: Oral .... Written .... (Get copy!)

7a. RENT: Present $.................... /week /month Rent when client first moved in $.................... /week /month
Is rent unpaid now? .... (Amounts and periods) ....
How much money does client have now? $............... If short, what money can client raise by what date(s)? ....
What happened to missing money? ....
Client's reason for not paying? .... Rent due on: ....
How usually paid: (a) Cash .... (b) Personal check ....
(c) Money order .... (d) Receipts? ....
Kind-Bank, Postal, etc.

CUESTIONARIO PARA INQUILINOS

1. FECHA........................ Nombre completo del entrevistador..

2. NOMBRE COMPLETO DEL CLIENTE ....
(ESCRIBA EN LETRA DE MOLDE) Pida al cliente que deletree su nombre ¡inclusive si sabe como se escribe!

...., Newark ....
Dirección Apto. # Zona Postal

de habitaciones en el Apto. .... Piso............... TELÉFONO (a)........................ casa (b)..................... trabajo

¿Cuándo se mudó el cliente al apto. ?..................................... Srta.
¿Desea mudarse el cliente? .... Sra.
Sr.

¿Ha hecho arreglos el cliente para mudarse?.............. (c) ....

¿Cuándo y para dónde? .... Vecino o pariente más cercano

¿Quién(es) vive(n) con usted?..

3. ...., ...
NOMBRE DEL PROPIETARIO Dirección

....Teléfono (a) .... (b)........................
Ciudad Estado Zona Postal casa trabajo

4. TIPO DE EDIFICIO (A) Casa.................................... # de Aptos. (B Multi Apto.. # de Aptos.

(C) Cooperativa .... (D) Condominio...

(E) Pensión... (F) Hotel ....

Llame a Newark License Division (733-3900) para confirmar (E) o (F).

5. SUPERINTENDENTE .... ¿Vive en ese mismo local?....................................
Nombre Teléfono

6. CONTRATO DE ARRENDAMIENTO: Oral................. Escrito................. (¡Consiga copias!)

7a. RENTA (alquiler): Actual $........................ /semanal /mensual ¿Cuánto pagó el cliente cuando se mudó al Apto.: .... /semanal /mensual

¿Está la renta sin pagar ahora?............... (Cantidades y períodos de tiempo) ....

¿Con cuánto dinero cuenta el cliente ahora? $................................. Si no tiene lo suficiente

¿cuánto dinero puede conseguir y para qué fecha(s)? $..

¿Qué pasó con el dinero que le falta?...

¿Razón por la cual el cliente no pagó?..........................La renta se venció el.........................

¿Cómo suele pagar: (a) En efectivo (cash)................... (b) Cheque personal ....

(c) Giro .... (d) ¿Recibos? ....
Clase-Bancario, Postal, etc.

7b. VERY IMPORTANT! ADVICE CLIENT: Begin paying only by personal check or *BANK* money order. (Specifically state no post office, drug store, grocery store, etc., money order.) Write on front *lower left hand corner* of money order or personal check "Payment in full for rent for month of .... 198.........."

Complaint to Newark Rent Control? .... (Use new sheet)

Past rent increases:	Date(s)	Amount of increase	New rent	Written notice of increase?
(Most Recent) (1)				
(2)				
Etc.				

8. Did landlord give you a tax refund or rent reduction?......................... How much?................

Call Newark Rent Control (733-6361) and ask: A. Amount of property tax reduction (from tax collecter's statement) .... B. Has landlord filed statement that tenant was paid?..............; Amount $...................... Date...............................

9. SECURITY DEPOSIT: (NJSA 46:8-19) Total required $.............. Amount paid $................. Date of last payment .... Receipt(s)?............................ Paid to present landlord? .... Did client receive written notice of where S.D. is deposited?...................... Did client receive interest on S.D. *each* year? .... Did client ever apply it to rent? (When?) .... Has client lost security deposit given to a former landlord? ....

10. WRITTEN NOTICE STATING NAMES AND ADDRESSES OF OWNERS, WHOM TO CONTACT IN EMERGENCY, *ETC.* (N.J.S.A. 46:8-27 et seq.)

Copy given to client?...................... Copy posted in building?...

Copy filed with city (call 733-3835)? .... (a) ....
Owner's name

(b) ....
Emergency person's name, phone

11. Did landlord inform client about obtaining apartment insurance (N.J.S.A. 46:3-38)?............. (A) Has client's apt. been robbed or burglarized?................................. (B) Has client been robbed outside of home?...............Details-Use new sheet.

12. (A) Has client ever received papers to go to court against present landlord?...................... (B) Did client go to court?.......................... Results: Are any agreements or stipulations still in effect?.................. Details & copies. (Use separate sheet).

7b. ¡MUY IMPORTANTE! ADVIÉRTALE AL CLIENTE: Empiece a hacer los pagos únicamente con cheque personal o giro *BANCARIO.* (Infórmele explícitamente que no compre giros en la oficina de correos, en las farmacias, ni en las tiendas de comestibles, etc.) Escriba en la parte inferior a la izquierda del giro bancario y cheque personal: "Payment in full for rent for month of........................ 198.........."

¿Se ha quejado al Control de Rentas de Newark?................................(Use una nueva hoja)

Aumento anteriores de la renta:	Fecha(s)	Cantidad del aumento	Renta después del aumento	Aviso por escrito del aumento
	....	....	....	....
(El más reciente) (1)	....	....	....	....
(2)	....	....	....	....
Etc.	....	....	....	....

8. ¿Le dió el dueño una devolución de impuestos o le redujo la renta? ....
¿Cuánto? ....

Llame a la Oficina de Control de Rentas en Newark (733-6361) y pregunte:

A. Cantidad de rebaja por impuestos sobre bienes (del estado de cuenta del recaudador de impuestos)...............................

B. ¿Ha presentado el dueño una declaración de que se le pagó al inquilino?.........................
Cantidad $....................................... Fecha...

9. FIANZA ("Security") (N.J.S.A. 46:8-19) Cantidad requerida $..
Cantidad pagada $.......................................
Fecha del último pago... ¿Recibo(s)?...
¿Se pagó al propietario actual? ....
¿Ha sido notificado por escrito el cliente del lugar en donde se ha depositado su depósito?
....
¿Recibió el cliente los intereses de su depósito *cada* año? ....
¿Lo usó alguna vez como parte de la renta? (¿Cuándo?) ....
¿Ha perdido algún depósito entregado a un propietario anterior?...........................

10. UN AVISO POR ESCRITO QUE INDIQUE NOMBRES Y DIRECCIONES DE LOS PROPIETARIOS, A QUIEN SE LE PUEDE NOTIFICAR EN CASO DE EMERGENCIA, ETC. (N.J.S.A., 46:8-27 et seq.)

¿Se le ha dado copia al cliente?...
¿Se colocó copia en el edificio?...
¿Se archivó copia en las oficinas de la ciudad (733-3835)? ....

(a) ....(b) ....
Nombre del propietario — Nombre y teléfono de la persona responsable en caso de emergencia

11. ¿Le avisó el propietario al cliente acerca de la posibilidad de obtener un seguro para su apartamento (N.J.S.A. 46:3-38)?.................(A) ¿Han robado o escalado alguna vez en el apto. del cliente?.................... (B) ¿Le han robado al cliente fuera de su casa?.......................... Detalles (Use una nueva hoja).

12. (A) ¿Ha recibido alguna citación para comparecer ante el tribunal en contra del propietario actual?............... (B) ¿Acudió el cliente al tribunal? .... Resultados:
¿Sigue en vigor algún acuerdo o estipulación?............Detalles y copias. (Use una hoja separada).

13. Is client on bad terms with landlord, superintendent or neighbor(s)? ....
Details on separate sheet.

14. Is client member/organizer of tenant association for their residence?...................................
Describe involvement on separate sheet.

15. Has there ever been a housing code inspection of premises? ....
Date(s) .... Inspector(s) Name(s)...

16. Are repairs to premises needed?........... Has client notified anyone about need for repairs?
.... Details (to whom, when, orally/writing? Use new sheet.

17. Notices from (or to) landlord?.....................How received/sent?.................. Get copies.
Use new sheet.

18. SUMMONS AND COMPLAINT: If client doesn't have a copy call Essex County District Court Tenant Dept. 961-7170; 961-7972. You must *give docket number* which is six digits preceded by a "T". It appears on lock out notice and court post card as well as summons and complaint.

Docket # T...................... Filling date.............................Return (Trial) Date...........................

SERVICE: (A) How client received papers.................. (B) Per Court records.......................

Caption of complaint.. vs. ....

Judge.............................. Grounds..
If "non-payment" give breakdown: by month(s)/
....
week(s) not just total sum

Judgment.. Warrant to issue ....

Warrant of removal: (a) Date issued............................ (b) Date executed.......................

(c) How received by client?..........................(d) Constable.......................... ....
Phone

Plaintiff: (a) Pro se?............. (b) Attorney's name...

.................., ...
Phone Address

13. ¿Tiene el cliente malas relaciones con el propietario, superintendente, vecino(s)?.................. Detalles en una hoja separada.

14. ¿Es el cliente miembro u organizador de alguna asociación de inquilinos en su vivienda? ....Describa su actividad en una hoja separada.

15. ¿Ha habido alguna inspección de acuerdo con el código de viviendas en el local donde vive?

.... Fecha(s) .... Nombre(s) de(l) (los) inspector(es) ....

16. ¿Hacen falta reparaciones al local? ....Ha avisado el cliente a alguien sobre la necesidad de reparaciones?...........Detalles (¿a quién, cuándo, oralmente/por escrito?) Use una nueva hoja.

17. ¿Avisos del (o para) el propietario?.............¿Cómo fueron recibidos o enviados?.................. Obtenga copias. Use una nueva hoja.

18. EMPLAZAMIENTO (Citación) Y DEMANDA: Si el cliente no tiene copia llame al Essex County District Court (Dept. Tenancy) 961-7170; 961-7962. Debe *darle el número del caso* que son seis dígitos precedidos por una "T". Aparece en el aviso de cierre ("lock-out") y en la tarjeta postal del tribunal tanto como en el emplazamiento y demanda. Caso # T..................

Fecha del registro.......................... Fecha de contestación (comparecencia) ....

CITACIÓN (Entrega de demanda): (A) ¿Cómo recibió el cliente los papeles?......................

(B) Según registros del tribunal....................................

Títulos de la demanda .... vs. ....

Juez................................ Bases de la acción..

Si es falta de pago ("non-payment") divídalo:

....

por mes(es)/semana(s) no solamente el total

Fallo.................................. Emisión de decreto (warrant) ....

Decreto de desalojo: (a) Fecha de emisión.............................. (b) Fecha de ejecutación

.... (c) ¿Cómo lo recibió el cliente?...................... (d) Alguacil ....

....

Teléfono

Demandante: (a) Pro se (sin abogado)?....................... (b) Nombre del abogado..................

..............................., ...

Teléfono Dirección

HOUSING REPAIR LIST

Date.............................. Certified mail # ....

Address ....Apt. # .... Newark, N.J. ....

Name ....

PROBLEM	Bath room	Kit-chen	1st Bed-room	2nd Bed-room	3rd Bed-room	Liv-ing room	Hall-way
CEILING-Peeling paint							
Falling plaster/Holes							
Water leaks							
WALLS-Peeling paint							
Falling plaster/Holes							
Water leaks							
FLOOR-Holes/Surface damaged							
"Gives"/Weak							
WINDOWS-Glass-Crack(s)/Holes/Loose							
Very drafty							
Can't open/close							
Won't stay open							
Locks-None/Broken							
No screens							
Screens-Poor fit/Holes/Etc.							
HEAT-None/never/sometimes							
Not enough							
Radiator-None							
Radiator-Can't turn on/off							
Radiator-Sections not hot							
Radiator-Leaks							
Space Heater-Broken/Dangerous							
ELECTRICAL-Outlets-None							
Outlets-Broken/Sparking							
Light Switches-Broken/Sparking							
Wires-"Wrapping"-None/Damaged							
WATER-None							
Not enough hot							
Not enough cold							
Not clean-sometimes/always							
PLUMBING-Pipes leak							
Faucets-Dripping-Running							
Faucets-Handles-Broken/None							
Drains-"Stopped up"/Slow draining							
Toilet-Broken/Leaks							
Toilet-Needs extra flushes							
Sink-Cracked/chipped							

LISTA DE REPARACIONES DE VIVIENDA

Fecha............................... Correo Certificado # ....

DIRECCIÓN ....Apto. #......................... Newark, N.J.....................

NOMBRE ....

PROBLEMA	Baño	Cocina	1er Dormitorio	2o. Dormitorio	3o. Dormitorio	Sala	Pasillo
TECHO-Pintura pelada							
Yeso caído/Agujeros							
Escape de agua/Goteras							
PAREDES-Pintura pelada							
Yeso caído/agujeros							
Escape de agua/Goteras							
PISO-Agujeros/Superficie dañada							
Flojo (se mueve al pisarse)/Débil							
VENTANAS-Cristal(es)-roto(s)/Con Agujero(s)/Flojo(s)							
Entra mucho aire frío (Invierno)							
No se pueden abrir/cerrar							
No se quedan abiertas							
Cerraduras-No hay/Rotas							
No hay tela metálica							
Tela metálica-Ajuste inadecuado/Agujeros/Etc.							
CALEFACCIÓN-No hay/nunca/a veces							
No hay suficiente							
Radiador-No hay							
Radiador-No se puede abrir/cerrar							
Radiador-Secciones no calientan							
Radiador-Escape							
Calentador eléctrico?/Roto/Peligroso							
ELECTRICIDAD-Toma corrientes-No hay							
Toma corrientes-Rotos/Echan chispas							
Interruptores-Rotos/Echan chispas							
Alambres eléctricos-"Envueltos"-Ningunos/dañados							
AGUA-No hay							
No hay suficiente agua caliente							
No hay suficiente agua fría							
No está limpia-a veces/nunca							
PLOMERíA-Escape en las tuberías (cañerías)							
Llaves (Plumas) (Pilas)-Gotean-Corre el agua							
Llaves (Plumas) (Pilas)-Tiradores rotos/no hay							
Desagüe-Tupido (No baja)/Baja despacio							
Inodoro-Roto/Escape							
Inodoro-Necesita descargarlo más de una vez							
Fregadero-(cocina/lavabo, lavatorio, baño)-Rajado/Saltada la porcelana							

	Bath room	Kitchen	1st Bedroom	2nd Bedroom	3rd Bedroom	Living room	Hallwal
MISCELLANEOUS							
Insects-Roaches/Other							
Mice/Rats							
Exterminating-None/Rarely							
Electrical-Fuses blow out							
Gas/Electric bill very high							
Apt. Entrance Door-Poor fit							
Little protection							
Lock-Hard to use/Broken							
APPLIANCES-If landlord's							
Stove-Gas odor							
Stove-Not Level							
Stove-Fix: Burners/Oven							
Fix: Handles/Knobs/Doors/Etc.							
Refrigerator-Not cold enough							
Fix: Handles/Door/Etc.							
Frexer-Not Cold Enough							
Freezer-Food-Can't keep long							
COMMON AREAS-Stairs-No light							
Stairs-Broken/Holes							
Stairs-Weak/Not safe							
Banister-Missing rungs/Weak							
Hallway-Light-None/Too little/Broken							
Fire Extinguisher-None/Broken							
Elevator-Doesn't work/Works wrong							
Fire Escape-Not safe/Needs painting							
Garbage Cans-Not enough							
Garbage Cans-Covers missing/Holes							
Incinerator-Broken/Smokes							
Mail Box-Can't lock, etc.							

	Baño	Cocina	1er. Dormitorio	2o. Dormitorio	3o. Dormitorio	Sala	Pasillo
MISCELÁNEA							
Insectos-Cucarachas/Otros							
Ratones/Ratas							
Fumigación-Nunca/Rara vez							
Electricidad-Fusibles quemados							
Cuenta de gas/electricidad muy alta							
Puerta de entrada al apto. Ajuste inadecuado							
Ofrece poca protección							
Cerradura-Difícil de usar/Rota							
UTENSILIOS (Aparatos)-Si son del dueño							
Estufa-Olor a gas							
Estufa-No está a nivel							
Estufa-Necesita arreglo: Hornillas/ Horno							
Necesita arreglo: Mangos/Botones/Puertas/Etc.							
Refrigerador (Nevera)-No enfría suficientemente							
Necesitan arreglo: Mangos/Puertas/Etc.							
Congelador-No congela suficientemente							
Congelador-No conserva los comestibles durante mucho tiempo							
LUGARES DE USO COMÚN-Escaleras-No hay luz							
Escaleras-Rotas/Agujeros							
Escaleras-Débiles/Inseguras							
Pasamano-Le faltan barrotes/Débil							
Luz en el pasillo-No hay/Muy poca/Bombillas rotas							
Extinguidor de fuego-No hay/Roto							
Ascensor (Elevador)—No funciona/Funciona mal							
Escalera de escape-Insegura/Necesita pintura							
Safacones (Latones de basura)-No hay suficientes							
Safacones (Latones de basura)-Les faltan tapas/Agujeros							
Incinerador-Roto/Humea							
Buzón-No cierra, etc.							

TENANT INTERVIEW

(Interpreter Susana Romero, a bilingual paralegal, is writing down all of the necessary information regarding Mrs. Juana Castro's tenant problem. At the beginning of the dialogue, she is making note of the last items which the attorney may want before interviewing the client. The interpreter writes down all information in English so that Miss Sloan, the non-Spanish-speaking attorney will have no difficulty in understanding.)

INTERPRETER: Diga, señora Castro, ¿en qué puedo ayudarla?

CLIENT: Tengo un problema con el dueño del apartamento donde vivo. Me ha pedido la casa para el mes que viene para un primo suyo que viene de la Argentina. Vendrá con su esposa y el nene y no tiene dónde quedarse. Como le he explicado, yo siempre pago la renta a tiempo y no hay razón de que me eche del apartamento. ¿Es cierto que el dueño tenga derecho de mandar que me vaya del apartamento?

INTERPRETER: Yo no puedo hacer más que tomar los datos. Un momento, señora Castro. Vamos a ver si la señora Sloan puede ayudarla. Ella es la abogada, y es la única persona que puede contestar preguntas legales.

(The interpreter rings the attorney on the intercom.)

INTERPRETER TO ATTORNEY: Ms. Sloan, Mrs. Castro arrived for her appointment a half hour ago. I have taken down some basic information. Can you see her now? Very good, we'll come in to your office in ten minutes.

INTERPRETER TO CLIENT: La abogada dice que tiene que hacer una llamada urgente pero que estará lista para hablar con usted en diez minutos.

(Ten minutes later, the interpreter again checks with the attorney and finds out that it is all right for her to bring Mrs. Castro into the attorney's office.

INTERPRETER TO MRS. CASTRO: Señora Castro, la señorita Sloan le va a hablar ahora.

(Interpreter and client enter the attorney's office. After initial greetings are courteously exchanged, the interpreter —who in this case is a bilingual paralegal— gives Miss Sloan the file on the case.)

INTERPRETER TO ATTORNEY: As you can see, all of the basic data is on the questionnaire. From what Mrs. Castro has explained to me, she has a problem with her landlord. He has told her to move next month, since he needs the apartment for his cousin who is coming from Argentina. The cousin's wife and children are coming along and they don't have any place to stay. Mrs. Castro asked me if the landlord has a right to order her to leave her appartment. I told her of course that only you could answer a question like that.

ATTORNEY TO INTERPRETER: Thanks, Susana.

ATTORNEY Ask her if she thinks that the landlord is just trying to get her out of the apartment?

INTERPRETER: ¿Cree Ud. que el propósito del dueño es de arreglar la situación para que Ud. tenga que mudarse?

CLIENT: No sé si es ésa su intención. Pero si me tengo que cambiar, el resultado es lo mismo.

INTERPRETER: She said: "I don't know if that is his intention. But if I have to move, the result is the same."

ATTORNEY: When did he inform her that he needs her apartment?

INTERPRETER: ¿Cuándo le ha hecho saber que necesita su apartamento?

CLIENT: A principios del mes pasado.

ATTORNEY: And why has she waited so long before asking for legal assistance?

INTERPRETER: ¿Y por qué ha esperado tanto tiempo para pedir ayuda legal?

CLIENT: Esperaba que a lo mejor cambiaría de parecer, pero ahora parece que definitivamente quiere el apartamento.

INTERPRETER: I hoped that he would change his mind, but now it seems that he definitely does want the apartment.

CLIENT: Explíquele a la abogada, por favor, que a mis hijos les conviene mucho este sitio porque está muy cerquita de la escuela. Y para mi marido, está muy a mano el autobús para ir a trabajar.

INTERPRETER: She says that it's a good place for her children because it's close to the school. And its handy for her husband because he can catch the bus for work.

ATTORNEY: Ask her how many families live in the building?

INTERPRETER: ¿Cuántas familias viven en el edificio donde Ud. vive?

CLIENT: Hay seis familias y el dueño vive en el primer piso.

INTERPRETER: She says that there are six families; in addition, the landlord lives on the first floor.

EXERCISE B

Reread the preceding dialogue carefully. As you read, note the presence and/or absence of the interpreting skills which have been studied. List your observations in the chart which follows, according to the line number of the dialogue (Column A); the skill which is present or absent (Column B); possible explanations (Column C). Compare your analysis with the commentary which follows.

(A) LINE NUMBER	(B) INTERPRETING SKILL (PRECENCE OR ABSENCE)	(C) POSSIBLE EXPLANATION

COMMENTARY

Lines 1-18 — This is an example of a hybrid informal interpreting situation. This part of the interview is conducted completely in Spanish, with the information written down in English for later use by non-Spanish-speaking professionals. The second interview, in the presence of the attorney, is an example of an informal interpreting situation, requiring the interpreter to orally convey all that is said between the Spanish-speaking client and the non-Spanish-speaking attorney.

Line 1 — In this case the interpreter is a bilingual paralegal. She could well be a receptionist, attorney, administrator, or any other staff member. The key is the combination of interpreting skills and a knowledge of the legal environment.

Lines 16-18 — Susana Romero clearly established and limited the interpreter's role, in a direct but tactful way, so that the client would know that she is not a person whom the client can consult for legal advice.

Lines 25-27 — The interpreter has explained to Mrs. Castro the reason for the extra ten-minute wait. Once a client knows what to expect, such an extra wait will seem more reasonable.

Lines 36-45 — During all of this summary of the case by the interpreter to the attorney, the interpreter has not bothered to explain to the uncomprehending client just what it is that she is saying to the attorney. The client may have no idea that the interpreter is only repeating the facts of the case. A few words of explanation, preferably before the interpreter begins a long discussion with the attorney, would prevent unwarranted concern on the part of the client.

Lines 48-49 — Here the attorney has used an idiomatic expression "to get her out of her apartment". Note that the translation does not correspond precisely. If the attorney were consciously trying to avoid the use of such idiomatic expressions, it would create a better situation for interpreting purposes.

The use of the third person "she" by the attorney makes it seem as if the client is being treated as a strange uncomprehending passive object, rather than as the very person whose problem is the reason for the entire interview. The attorney should be made aware of the need to pose questions as if speaking directly with the client, thus approximating, as closely as possible, a normal dialogue.

Line 54 — The use of the phrase "She said" as an introduction to the sentences interpreted is another undesirable way of turning a direct dialogue into a discussion *about* someone.

Lines 56-57 — The interpreter and the attorney used two different tenses. The attorney said "When DID he let her know?" The interpreter said: ¿Cuándo le HA HECHO saber?"

Lines 69 — The interpreter has now lapsed into the third person "she", which is just as wrong as in the case of the attorney (Line 54).

Lines 74-76 — The interpreter has presumed something which may be an error in translation. The client said "*y* el dueño vive en el primer piso." The interpreter has assumed that this means that there are six families *in addition to* the landlord. This may prove to be important, since rent laws in certain states are different for apartment buildings where there are more than a certain number of families residing. If the client's statement is unclear, the interpreter should ask for a clarification *before* making a presumption of this kind.

All of these errors on the part of the interpreter point out that, hand in hand with linguistic expertise, *the interpreter must have a good grasp of the legal concepts involved in the material which he or she will be interpreting.*

SITUATION C: CRIMINAL LAW — MIRANDA WARNINGS

The criminal law area is the one in which interpreters are most frequently required by law because a person's life or freedom may be at stake. The first time in a given case that the need for an interpreter may arise is when an officer of the law seeks to interrogate a non-English-speaking person who is in custody. The Federal law of the United States requires that a person who is about to undergo custodial interrogation be given a series of warnings. If that person is non-English-speaking, the warnings must be given in a language which that person can understand. The warnings are called "Miranda warnings" because the need to give these warnings was established in the case of a Spanish-speaking defendant named Miranda.

MIRANDA WARNINGS

1. You have the right to remain silent.
2. Anything that you say can and will be used against you in a court of law.
3. You have the right to talk with an attorney and to have an attorney present to advise you prior to or during any questioning.
4. If you are unable to pay an attorney, you have the right to have an attorney appointed to counsel you prior to or during any questioning.

SPANISH VERSION OF MIRANDA WARNINGS

1. Usted tiene el derecho de guardar silencio (quedarse callado).
2. Cualquier cosa que diga (cualquier declaración que hace) puede emplearse (usarse) y se empleará (se usará) en contra de usted en el juicio (juzgado).
3. Usted tiene el derecho de hablar con un abogado y de pedirle a un abogado que esté presente para que le aconseje, antes de que usted sea interrogado o mientras lo interrogan a usted.
4. Si usted no puede pagar un abogado, tiene el derecho de que se le nombre un abogado para que le aconseje antes de que usted sea interrogado o mientras lo interrogan a usted.

It is necessary that any person who is about to be interrogated affirm that he or she understands the Miranda warnings *before* the interrogation begins. Therefore, the person to be questioned must respond affirmatively to the following questions, which constitute a waiver:

WAIVER

1. Do you understand each of these rights which I have explained to you?
2. Keeping in mind these rights, do you want to speak with us now?

SPANISH VERSION OF WAIVER

1. ¿Entiende usted cada uno de estos derechos que le he explicado?
2. ¿Teniendo en cuenta estos derechos, quiere usted hablar con nosotros ahora?**

The following alternative translation for the Miranda Warning and Waiver was provided by Carlos B. Vega.

**Spanish versions of the Miranda Warnings used by the District Attorney of El Paso County, Texas, and by the Law Enforcement and Security Training Division of the Texas Engineering Extension Service at Texas A & M University were consulted in preparing the Spanish versions of the Miranda warnings.

ADVERTENCIA MIRANDA

(Miranda Warning)

1. Está Vd. en derecho de permanecer callado.
2. Lo que diga puede y de hecho será adversamente empleado ante un tribunal.
3. Está Vd. en derecho de consultar con un abogado, así como pedirle que le acompañe y esté presente mientras se le interroga.
4. Caso de que Vd. no pueda pagar un abogado, y si lo desea, se le podrá asignar uno que le acompañe y esté present durante cualquier interrogatorio.

RENUNCIA

(Waiver)

Una vez hecha la advertencia, y con el fin de obtenerse una renuncia, se harán las preguntas que siguen, procurando una respuesta afirmativa a cada una de ellas:

1. ¿Entiende Vd. cada uno de estos derechos como le han sido explicados?
2. Teniendo presentes estos derechos, ¿desea Vd. hablarnos ahora?

As can be seen from the Miranda warnings, elaborate precautions must be taken to guard the rights of a defendant or potencial defendant in a criminal case. A very sad example of the heavy responsibility weighing upon an interpreter in a criminal case occurred during a preliminary hearing involving a man who had been unjustly accused of shoplifting. The judge at the hearing said to the interpreter: "Tell Mr. X that I am entering a not guilty plea for him." The interpreter told Mr. X: "El juez lo declara no culpable." The judge had *not* adjudged Mr. X to be innocent. Rather, he had entered a not guilty plea for Mr. X, but a trial would still be necessary to decide the merits of the case. Because of this misunderstanding, Mr. X thought that he had been adjudged not guilty, and never returned for trial. Although the mistake was clearly that of the interpreter, Mr. X suffered the penalties as a fugitive from justice until the misunderstanding was cleared up.

Many defendants are not so lucky. Since the only records of a proceeding are in English, the interpreter's errors can seldom be rectified.

The same kind of extra caution and precision should apply to interviews in the criminal sphere of the law as well as to *all* interpreting situations. It is not that criminal law situations require greater care or expertise on the part of the interpreter. It is just that the criminal sphere helps to emphasize the potentially serious dangers of inaccurate or careless interpreting.

RECOUNTING A DISPUTE AT THE PUBLIC DEFENDER'S OFFICE

In the following interview, Pablo Rodríguez recounts to an attorney at the Public Defender's Office what happened during a dispute with his neighbor, James Borden. Pablo has never learned standard Spanish and his Spanish is heavily influenced by anglicisms. The interpreter here is a friend of Pablo's who has no special training or expertise in interpreting. In commenting upon the interview in the exercise following the conversation, pay particular attention to how the interpreter dealt with specific vocabulary words and expressions. Compare your observations with the commentary following the exercise.

INTERVIEW AT THE PUBLIC DEFENDER'S OFFICE

After a dispute with his neighbor James Borden, Pablo Rodríguez visits the Office of the Public Defender, seeking assistance. Since Pablo cannot afford a private attorney he must seek assistance at the Public Defender's Office. He is seated in a room with an attorney and with a friend of his, whom he has brought along to serve as interpreter. Comments and directions are omitted from the interview itself, since the purpose of the exercise which follows is to concentrate upon the linguistic weaknesses and strengths of the interpreter's version of the events.

LAWYER: Pablo, would you please tell us in your own words
exactly what happened at 7:30 P.M. on June 5 of this
year between you and your neighbor, James Borden.

INTERPRETER: Pablo, dinos en tus propias palabras exactamente lo
que pasó el 5 de junio de este año a las siete y media
de la noche entre ti y tu vecino, Jaime Borden.

PABLO: ¿Quiere saber por qué me peleé con él?

INTERPRETER: Sí, lo que pasó entre ustedes dos.

PABLO: Bueno, pa' empezar, Jimmy vio que había pasao toa la
talde limpiando el carro y cuando ehtaba a punto de
terminar vino con una lata de pintura, de espray. Coño,
cuando echó la pintura en el cristal le di un golpe
en la barriga y se cayó pa' trás. Luego se levantó y
echó mano a un cacho de madera y me dio un golpe a mí.
Como mi papá nos oyó dando voces me dijo que entrara
en la casa y eso eh lo que hice. Pero Jimmy seguía
echando pintura en el carro. Yo no podía má. Salí
corriendo de la casa. Cuando me vio cogió el cacho
de madera otra veh. Pero esa veh ya ehtaba yo
preparao y cogí el martillo. Cuando trató de darme
otra veh di en el hombro con el martillo y se cayó
pa' trás.

INTERPRETER: Well, to start with Jimmy saw that I had spent all
afternoon cleaning the car and when I was nearly
finished he came over with a can of paint, spray
paint. Boy, when he threw the paint on the crystal
I gave him a blow on the stomach and he fell down.
Then, he got up and put his hand on a piece of wood
and hit me. As my father heard us shouting he told
me to come into the house and that's what I did.
But Jimmy kept throwing paint on the car. I
couldn't do any more. I went running out of the
house. When he saw me he grabbed the piece of
wood again. But that time I was ready and I grabbed
the hammer. When he tried to hit me again, I hit
him on the shoulder with the hammer and he fell
down.

EXERCISE C

Reread the preceding dialogue carefully. As you read, note the presence and/or absence of the interpreting skills which have been studied. List your observations in the chart which follows, according to the line number of the dialogue (Column A); the skill which is present or absent (Column B); possible explanations (Column C). Compare your analysis with the commentary which follows.

(A) LINE NUMBER	(B) INTERPRETING SKILL (PRESENCE OR ABSENCE)	(C) POSSIBLE EXPLANATION

COMMENTARY

In Line 4, the interpreter addresses Pablo in the familiar *"tú"* form. It would be hard to imagine him doing otherwise, since he is a friend of Pablo's. Yet, the very use of the familiar form points out the impartiality and objectivity problems which will arise if a friend serves as interpreter.

In lines 7 and 8 Pablo asks the interpreter if what the attorney really wants is to know why he fought with James Borden. That is slightly different than the interpreter's "clarification" of "Yes, what happened between you two?" This kind of subjective dialogue between client and interpreter should be avoided. It should be explained to the attorney that the client has asked for a clarification. Every word that is spoken between Pablo and the interpreter should be related to the attorney.

In line 11 the interpretation of *coño* as *boy* is also incorrect. When vulgar Spanish expressions come up in interpreting, expressions which convey the same tone and level in English should be used. Even in a informal interpreting situation, the softening of this expression in English could give a false impression to an attorney who might miss the feeling of urgency or frustration which has been expressed through Pablo's use of this word.

In line 12 *cristal* should be translated as *window* or *car window* but not crystal. The inexperienced interpreter looked for the literal meaning rather than the true idea.

In line 13, the expression *se cayó pa'trás* or *para atrás* is incorrectly rendered into English as *fell down,* the correct interpretation being *fell backwards.* This may seem to a person to be an insignificant detail, but it may very well be of extreme importance at a later date. By interpreting *se cayó pa'trás* as *he fell down* and not *backwards,* the interpreter has taken it upon himself, whether he did so knowingly or not, to totally change the result of actions. The type of possible injury which could have been sustained by the blow which Pablo gave to Jaime Borden could significantly change if Jaime fell *down* rather than *backwards.* Of course it is quite possible that the interpretation, though incorrect, may have no bearing on the problem at hand. Yet it is not up to the interpreter to alter in any way what he is interpreting. This is a value judgement by the interpreter which could prove to be very damaging to as dangerous for the client.

In line 14, *echó mano a* does not mean *he put his hand on* but rather *he got hold of.* The untrained interpreter is again inaccurate.

In line 17, *Yo no podía má* would better be interpreted as *I couldn't take any more* rather than *I couldn't do any more.* Here Pablo's emotional state would have been accurately captured through the correctly interpreted phrase. Whether interpreting in an agency office or in court, accuracy and attention to detail must always be stressed.

In lines 35-36, the phrase *se cayó pa' trás* comes up once more and here again it is misinterpreted.

SITUATION AND PRACTICE D:
APPLICATION AND AFFIDAVIT FOR WELFARE ASSISTANCE

Excerpts from the application and affidavit for AFDC, MA, CRA, IRP and Food Stamps used by the New Jersey Department of Human Services-Division of Public Welfare are found, in English and Spanish, on the following pages of the text. The applicant, with the help of the intake worker, fills out the initial items and then returns the form to the Welfare worker who will continue to fill it out during the interview with the applicant. As you read the English version of the form, visualize that you are the interpreter in an interview situation where this questionnaire is the basis for receiving information from a client seeking public assistance and that you must render an accurate version of the questions into Spanish for a Spanish-speaking client who requires Welfare assistance.

Translate the English version of the questionnaire in Spanish and compare your Spanish version with the one which is reproduced next to each page of the English version.

APPLICATION AND AFFIDAVIT FOR AFDC, MA, CRA, IRP AND FOOD STAMPS (EXCERPTS)

NEW JERSEY DEPARTMENT OF HUMAN SERVICES - DIVISION OF PUBLIC WELFARE

APPLICANT: *PLEASE COMPLETE SECTIONS II AND III OF THIS FORM CAREFULLY AND ACCURATELY. IF YOU HAVE ANY QUESTIONS, ASK THE COUNTY WELFARE WORKER.*

SECTION II PERSON(S) APPLYING FOR ASSISTANCE

1) NAME OF APPLICANT ....
(Last) (First) (Initial) (Maiden)

CO-APPLICANT'S NAME ....
(Last) (First) (Initial) (Maiden)

WHERE DO YOU LIVE? ....
(Number) (Street or Road) (Apt. No.)

....
(City, Town or Township) (Zip Code)

MAILING ADDRESS *(If Different)* ....
(Zip Code)

PREVIOUS ADDRESS ....
(Zip Code)

DATE MOVED ....
Signature Of Person Initiating Application

PHONE NUMBER.................................... RENT/MORTGAGE AMOUNT $............................( ) MONTHLY ( ) WEEKLY
( ) OTHER-SPECIFY

DO YOU PLAN TO CONTINUE LIVING IN N.J.? ( ) YES ( ) NO. IF "NO" EXPLAIN.

2) FOR WHICH PROGRAMS(S) DO YOU WISH TO APPLY OR REAPPLY?

( ) AID TO FAMILIES WITH DEPENDENT CHILDREN (INCLUDING MEDICAID)	(YOU ARE NOT ABLE TO SUPPORT YOUR CHILDRREN OR THE CHILDREN WHO ARE IN YOUR CARE.)
( ) MEDICAL ASSISTANCE ONLY (MEDICAID FOR YOUR FAMILY)	(YOU DO NOT WANT MONEY FOR DAILY EXPENSES BUT YOU DO NOT HAVE ENOUGH MONEY TO PAY MEDICAL BILLS.)
( ) MEDICAL ASSISTANCE ONLY (PENDING BIRTH OF CHILD)	(YOU ARE PREGNANT AND YOU DO NOT HAVE ENOUGH MONEY TO PAY MEDICAL BILLS.)
( ) CUBAN REFUGEE ASSISTANCE (INCLUDING MEDICAID)	(YOU ARE A REFUGEE FROM CUBA AND YOU ARE REGISTERED AT THE CUBAN REFUGEE CENTER IN MIAMI, FLORIDA.)
( ) INDO-CHINESE REFUGEE PROGRAM (INCLUDING MEDICAID)	(YOU ARE A REFUGEE FROM VIETNAM, CAMBODIA OR LAOS WHO ENTERED THE UNITED STATES AFTER ABRIL 8, 1975.)

DO YOU WISH TO APPLY FOR THE FOOD STAMP PROGRAM? ( ) YES ( ) NO	(YOU NEED FOOD STAMPS TO HELP BUY FOOD)

---

3) BASIC INFORMATION: *(LIST EACH PERSON FOR WHOM THIS APPLICATION IS BEING MADE. LIST ADULTS FIRST, THEN THE OLDEST TO THE YOUNGEST CHILD. IF MORE SPACE IS NEEDED, USE THE REVERS SIDE.)*

List Only Those Individual Applying For Both Public Assistance and Food Stamps

NAME	AGE	BIRTH DATE & BIRTHPLACE	RELATIONSHIP	SOCIAL SECURITY NUMBER	GRADE AND SCHOOL

SOLICITUD Y AFIDÁVIT PARA AFDC, MA, CRA, IRP Y CUPONES DE ALIMENTOS
DEPARTAMENTO DE SERVICIOS HUMANOS DE NUEVA JERSEY
DIVISIÓN DE BIENESTAR PÚBLICO

SOLICITANTE: POR FAVOR COMPLETE SECCIONES II Y III DE ESTA SOLICITUD CON CUIDADO Y CORRECTAMENTE. SI USTED TIENE ALGUNAS PREGUNTAS, PREGÚNTE AL(A LA) TRABAJADOR(A) DEL BIENESTAR DEL CONDADO.

SECCIÓN II PERSONA(S) SOLICITANDO ASISTENCIA

1) NOMBRE DEL SOLICITADOR ....
(Apellido) (Nombre) (Nombre del Medio) (Apellido de Soltera)

NOMBRE DEL CO-SOLICITADOR ....
(Apellido) (Nombre) (Nombre del Medio) (Apellido de Soltera)

¿DÓNDE VIVE USTED? ....
(Nombre) (Calle o Camino) (Num. de Apto.)

....
(Ciudad o Municipio) (Zip Code)

DIRECCIÓN POSTAL (SI ES DIFERENTE) ....
(Zip Code)

DIRECCIÓN ANTES DE LA PRESENTE ....
(Zip Code)

FECHA CUANDO SE MUDÓ ....
Firma de la Persona Iniciando la Solicitud

NÚMERO DE TELÉFONO.................................. RENTA/HIPOTECA $.................................. ( ) MENSUAL ( ) SEMANAL
( ) OTRO - ESPECIFIQUE

¿PLANEA USTED SEGUIR VIVIENDO EN N.J.? ( ) SÍ ( ) NO SI INDICA "NO" EXPLIQUE.

2) PARA CUÁ(ES) PROGRAMA(S) DESEA USTED SOLICITAR O RE-SOLICITAR?

( ) AYUDA PARA FAMILIAS CON NIÑOS DEPENDIENTES (INCLUYENDO ASISTENCIA MÉDICA — MEDICAID)	(USTED NO PUEDE MANTENER A SUS HIJOS O LOS NIÑOS BAJO SU CUIDADO.)
( ) ASISTENCIA MÉDICA SOLAMENTE (MEDICAID) (ASISTENCIA MÉDICA PARA SU FAMILIA)	(USTED NO DESEA DINERO PARA GASTOS DIARIOS, SINO QUE USTED NO TIENE SUFICIENTE DINERO PARA PAGAR CUENTAS MÉDICAS.)
( ) ASISTENCIA MÉDICA SOLAMENTE (PENDIENTE EL NACIMIENTO DEL HIJO)	(USTED ESTÁ ENCINTA Y NO TIENE SUFICIENTE DINERO PARA PAGAR CUENTAS MÉDICAS.)
( ) ASISTENCIA PARA REFUGIADOS CUBANOS (INCLUYENDO ASISTENCIA MÉDICA)	(USTED ES UN REFUGIADO DE CUBA Y ESTÁ REGISTRADO EN EL CENTRO DE REFUGIADOS CUBANOS EN MIAMI, FLORIDA.)
( ) PROGRAMA DE REFUGIADOS INDOCHINOS (INCLUYENDO ASISTENCIA MÉDICA)	(USTED ES UN REFUGIADO DE VIETNAM, CAMBODIA O LAOS QUIEN ENTRÓ EN LOS ESTADOS UNIDOS DESPUÉS DE ABRIL 8, 1975.)

¿DESEA USTED SOLICITAR PARA EL PROGRAMA DE CUPONES DE ALIMENTOS? (USTED NECESITA CUPONES DE ALIMENTOS PARA AYUDARLE A COMPRAR ALIMENTOS)

( ) SÍ ( ) NO

---

3) INFORMACIÓN BÁSICA: (NOMBRE CADA PERSONA PARA QUIEN SE SOLICITA ASISTENCIA. NOMBRE ADULTOS PRIMERO, DESPUÉS, DEL MAYOR HASTA EL MENOR. SI NECESITA MÁS ESPACIO, USE EL REVERSO DE ESTA PÁGINA.)

NOMBRE SOLAMENTE A ESOS INDIVIDUOS QUE SOLICITAN ASISTENCIA PÚBLICA Y CUPONES DE ALIMENTOS

NOMBRE	EDAD	FECHA Y LUGAR DE NACIMIENTO	RELACIÓN AL SOLICITADOR	NÚMERO DEL SEGURO SOCIAL	GRADO Y ESCUELA

4) **PREGNANT FEMALE SEEKING AID FOR UNBORN CHILD** *(Please Complete The Following.)*

EXPECTED DATE OF BIRTH ....

VERIFICATION RECEIVED DATE

DOCTOR'S NAME ....

ADDRESS ....

5) **LIST ANY PERSONS IN THE HOME WHO IN ADDITION TO THOSE IDENTIFIED IN ITEM 3 ARE APPLYING FOR FOOD STAMPS.**

NAME	AGE	BIRTHDATE & BIRTHPLACE	SOCIAL SECURITY NUMBER	RELATIONSHIP TO HOUSEHOLD	EDUCATION AND GRADE LEVEL

* * *

ADDITIONAL AFDC INFORMATION

35) **DO YOU OR ANYONE MAKING APPLICATION HAVE ANY PENDING CLAIMS, SUCH AS LAW SUITS, SALE OF PROPERTY OR DOES ANYONE OWE YOU MONEY?**

TYPE OF CLAIM:

36) **OTHER PERSONS LIVING IN THE HOME** *(Not Listed In Item 3 or Item 5)*

37) **LEGALLY RESPONSIBLE RELATIVES** *(Do Not Include Those Parents Listed In Section VI Below)*

NAME	ADDRESS	RELATIONSHIP	AGE

***Questions 6 through 34 have been omitted.

4) MUJER ENCINTA SOLICITANDO ASISTENCIA PARA NIÑO INNATO
(Favor de Completar Lo Siguiente.)

FECHA QUE SE ANTICIPA EL NACIMIENTO .... VERIFICACIÓN RECIBIDA

NOMBRE DEL MÉDICO .... FECHA: ....

DIRECCIÓN ....

---

5) NOMBRE A LAS PERSONAS EN EL HOGAR QUIENES, ADEMÁS DE ESOS IDENTIFICADOS EN ÍTEM 3, ESTÁN SOLICITANDO LOS CUPONES DE ALIMENTOS.

NOMBRE	EDAD	FECHA Y LUGAR DE NACIMIENTO	NÚMERO DEL SEGURO SOCIAL	RELACIÓN AL HOGAR	NIVEL DE EDUCACIÓN Y GRADO

* * *

INFORMACIÓN ADICIONAL DE AFDC

35) ¿TIENE USTED O QUIENES SOLICITAN ASISTENCIA DEMANDAS PENDIENTES COMO PLEITO LEGAL, VENTA DE PROPIEDAD O HAY ALGUIEN QUIEN LE DEBE DINERO?

Clase de demanda pendiente:

36) OTRAS PERSONAS QUE VIVEN CON USTED EN EL HOGAR (Quienes No Están Mencionadas En Ítem 3 o Ítem 5)

37) PARIENTES LEGALMENTE RESPONSABLES (No Incluya a Esos Padres Mencionados en la Sección VI, abajo)

NOMBRE	DIRECCIÓN	RELACIÓN	EDAD

***De la pregunta 6 a la 34 se han omitido.

SECTION VI MARITAL STATUS AND DEPRIVATION FACTOR

38) MARITAL STATUS: ( ) SINGLE ( ) MARRIED ( ) SEPARATED
( ) DIVORCED ( ) WIDOWED

NAME OF PRESENT HUSBAND/WIFE ....

NAME AND PLACE OF MARRIAGE ....

DATE OF SEPARATION ....

NAME OF FORMER HUSBAND/WIFE ....

DATE AND PLACE OR DIVORCE ....

DATE AND PLACE OF DEATH ....

39) DEPRIVATION FACTORS: A—ABSENT PARENT D—DEATH I—INCAPACITY X—DESERTION

CHILD'S NAME	CODE	PARENT'S NAME	ADDRESS OR EMPLOYER	PARENT'S SOCIAL SECURITY/ VA NUMBER

A) APPLICANT STATES THAT THE CHILDREN AS IDENTIFIED BY "X" ABOVE WERE DESERTED BY THE ABSENT PARENT. ( ) YES ( ) NO

B) DID APPLICANT HAVE CSP GOOD CAUSE RIGHTS EXPLAINED. ( ) YES ( ) NO

* * *

SECTION IX FOOD STAMP INFORMATION

42) SHELTER COSTS *(List Household Expense For The Following Items)*

SHELTER EXPENSE	AMOUNT	HOW OFTEN PAID
RENT/MORTGAGE		
PROPERTY TAXES		

***Questions 40 and 41 have been omitted.

SECCIÓN VI ESTADO MARITAL Y FACTOR DE PRIVACIÓN/ABANDONO

38) ESTADO MARITAL: ( ) SOLTERO(A) ( ) CASADO(A) ( ) SEPARADO(A)
( ) DIVORCIADO(A) ( ) VIUDO(A)

NOMBRE DEL (DE LA) ESPOSO (A) PRESENTE ....

FECHA Y LUGAR DEL MATRIMONIO ....

FECHA DE SEPARACIÓN ....

NOMBRE DEL(DE LA) ESPOSO(A) ANTERIOR ....

FECHA Y LUGAR DE DIVORCIO ....

FECHA Y LUGAR DE MUERTE ....

---

39) FACTOR DE PRIVACIÓN/ABANDONO: A—AUSENCIA DEL(DE LA) PADRE/MADRE D—MUERTE I—INCAPACIDAD

NOMBRE DEL (DE LA) NIÑO(A)	CÓDIGO	NOMBRE DE LOS PADRES	NÚMERO DE SEGURO SOCIA/VETERANO DE LOS PADRES	DIRECCIÓN O PATRÓN

A) EL SOLICITADOR DECLARA QUE LOS NIÑOS, LOS QUE ESTÁN IDENTIFICADOS CON UNA "X" ARRIBA, FUERON ABANDONADOS POR EL(LA) PADRE (MADRE). ( ) SÍ ( ) NO

B) SE LE EXPLICÓ AL SOLICITADOR LOS DERECHOS DE CAUSA BUENA DE CSP. ( ) SÍ ( ) NO

* * *

SECCIÓN IX INFORMACIÓN SOBRE LOS CUPONES DE ALIMENTOS

42) GASTOS INCURRIDOS EN EL(LA) HOGAR/CASA (Mencione Los Gastos De Casa Para Los Siguientes Artículos:)

GASTO DE CASA/HOGAR	CANTIDAD	¿FRECUENCIA CON QUE SE PAGA?
RENTA/HIPOTECA		
IMPUESTOS DE PROPIEDAD		

***Se han omitido las preguntas 40 y 41.

INSURANCE ON HOME

....

TELEPHONE

....

ELECTRICITY

....

GAS

....

OIL

....

WATER AND SEWAGE

....

GARBAGE/TRASH

....

COST OF INSTALLATION OF UTILITIES

....

OTHER (COAL, WOOD, KEROSENE)

....

A) DOES ANYONE OUTSIDE OF THE HOUSEHOLD PAYMENTS OF ANY HOUSEHOLD EXPENSES?
( ) YES ( ) NO *If "YES" complete below.*

TYPE OF SHELTER EXPENSE	PAID TO WHOM	PAID BY	HOW OFTEN PAID

* * *

46) AUTHORIZED REPRESENTATIVE *You Can Authorize Someone Outside Your Household To Apply For Food Stamps For You, To Obtain Food Stamps For You, Or To Use Them To Purchase Food For You. If You Wish To Designate Such A Person, Complete The Following Information:*

NOTE: THIS DESIGNATED PERSON MAY LIVE WITH THE ELIGIBLE HOUSEHOLD OR SOMEWHERE ELSE.

NAME .... TELEPHONE NUMBER ....

ADDRESS ....

....

....

SECTION X SOCIAL SERVICES

47) CHECK ANY ITEMS THAT THE CLIENT WISHES TO DISCUSS WITH COUNTY WELFARE WORKER

( ) JOB TRAINING
( ) EMPLOYMENT
( ) EDUCATION
( ) LEGAL SERVICES
( ) MONEY MANAGEMENT
( ) FAMILY PLANNING
( ) CHILDREN
( ) HOUSING
( ) HOME MANAGEMENT
( ) MEDICAL, DENTAL and/or EYE CARE
( ) DAY CARE
( ) HOMEMAKER SERVICE
( ) OTHER PROBLEMS
( ) TRANSPORTATION
( ) NONE

***Questions 43 through 45 have been omitted.

SEGURO DE LA CASA

....

TELÉFONO

....

ELECTRICIDAD

....

GAS

....

ACEITE/PETRÓLEO

....

AGUA Y ALCANTARILLADO (Drenaje)

....

DESPERDICIO/BASURA

....

COSTO DE LA INSTALACIÓN DE UTILIDADES

....

OTROS (Carbón, Leña, Querosina)

....

A) ¿HAY ALGUNA PERSONA, AFUERA DEL HOGAR, QUIEN PAGA O AYUDA A PAGAR ALGUNOS DE LOS GASTOS DEL(DE LA) HOGAR (CASA) ( ) SÍ ( ) NO, Si La Respuesta Es Sí, Complete Lo Siguiente.

CLASE DE GASTO DE CASA/HOGAR	¿A QUIÉN FUE PAGADO?	PAGADO POR	¿FRECUENCIA CON QUE SE PAGA?

* * *

46) REPRESENTANTE AUTORIZADO Usted Puede Autorizar A Una Persona De Su Hogar, Como Su Representante, Para Solicitarle Los Cupones De Alimentos, Canjearle Los Cupones De Alimentos, O Para Comprar Alimentos Para Usted. Si Usted Desea Designar Tal Persona, Complete La Siguiente Información:

NOTA AVISO: ESTA PERSONA DESIGNADA PUEDE VIVIR EN EL HOGAR ELEGIBLE O EN ALGUNA OTRA PARTE (Afuera Del Hogar).

NOMBRE .... NÚMERO DE TELÉFONO ....

DIRECCIÓN ....

....

SECCIÓN X SERVICIOS SOCIALES

47) INDIQUE CON UNA "X" SOBRE QUÉ ASUNTO(S) EL CLIENTE DESEA HABLAR CON UN(A) TRABAJADOR(A) DE LA AGENCIA DE BIENESTAR DEL CONDADO.

( ) ENTRENAMIENTO PARA EMPLEO
( ) EMPLEO
( ) EDUCACIÓN
( ) SERVICIOS LEGALES
( ) MANEJO DE DINERO
( ) PLANIFICACIÓN FAMILIAR
( ) NIÑOS
( ) VIVIENDA
( ) MANEJO DOMÉSTICO
( ) CUIDO MÉDICO, DENTAL Y/U OCULAR
( ) SALÓN DE CUIDO PARA NIÑOS DURANTE EL DÍA
( ) SERVICIO DE CUIDO EN EL HOGAR
( ) TRANSPORTACIÓN
( ) OTROS PROBLEMAS
( ) NINGUNO

***De la pregunta 43 a la 45 se han omitido.

AUTHORIZATION TO EXAMINE INCOME TAX RECORDS

I (We) hereby authorize the New Jersey Division of Taxation to permit the Division of Public Welfare and/or the local welfare agency to examine State income tax records submitted in my (our) name(s) for the sole purpose of obtaining information relative to job history and earnings.

....	....
Applicant Signature	**Co-Applicant Signature**
....	....
Date	**Date**

BEFORE YOU SIGN, READ THE STATEMENTS BELOW. IF YOU DO NOT UNDERSTAND OR HAVE ANY QUESTIONS, PLEASE ASK.

- I (we) agree that the statements made on this form are true and complete to the best of my (our) knowledge. I (we) know that lying about my (our) situation, failing to give necessary information or causing others to hold back information is against the law and may subject me (us) to prosecution.
- I (we) understand that any information I (we) give is subject to verification by the County Welfare Agency and/or the Division of Public Welfare.
- I (we) hereby authorize the County Welfare Agency to contact, for the sole purpose of verifying the statements I (we) have made, any individual or other source who may have knowledge about my (our) circumstances.
- I (we) know that any information I (we) give will be used only in connection with my (our) application for public assistance and Food Stamp benefits.
- I (we) have received and had explained to me (us), if necessary, a copy of the pamphlet, YOUR RIGHTS AND RESPONSIBILITIES.
- I (we) agree to let the County Welfare Agency know immediately of any change in living conditions, family situation or money received from any source. (See YOUR RIGHTS AND RESPONSIBILITIES.)
- I (we) understand that I (we) may request a fair hearing, if I (we) am (are) not satisfied with any action taken by the County Welfare Agency.
- I (we) understand that I (we) will not be discriminated against because of race, age, color, creed, sex, national origin, marital status, handicap or political belief.

Have you received an EPSDT pamphlet which explains the Early and Periodic Screening Diagnosis and Treatment Program (EPSDT)? ( ) YES ( ) NO.

I (we) .... attest that I (we) have read and agree to these statements and fully realize that the County Welfare Agency relies upon the truth and accuracy of my (our) statements.

....		....	
Applicant Signature	*Date*	*Co-Applicant Signature*	*Date*

....
Agency Representative Sworn and subscribed before me this ....day........................19....

AUTORIZACIÓN PARA EXAMINAR REGISTROS DE IMPUESTOS SOBRE LA RENTA

YO(NOSOTROS) POR ESTE MEDIO AUTORIZO(AUTORIZAMOS) A LA DIVISIÓN DE CONTRIBUCIONES/IMPUESTOS DE NUEVA JERSEY A PERMITIR LA DIVISIÓN DE BIENESTAR PÚBLICO Y/O LA AGENCIA LOCAL DE BIENESTAR A EXAMINAR LOS REGISTROS DE IMPUESTOS SOBRE LA RENTA DEL ESTADO SOMETIDOS EN MI(NUESTROS) NOMBRE(S) CON EL PROPÓSITO EXCLUSIVO DE OBTENER INFORMACIÓN PERTINENTE A LA HISTORIA DE EMPLEO Y SALARIOS/GANANCIAS.

.... FIRMA DEL SOLICITADOR .... FIRMA DEL CO-SOLICITADOR

.... FECHA .... FECHA

ANTES DE FIRMAR, LEA LAS SIGUIENTES DECLARACIONES. SI NO LAS ENTIENDE O TIENE ALGUNAS PREGUNTAS, FAVOR DE PREGUNTARNOS.

- YO (NOSOTROS) ESTOY(ESTAMOS) DE ACUERDO QUE LAS DECLARACIONES HECHAS EN ESTA SOLICITUD SON VERDADERAS Y COMPLETAS SEGÚN MI(NUESTRO) SABER Y CONOCIMIENTO. SÉ(SABEMOS) QUE EL MENTIR SOBRE MI(NUESTRA) SITUACIÓN, NO DAR INFORMACIÓN NECESARIA O CAUSAR QUE OTROS OCULTEN INFORMACIÓN ES CONTRA LA LEY Y ME(NOS) PUEDE SUJETAR A PROCEDIMIENTOS DE PROSECUCIÓN.
- YO(NOSOTROS) ENTIENDO(ENTENDEMOS) QUE CUALQUIER INFORMACION QUE YO(NOSOTROS) DOY(DAMOS) ESTÁ SUJETA A INVESTIGACIÓN POR LA AGENCIA DE BIENESTAR DEL CONDADO Y O POR LA DIVISIÓN DE BIENESTAR PÚBLICO.
- YO(NOSOTROS) POR ESTE MEDIO AUTORIZO (AMOS) A LA AGENCIA DE BIENESTAR DEL CONDADO A PONERSE EN CONTACTO CON CUALQUIER INDIVIDUO U OTRO MEDIO DE INFORMACIÓN QUE TENGA CONOCIMIENTOS DE MIS(NUESTRAS) CIRCUNSTANCIAS, CON EL PROPÓSITO EXCLUSIVO DE VERIFICAR LAS DECLARACIONES QUE YO(NOSOTROS) HE(MOS) HECHO.
- YO(NOSOTROS) SÉ(SABEMOS) QUE CUALQUIER INFORMACIÓN QUE YO(NOSOTROS) DÉ(MOS) SERÁ USADA SOLAMENTE EN CONEXIÓN CON MI(NUESTRA) SOLICITUD PARA ASISTENCIA PÚBLICA Y LOS BENEFICIOS DE CUPONES DE ALIMENTOS.
- YO(NOSOTROS) HE(MOS) RECIBIDO Y ME(NOS) HAN EXPLICADO, SI ES NECESARIO, UNA COPIA DEL FOLLETO **SUS DERECHOS Y RESPONSABILIDADES.**
- YO(NOSOTROS) ESTOY(ESTAMOS) DE ACUERDO A INFORMAR INMEDIATAMENTE A LA AGENCIA DE BIENESTAR DEL CONDADO DE CUALQUIER CAMBIO DE CONDICIONES DE VIVIENDA, SITUACIÓN DE FAMILIA O DINERO RECIBIDO DE CUALQUIER ORIGEN. (VEA **SUS DERECHOS Y RESPONSABILIDADES,** PÁGINAS 6 Y 7.)
- YO(NOSOTROS) ENTIENDO(ENTENDEMOS) QUE YO(NOSOTROS) PUEDO(PODEMOS) PEDIR UNA AUDIENCIA IMPARCIAL SI NO ESTOY(ESTAMOS) SATISFECHOS(S) CON CUALQUIERA ACCIÓN TOMADA POR LA AGENCIA DE BIENESTAR DEL CONDADO.
- YO(NOSOTROS) ENTIENDO(ENTENDEMOS) QUE NO HABRÁ DISCRIMINACIÓN CONTRA MÍ(NOSOTROS) POR RAZONES DE EDAD, RAZA, COLOR, CREDO, SEXO, ORIGEN NACIONAL, ESTADO MARITAL, IMPEDIMENTO O CREENCIA POLÍTICA.

¿HA RECIBIDO USTED UN FOLLETO DE EPSDT QUE EXPLICA EL PROGRAMA DE TRATAMIENTO Y DESCUBRIMIENTO DIAGNÓSTICO ANTICIPADO Y PERIÓDICO (EPSDT)? ( ) SÍ ( ) NO.

YO(NOSOTROS) .... ATESTIGUO(AMOS) QUE

HE(HEMOS) LEÍDO Y ESTOY(ESTAMOS) DE ACUERDO CON ESTAS DECLARACIONES Y ME DOY(NOS DAMOS) CUENTA COMPLETAMENTE QUE LA AGENCIA DE BIENESTAR DEL CONDADO DEPENDE DE LA VERDAD Y LA EXACTITUD DE MIS(NUESTRAS) DECLARACIONES.

....

FIRMA DEL SOLICITADOR FECHA FIRMA DEL CO-SOLICITADOR FECHA

....

REPRESENTANTE DE LA AGENCIA JURADO Y SUSCRITO ANTE MÍ ESTE..............................DÍA DE.....................DE 19........

NOTES — NOTAS

SITUATION AND EXERCISE E: CHANGE OF NAME

The questionnaire found on the following pages is a change of name form as used at Essex-Newark Legal Services, Newark, New Jersey. Visualize that you are the interpreter in an interview situation where this questionnaire is the basis for receiving information from a client. On the page facing the English version of the questionnaire, translate it into Spanish, just as if you were interpreting the questions during an oral interview.

NAME CHANGE FORM

Full name ....
Address ....
date of birth ....
place of birth ....
citizenship ....
occupation ....
marital status ....
name of spouse ....

Have you any unsatisfied judgments or suits pending?
Name of action: ....v. ....
Docket No. ....
Court: ....
Type of proceeding: ....
Stage of proceeding: ....
Amount of Judgement: ....

Have you ever been involved in a bankruptcy proceeding? ....
Docket Number: ....
Stage of proceeding: ....
Date of Discharge: ....

Has there ever been a bankruptcy or insolvency proceding instituted against you? If so, please explain.) ....
....

Have you been convicted of a crime within the past ten years? ....
Nature of crime: ....
Docket No.: ....
Date of conviction: ....
Place of conviction: ....

Are there any criminal charges pending against you? ....
Nature of charges: ....
Indictment or complaint number: ....
Date of arrest: ....
Place of arrest: ....

Is this action being instituted with the intent to avoid creditors or criminal prosecution or for any other fraudulent purpose?
....

Have you ever made an application to assume another name? (If so, please explain.) ....
....

What is the reason you wish to change your name? ....
....

What name do you wish to assume? ....
Is that the name of any other person you know? ....
If so, do you have the consent of the person? ....
If so, can you get the consent in writing? ....
If no, what is the person's address? ....
....

SPANISH VERSION OF NAME CHANGE FORM

SITUATION AND EXERCISE F: IMMIGRATION VISA APPLICATION

The following is an excerpt from the application for an immigration visa used by the U.S. State Department. Visualize that you are the interpreter in an interview situation where this questionnaire is the basis for receiving information from a client. On the pages facing the English version of the questionnaire, translate it into Spanish, just as if you were interpreting the questions during an oral interview.

EXCERPT FROM IMMIGRATION FORM

STATE DEPARTMENT

APPLICATION FOR IMMIGRANT VISA

1. Family name First name Middle name

....

2. Other names used or by which known (if married woman, give maiden name)

....

3. Full name in native alphabet (if Roman letters not used)

....

4. Date of birth
   Day Month Year

....

5. Age

....

6. Place of birth
   City or town Province Country

....

7. Nationality

....

8. Sex
   Male Female

....

9. Marital Status
   Single (never married) Married Widowed Divorced Separated
   Including my present marriage, I have been married ....times.

SPANISH VERSION OF EXCERPT FROM IMMIGRATION FORM

10. Occupation

....

11. Present address

....

12. Purpose in going to the United States

....

13. Name and address of wife/husband
(give maiden name of wife)

....

14. Names and addresses of children under 21 years of age

....

15. Person(s) named in 13 and 14 (will) (will not) accompany or follow me to the United States (Cross out words that do not apply)

....

16. Length of intended stay (if permanently, so state)

....

17. Intended port of entry

....

18. Final address in the United States

....

19. Do you have a ticket to final destination?

....

20. Person you intend to join (Give name, address and relationship, if any)

....

21. Name and address of sponsoring person or organization
(if different from 20)

....

22. Personal description

a) Color of hair

c) Height
.... ft. ....in.

b) Color of eyes

d) Complexion

....

23. Marks of identification

....

24. The following documents are submitted in support of this application
Police record Divorce decree Affidavit Photographs of support

....

25. Mother's maiden name and addresss (If deceased, so giving year of death)

....

26. Name and address of next of kin in home country (if neither parent is living)

....

27. List all places of residence for six months or more since your sixteenth birthday

City or town	Province	Country	Dates from-to	Calling or occupation

28. List all organizations you are now or have been a member of or affiliated with since your sixteenth birthday

Name and address	Dates from-to	Type of membership and office held, if any

29. List all languages, including your own, that you can speak, read and write

Language	Speak	Read	Write

30. Inclusive dates of previous residence in or visits to the United States (Give type of visa or status) (If never, so state)

....

31. Have your ever been treated in a hospital, institution or elsewhere for a mental disorder, drug addiction or alcoholism? (If answer is Yes, explain) Yes No

....

32. Have you ever been arrested, convicted or confined in a prison, or have you ever been placed in a poorhouse or other charitable institution? (If answer is Yes, explain) Yes No

....

33. Have you ever been the beneficiary of a pardon, amnesty, rehabilitation decree, other act of clemency or similar action? (If answer is Yes, explain) Yes No

....

34. Have you ever applied for a visa to enter the United States? (If answer is Yes, state where and when, whether you applied for a non-immigrant or an immigrant and whether the visa was issued or refused) Yes No

SPANISH VERSION OF EXCERPT FROM IMMIGRATION FORM

35. Have you been refused admission to the United States during the last twelve months? (If answer is Yes, explain) Yes No

....

36. Have you ever registered with a draft board under United States Selective Service Laws? (If answer is Yes, explain) Yes No

....

37. Have you ever applied for relief from training and service in the United States armed forces or departed from or remained outside the United States to avoid or evade military service? (If answer is Yes, explain) Yes No

....

38. Do you intend to enter the United States from Canada, Mexico or an island adjacent to the United States within two years after arrival in Canada, Mexico or such adjacent island? (If answer is Yes, give the name of the transportation company by which you entered or intend to enter Canada, Mexico or such island) Yes No

....

DO NOT WRITE BELOW THE FOLLOWING LINE
The consular officer will assist you in answering parts 39 and 40

....

39. I claim to be exempt from ineligibility to receive a visa and exclusion under item ....in part 41 for the following reasons:

....

....

....

....

40. I claim to be a
.... preference immigrant subject to the numerical limitation for .... (foreign state or dependent area)
Special immigrant subject to Western Hemisphere numerical limitation
Special immigrant not subject to limitation
Immediate relative of a United States citizen
My claim is based on the following facts:

Signature of Applicant

....

Subscribed and sworn to before me this .... day of ....19......at ....

....

Consular Officer

SPANISH VERSION OF EXCERPT FROM IMMIGRATION FORM

CHAPTER 6

FORMAL INTERPRETING SITUATIONS

The interpreting skills developed through Chapters 4 and 5 in dealing with informal interpreting situations are certainly applicable to formal interpreting situations. A formal interpreting situation such as a courtroom is distinguished from an informal situation by the setting and by the fact that there are set rules and procedures governing the conduct and role of interpreters. Before continuing with this chapter, review the section of Chapter 1 of this part of the text which deals with the role of the interpreter in formal interpreting situations.

GUIDELINES FOR INTERPRETERS: FORMAL INTERPRETING SITUATIONS

You may recall from Chapter 1 that an interpreter may be appointed by the court, or else the plaintiff, defendant, or a witness may bring along an interpreter. In the latter instances, the interpreter is frequently a bilingual staff member of the office or agency of the attorney for the plaintiff or defendant. No matter who appoints an interpreter or what office the interpreter works for, ALL INTERPRETERS must follow the rules of the court regarding interpreters. *The interpreter's primary allegiance is to convey an accurate and complete version of what is originally said in the source language into the target language.*

An interpreter should always be *on time.* Upon arriving, the interpreter should give his or her full name to the court clerk, as well as the language or languages in which he or she is competent to interpret. If the interpreter's words are "on the record", that is to say as interpreter for a witness, then the interpreter is sworn in at the beginning of the testimony to be given by the non-English-speaking witness. The interpreter swears to give a true and faithful rendering of all that is to be translated. For example, the interpreter may be asked to raise his or her right hand and be sworn in as follows:

> Do you solemnly swear that you will well and truly interpret English into Spanish and Spanish into English to the best of your ability in the cause now pending before this court, so help you God.

After the interpreter says "I do", he or she is asked to formally state and spell his (her) full name for the record.

During the course of testimony, the interpreter for a witness generally stands near the witness stand, speaking in a clear voice, loud enough for all to hear what he or she is saying. In the case of an interpreter for a party, the interpreter sits near the party at counsel table, speaking just loudly enough to be heard only by the person for whom he or she is interpreting.

When a non-English-speaking witness is sworn in, the interpreter administers the oath to the witness in Spanish. The oath will usually be one of the following:

> ¿Jura ante Dios decir la verdad, solamente la verdad y nada más que la verdad?

> ¿Jura que en su testimonio dirá la verdad, solamente la verdad y nada más que la verdad?

All court interpreting should be done in the first person. *The interpreter must speak as if he or she is the mirror image of the witness.* If a question or answer is too lengthly to be interpreted at once, the interpreter should use hand signals to indicate to the speaker that there is a need for a pause. Hand signals should also be used to indicate when the speaker can again begin to speak.

The interpreter should develop a list of standard terminology common to court proceedings. Whenever the interpreter knows in advance what the subject matter of the trial will be, he or she should study the particular type of vocabulary involved. This is especially true in areas where non-standard terms are used, such as in narcotics trials.

Just as in informal interpreting situations, the interpreter must always strive to provide the *most accurate* rendering of the testimony of a witness. Vulgar expressions, pejorative exclamations, slang, and foul language must *all* be translated using the same tone and choice of vocabulary of the speaker. Remember that the interpreter has no right to edit or change the content or tone of the testimony of a witness. A "correction" of a mistake by the witness is violation of the interpreter's duty. The interpreter must stay as close as possible to the original words of the witness.

The question of *interpreter competence* can never be forgotten. Remember that, at times, the interpreter is the only bilingual person in the courtroom. If the interpreter does not feel competent to interpret the testimony of a given witness or witnesses, then the interpreter must *immediately* bring this fact to the attention of the presiding judicial officer, so that a replacement can be found. On the other hand, at times an interpreter may simply not understand a given question or reply. The interpreter should also ask the presiding judicial officer directly for permission to get a clarification or repetition. *Since it is only the words of the interpreter and not the words of the witness in the source language which go on the record, it is almost impossible to later correct an interpreter's errors.*

THE PRE-APPEARANCE INTERVIEW

If possible, the interpreter should have the opportunity to converse briefly with the non-English-speaking witness or party before interpreting for that person in court. This brief conversation may be called a "pre-appearance interview". It is, however, much briefer and more superficial than a client interview. A pre-appearance interview gives the interpreter the opportunity to become accustomed to the non-English-speaking person's individual speech pattern as well as to any dialectical or regional characteristics of the non-English-speaking person's speech. By the same token, it also gives the non-English-speaking person the opportunity to become accustomed to the interpreter's speech.

This pre-appearance interview does *not* conflict with the precautions given throughout these materials regarding idle conversations between the interpreter and the non-English-speaking person or conversation in the hallways or out of the hearing of the attorney. Rather, this is comparable to the suggestions given in the preceding chapter dealing with in-person interviews; the interpreter should exchange greetings and perhaps a brief word of explanation regarding the interpreting process, the use of hand signals, etc. *Conversation between client and interpreter outside of the actual in-court interpreting process should be limited to what is suggested here.* Other types of discussion *are* inappropriate to the interpreter's role and may even be unethical.

The presiding judicial officer should be consulted if the interpreter or one of the attorneys desires a pre-appearance interview for a non-English-speaking party or witness. Otherwise it will seem as if the interpreter and the non-English-speaking person are consulting in an impermissible manner.

FORMAL INTERPRETING SITUATIONS: SOME EXAMPLES

SITUATION A: DIVORCE PROCEEDINGS

The following series of questions, in English and Spanish, represents the questions most frequently asked of a client at a court hearing to grant an uncontested divorce. When the plaint-tiff, the person seeking the divorce, is on the witness stand, his or her attorney will generally ask the series of questions. Sometimes the attorney for the plaintiff will ask the entire series of questions, and the judge may ask questions of the witness afterwards. At other times the judge will interject questions while the attorney is questioning the plaintiff. The interpreter, of course, translates questions posed by both judge and attorneys.

Before interpreting at a divorce hearing an interpreter should be thoroughly familiar with these questions in English and Spanish.

DIVORCE QUESTIONS

1. Where do you reside? How long have you lived there?
2. When, where and by whom were you married?
   (I show you what purports to be your marriage certificate. Can you identify it?)
3. Are you living with your wife/husband?
4. When did you and your wife/husband last live together? Date of Separation?
5. Since that date, have you and your wife/husband ever resumed living together?
6. Is there any reasonable prospect of reconciliation?
7. Were there any children born of the marriage?
8. State their names and ages.
9. Do you wish custody of these children?
10. Are the children presently in your custody?
11. Are you asking for child suport?
12. Are you asking for alimony?
13. Have there been any previous proceedings between you and your wife/husband for di-vorce, annulment, separation or support?
14. Do you wish to resume your maiden name?
15. What is your maiden name?

SPANISH TRANSLATION OF DIVORCE QUESTIONS

1. ¿Dónde reside (vive) usted? ¿Cuánto tiempo tiene usted de residir (vivir) allí?

2. ¿Dónde se casó usted? ¿Cuándo se casó usted? ¿Por quién fue usted casado(a)?

   (Le muestro lo que, según las indicaciones, es su partida de casamiento. ¿La puede usted identificar?)

3. ¿Vive usted con su esposo/esposa?

4. ¿Cuándo convivieron usted y su esposo (a) por última vez? ¿Cuál fue la fecha de la separación?

5. Desde esa fecha, ¿han vuelto a convivir usted y su esposo/esposa?

6. ¿Hay alguna posibilidad de reconciliación?

7. ¿Nacieron hijos del matrimonio?

8. Diga los nombres y las edades de sus hijos.

9. ¿Desea usted patria potestad sobre (custodia de) sus hijos?

10. ¿Actualmente, están los hijos bajo su tutela?

11. ¿Pide usted sostenimiento (mantenimiento) para sus hijos?

12. ¿Pide usted pensión alimenticia?

13. ¿Ha habido entre usted y su esposo(a) procedimientos previos de divorcio, anulación, separación o mantenimiento?

14. ¿Desea usted volver a usar su apellido de soltera?

15. ¿Cuál es su apellido de soltera?

SITUATION B: ADOPTION PROCEEDINGS

The following series of questions, in English and Spanish, represents the questions typically asked of prospective adoptive parents at an adoption hearing. When a prospective adoptive parent is on the witness stand, his or her attorney will generally ask the series of questions. Sometimes the attorney for the petitioner will ask the entire series of questions, and the judge may ask questions of the witness afterwards. At other times the judge will interject questions while the attorney is questioning the plaintiff. The interpreter, of course, translates questions posed by both judge and attorneys.

Before interpreting at an adoption hearing an interpreter should be throughly familiar familiar with these questions in English and Spanish.

ADOPTION QUESTIONS

1. Have you and your wife (husband) presented to this court a complaint applying for the adoption of ....?
2. What is your name?
3. Where do you reside?
4. How old are you? How old is your wife (husband)?
5. Are you a citizen of the United States?
6. How long have you resided in the State of (New Jersey)?

   (At this time the attorney introduces into evidence the surrender of the child.)
7. What is the name of the child?
8. When and where was he (she) born, if you know?
9. Do you have any natural children?
10. Do you have any other adopted children?
11. This child was received by you from (Name of Agency), was it not?
12. When was this child received by you?
13. Has he (she) been under your continuous care from that date to the present?
14. Do you know the natural parents of the child, or either of them?
15. Do you know the marital status of the natural parents of the child?
16. Does the child have any property?
17. By what name do you desire the child to be known if he (she) is adopted by you?
18. Where are you employed?
19. How long?
20. Are you able to support the child?
21. Will you take the same responsibilities (treat the child) as if he (she) were your natural child?

SPANISH TRANSLATION OF ADOPTION QUESTIONS

1. ¿Han presentado usted y su esposa/esposo una demanda a este tribunal para solicitar la adopción de ....?
2. ¿Cómo se llama usted?
3. ¿Dónde reside (vive) usted?
4. ¿Cuántos años tiene usted? ¿Cuántos años tiene su esposo/esposa?
5. ¿Es usted ciudadano(a) de los Estados Unidos?
6. ¿Cuánto tiempo hace que Ud. reside (vive) en el estado de (Nueva Jersey)?

   (En este momento, el abogado (la abogada) presenta prueba de la entrega del niño/de la niña.)
7. ¿Cómo se llama el niño/la niña?
8. Si lo sabe, ¿cuándo y dónde nació él/ella?
9. ¿Tiene usted hijos no adoptivos?

   (***Note: DO NOT use "hijos naturales", which means illegitimate children.)
10. ¿Tiene usted otros hijos adoptivos?
11. La Agencia (Nombre de la Agencia) le entregó a usted este niño/esta niña, ¿no es verdad?
12. ¿Cuándo recibió usted este niño/esta niña?
13. ¿Ha estado él/ella bajo su cuidado continuo desde esa fecha hasta el presente?
14. ¿Conoce usted a los padres por nacimiento, o a uno de ellos?
15. ¿Está enterado(a) usted del estado civil de los padres por nacimiento del niño/de la niña?
16. ¿Es propietario el niño/la niña de algunos bienes?
17. ¿Bajo qué nombre desea usted que se conozca al niño/a la niña si él/ella es adoptado(a) por usted?
18. ¿Dónde trabaja usted?
19. ¿Cuánto tiempo hace que usted trabaja en este lugar?
20. ¿Tiene usted los recursos económicos para mantener al niño/a la niña?
21. ¿Se hará usted responsable del niño/de la niña como si fuera su hijo/hija por nacimiento?

SITUATION C: DEPOSITIONS

"Taking a deposition" refers to the process of taking a witness's sworn testimony outside of court. The witness whose testimony is taken is called the deponent. All parties who are normally present in the courtroom situation —plaintiff, defendant, and their attorneys— must be notified of a deposition so that they have the right to be present if they want to attend and participate. Unless all parties are notified, a deposition cannot be used in court to replace live testimony. Even if all parties are present, there are limitations to the use of depositions in court. These limitations are determined by the rules of a particular court system.

To an interpreter who is present at a deposition, there is little change from the courtroom situations described previously in this chapter. The major difference is that, given the absence of a presiding judicial officer, any objections or comments must be noted for later consideration by a judge, rather than considered immediately as in open court. As in the case of testimony given in open court, precision in interpreting is of paramount importance, since only the English words of the interpreter go into the formal record of the deposition. The testimony in the source language, Spanish, is not formally preserved.

At times, when an interpreter cannot be present, a witness's testimony in Spanish will be taken on tape, for an interpreter to translate into written English at a later time. The product of this written translation, as in the case of the product of the oral testimony, is called the "deposition".

EXERCISE 1C

The following deposition represents a written transcription of the Spanish narration of an incident as related by a person whose Spanish has been heavily affected by anglicisms. In addition, the deponent has never learned standard Spanish. Assume that you are hearing the deponent and orally interpreting at the taking of a deposition. Try to render the passage directly into English in the space provided underneath the Spanish version. *Recall that the Spanish of the deposition represents phonetic pronunciation rather than standard Spanish spelling.*

If possible, as a second exercise, try to work on this deposition *orally* with another person. One person functions as the deponent and the other as the interpreter. It would be best if the entire proceeding could be taped, for review and critique.

Deposition

Había un grupo de muchachah allí en la calle cuando vino Ramíreh preguntando por Tomáh. Leh preguntó si lo habían vihto y una de lah muchachah se rió dél, de Ramíreh, porque el goldo tropezó con algo allí en la acera y se cayó. Cuando se levantó ehtaba enfogonao porque se ensució loh pantaloneh.

Como es carvo lleva peluca y se le cayó, digo la peluca. Luego, le dio una patá al perro y eh por eso que el perro le mordió. Tó pasó con tanta prisa que no había ná que hacer. Eso de que el perro le mordió sin haberle hecho ná eh mentira. Ehtá mintiendo. Pero de lah cinco chicah que habían en la calle, como naide quiere cuenta con la policía, no quieren ayudarme en eso. Pero eso de que tropezó con algo allí en la acera, eso sí que eh verdah. Entre la marqueta y la lavandería vi una paipa de doh o treh pieh. No tengo ni la menor idea de quien la había dejao allí. Coño, cuando se levantó el tío ese ehtaba pero que trina, y lah chicah se paniquearon y se fueron corriendo.

Pero eso de que se dañó la esparda tropezando con el cacho de tubo son cuentoh suyoh. Porque cuando le dio la patá a mi perro no dijo ná de su ehparda. Sí que ehtaba enfogonao con el perro y con la Rosa —así se llama una de lah chicah que se ehtaba riendo a carcajá de él. Empezó a correr trah ella —la Rosa— pero no la alcanzó.

Dehpuéh, volvió la Rosa, digo Ramíreh, y comenzó de nuevo con eso del perro. Entonceh, yo le dije que ehtaba harto y que no quería ehcucharlo má. Güeno, ehtaba tan enfogonao que trató de pegarme pero falló y se ehcurrió y se cayó en la calle. Trató de levantarse pero no pudo. Ni podía mover lah piernah. Así eh como se dañó la ehparda y no cuando tropezó con la paipa entre la marqueta y la lavandería.

EXERCISE 2C ENGLISH VERSION OF DEPOSITION

OTHER FORMAL INTERPRETING SITUATIONS

Although the most frequently encountered formal interpreting situation may be a judicial trial, interpreters are frequently required at other formal proceedings. A deposition, as just seen, is one example. In the criminal law area, interpreters are frequently needed at hearings during other phases of the criminal justice process such as detention hearings, arraignments, grand jury hearings, post-trial appeals, and parole hearings.

Interpreters are also frequently needed at administrative agency hearings, such as Welfare, Social Security, Worker's Compensation, and the like. At an administrative agency hearing, the presiding judicial officer will be a hearing examiner or an administrative law judge rather than a trial court judge. The hearing process is similar to a judicial trial. Just as each court system has its own rules, so administrative agencies have their own rules to govern hearings. Some administrative agencies and their rules are governed by the law of an individual state. Other agencies are federally controlled, with rules standardized for the entire nation. Thus, the amount of interpreter assistance required by law may vary from agency to agency and from state to state.

For the interpreter, the setting where the formal proceedings take place may vary, but the role, the responsibilities, and the ethical considerations cannot change. Confidentiality, high standards, and precision are always key parts of the interpreting process.

GLOSSARY OF TERMS ENGLISH-SPANISH

The following glossary contains many terms which may be useful to an interpreter in a variety of situations within the legal environment. These include: domestic relations, criminal law, landlord-tenant law, personal injury, and procedural terms, as well as many expressions which may be employed during interviews, telephone conversations, and formal interpreting situations. In the glossary, verbs are listed in the infinitive form while nouns and adjectives are generally listed in the masculine singular form, with the feminine given in parenthesis when appropriate. The only exception to this pattern occurs in the case of an idiomatic expression or a special usage of a given word or phrase. The glossary is arranged alphabetically according to the English. In contrast to the Spanish-English Legal Terminology presented in the companion volume to this text, the glossary presented here is intended to be a quick reference tool for interpreters. Therefore, it must be borne in mind that the expressions listed below, like all words and phrases, may have different meanings in different contexts. If there is doubt about the use of an expression in a given context, an appropriate dictionary should be consulted. The lists of reference works found at the end of the three parts of this text include many such dictionaries.

abduction	rapto
accomplice	cómplice
accused	acusado (a); procesado (a)
to acquit	absolver
acquittal	absolución, sentencia absolutoria
acquitted	absuelto (a)
adjustment	ajuste
admission of guilt	confesión de culpabilidad
adultery	adulterio
advance payment	pago adelantado
advertisement	propaganda
affidavit	declaración jurada
aforementioned	antes mencionado
aforethought	con premeditación
alien	extranjero (a)
alimony	pensión alimenticia
to allege	alegar
annulment	anulación
answer (to a complaint)	contestación (a una demanda)
appeal (noun)	apelación
to appeal	apelar
appeal for reconsideration	recurso de suplicación
appeal for reversal	recurso de reposición
appeal hearing	audiencia de apelación
to appear	comparecer
appellant	apelante; recurrente
appellate court	tribunal de apelación
applicant	solicitante
application	solicitud
armed robbery	robo a mano armada
arraignment	acusación
arrears	atrasos
arrest (noun)	arresto; detención
to arrest	detener

English	Spanish
assault and battery	asalto y agresión
assistance	ayuda; asistencia
association	sociedad
to attest; to certify	dar fe
attorney; lawyer	abogado (a); licenciado (a)
attorney general	procurador general
award	fallo; adjudicación
bail	fianza
on bail	bajo fianza
bailiff	alguacil, márshal (P.R.)
bailor	fiador
bankrupt	quebrado (a)
bankruptcy	bancarrota
baptismal certificate	fe de bautismo
bar association	asociación de abogados; colegio de abogados
bargain	negociación; contrato
basic standard of adequate care	criterio básico de cuidado adecuado
being duly sworn	habiendo prestado juramento
belief	creencia
bench warrant	orden de arresto
beneficiary	beneficiado (a)
benefit payments	pagos beneficiales
beneficial owner	dueño útil
best evidence	la mejor prueba
beyond a reasonable doubt	fuera de duda razonable
bill	proyecto de ley; cuenta
bill of rights	garantías individuales
bill of sale	escritura de venta
bi-monthly (every 15 days)	quincenales
birth certificate	partida de nacimiento
birth control	control de la natalidad
birth record	certificado de nacimiento
bonds	vínculos
boss	jefe
breaking and entering	escalamiento
to bring a suit	entablar iniciar presentar una queja, un pleito, un litigio
broken English	inglés chapurreado interrumpido imperfecto
budget	presupuesto
burden of proof	obligación de comprobar
calendar	lista de pleitos, juicios, señalamientos
capital crime	crimen sancionable con pena de muerte
capital punishment	pena de muerte
case (noun)	caso; pleito; acción; causa
cash	al contado; dinero en efectivo
cash refund	reembolso en efectivo
ceiling	techo

English	Spanish
chamber of commerce	cámara de comercio
to charge	acusar
to charge the jury	instruir al jurado
chief referee	jefe de árbitros
child support	mantenimiento para el hijo
circumstancial evidence	prueba circunstancial
civil register	registro civil
to claim	alegar, reclamar
claimant	reclamante
coalition	liga
code	código
collected amount	cantidad cobrada
to come into force	entrar en vigor
commercial paper	documentos mercantiles
community property	propiedad común
complaint	demanda; queja
to condone	perdonar
constable	alguacil
contempt	desacato
to contest	disputar
continued absence	ausencia continuada
conviction	condena
corporation	sociedad anónima
costs and attorneys fees	costos y honorarios
count (noun)	cargo; acusación
county	condado
court, court of law	tribunal; juzgado
(awaiting) court action	(esperando) la acción del tribunal
court clerk	escribano del tribunal
court costs	costos procesales
courthouse	corte, edificio de los tribunales
courtroom	sala del tribunal
criminal law	derecho penal
criminal prosecution	prosecución criminal
crime	crimen; delito
cruel and unusual punishment	castigo cruel y no aplicado corrientemente
custody	custodia; tutela; patria potestad
damages	daños y perjuicios
to debate	disputar
debt	deuda
deduction	deducción
default (noun)	incumplimiento; defecto
defendant	demandado; acusado
defense counsel	abogado (a) defensor (a)
to defraud	engañar, estafar, defraudar
demand for payment	demanda para reembolso
denial	negación
to deny (paternity)	negar (la paternidad)
Department of Health	Departamento de Salud; Ministerio de Salubridad
Department of Public Works	Departamento (Ministerio) de Obras Públicas

deprivation	privación
desertion	abandono
determination	decisión; fallo
diagnosis	diagnosis
disability benefits	beneficios de incapacidad
discharge (noun)	liberación; descargo; cumplimiento
to discharge	despedir
discretion	discreción
to dismiss	dar por terminado (a); despedir
district attorney	fiscal
Division of Small Claims	División de Pequeñas Reclamaciones
divorce	divorcio
to sue for divorce	pedir el divorcio
no fault divorce	divorcio sin culpa
divorce decree	sentencia de divorcio
docket number	número de presentación; número del acta
documentary proof	constancia
drain	desagüe
drunken driving	manejar borracho, en estado de embriaguez
due process of law	debido y adecuado proceso legal
duly sworn	debidamente juramentado (a)
earned income	ingresos de trabajo
eligible	elegible
embezzlement	desfalco
emergency loan program	programa de préstamos de emergencia
employee	empleado (a)
to endorse	endosar
endorsement	endoso
enforce	hacer valer, poner en vigor
equitable distribution	distribución equitativa
estimate	presupuesto
eviction	desalojo
evidence	evidencia; prueba (s)
ex-convict	ex-penado; ex-presidiario
exempted	exonerado (a)
exemption	exención
expenses	gastos
to expunge	borrar; cancelar
extenuating circumstances	circunstancias atenuantes
eye witness	testigo presencial
fact	hecho
false arrest	arresto ilegal
false statement	declaración falsa
faucet	grifo
felony	delito grave
fictitious plates	placas ficticias
Fifth Amendment	quinta enmienda (constitucional)
files	archivos
final grades	calificaciones finales
financial eligibility	elegibilidad financiera
fine	multa

fingerprints	impresiones digitales; huellas digitales
to fire; to dismiss	despedir
food coupons	estampillas para comida; cupones
food stamp program	programa de estampillas para comida
form	formulario
forthwith	en seguida; inmediatamente
forward adjustment	ajuste adelantado
foster care	cuidado de crianza
fraud	fraude
freedom	libertad
freedom of speech	libertad de palabra
to give advice	dar aviso de antemano
grand jury	jurado de acusación; gran jurado; jurado mayor
grievance	agravio
grounds	causa
guilt	culpa
guilty	culpable
guilty plea	declaración de culpabilidad
handwriting comparison	comparación manuscrita
hearing	vista; audiencia
hearing officer	árbitro
hearsay	prueba de oídos
heat	calefacción
height	estatura
heir	heredero (a)
hereafter	en adelante
hereinafter	más adelante
hereby	por el presente
heretofore	anteriormente
hereunder	bajo esto
herewith	con el presente
hold-up	salteo
homicide	homicidio
excusable homicide	homicidio inculpable
hospitalization	hospitalización
hostile witness	testigo desfavorable
household	hogar
housing authority	autoridad de vivienda
hung jury	jurado sin veredicto
identification card	cédula de identificación
identifying marks	señas de identidad
impeachment	desacreditación
impounded	bajo la custodia del tribunal de justicia
incapacity	incapacidad
income	ingresos
income tax	impuesto sobre los ingresos
incriminating evidence	prueba acusadora
indictment	procesamiento; informe del fiscal; acusación por el gran jurado
infant	criatura

inheritance	herencia
injury	herida; perjuicio; lesión; daño; agravio
in-kind income	ingresos no en efectivo
insanity	locura
intake worker	entrevistador (a)
intent	intención
Internal Revenue Service	El Servicio de Impuestos Internos
interpreter	intérprete
interrogatory	interrogatorio
invoice	factura
irrelevant	inaplicable
issued	expedido (a)
job	empleo
judge	juez
judgment	juicio; sentencia
judiciary	poder judicial
to jump bail	quebrar la fianza
juror	jurado; miembro del jurado
jury	jurado
juvenile court	tribunal de menores
key	llave
landlady	dueña
landlord	dueño
law	ley
to bring a lawsuit; to institute proceedings	presentar una demanda
law in force	ley vigente
lawyer; attorney	abogado (a); licenciado (a)
layoff	cesantía
leading question	pregunta que insinúa la respuesta
lease (noun)	contrato de arrendamiento
legal stamps	sellos legales
lenient	indulgente
let the record stand	que quede establecido en el Registro Oficial
letterhead	membrete
liability	obligación
literally	al pie de la letra
litigation	litigio
loan agreement	contrato de préstamo
lock (noun)	cerradura; candado
lump-sum payment	pagos globales
maiden name	apellido de soltera
mailbox	buzón de correo
malice	malicia
manager	gerente
mandatory jail sentence	cárcel mandatario; condena mandatoria
manslaughter	homicidio sin premeditación
marital status	estado civil
married (adjective)	casado (a)
married couple	matrimonio

marshal (noun)	alguacil; oficial de los tribunales de justicia
material witness	testigo esencial
matrimonial bond	vínculo matrimonial
mental disability	incapacidad mental
mental health	salud mental
mental hospital	hospital mental, manicomio
mentally retarded	mentalmente atrasado (a)
mercy	gracia
misdemeanor	pequeño delito
mistrial	juicio nulo
money management	manejo de dinero
money order	giro
monopoly	monopolio
mortgage (noun)	hipoteca
motion	petición
murder	asesinato
to murder	asesinar
murder weapon	arma de asesinato
name (noun)	nombre
first name	primer nombre nombre de pila nombre cristiano
last name	apellido
nickname	apodo
negligence	descuido; negligencia
not guilty	no culpable
notarial deed	escritura notarial
notice	aviso
notice of action	notificación de acción
oath	juramento
objection	objeción; oposición
to obstruct	obstruir
offense	ofensa; delito
on the grounds of (desertion)	por causa de (abandono)
on your behalf	en su nombre
opening statement	declaración inaugural
order	decreto; orden
final order	orden final decreto
ordinance	estatuto; reglamento; ordenanza
outcome	resultado
overcharge	cargo excesivo
overpayment	pago de más; pago excesivo
to overrule	denegar; declarar sin lugar; no aceptar la objeción del abogado
pardon	absolución; perdón; indulto; remisión de delito
parole	libertad condicional
parties (plaintiff and defendant)	las partes (demandante y demandado)

opposing party; other side	la parte contraria
to pass	quedar aprobado; aprobar
paternity	paternidad
payee	cobrador
payment	pago
to penalize	castigar
penalty	castigo; condena
pending court action	acción pendiente
penitentiary	penitenciaría
period	plazo
certification period	plazo de certificación
perjury	falso testimonio
personal property	propiedad personal
pickpocket	ratero, carterista
plaintiff	demandante
plaster	yeso
plea	alegación; petición
to plead	alegar
to plead guilty	declararse culpable
pleadings	alegaciones
policy	póliza
life insurance policy	póliza de seguros de vida
postal authority	autoridad postal
to postpone	aplazar
postponement	aplazamiento
to pay for a judgment	pedir una sentencia
to prejudice	perjudicar
to press charges	levantar cargos
pre-trial intervention program	programa de intervención antes del juicio
printed	impreso (a)
probation	libertad condicional vigilada a prueba
probation officer	oficial probatorio
proceedings	procedimientos
to pronounce sentence	pronunciar un fallo
proof	prueba; comprobación
to prosecute	procesar
prosecuting attorney	abogado acusador
prosecutor	fiscal
provisions	disposiciones
psychiatrist	psiquiatra
public defender	(abogado) defensor público
pursuant to	de acuerdo con
to question	interrogar; preguntar
quota system	sistema de cuota
race	raza
to rape (rape)	violar (violación)
rate	interés
real estate	bienes raíces, bienes inmuebles
real property	propiedad inmueble; inmobiliaria

rebuttal	refutación
receipt	recibo
recipient	recipiente
records	actas
referee	árbitro
refugee	refugiado (a)
registration	matrícula
rehabilitation	rehabilitación
release (noun)	descargo; liberación
rent (noun)	alquiler; renta (Americano — en general, renta significa lo que se gana de una inversión)
to reimburse; to repay	reembolsar
reprieve	suspensión temporal
reputed	supuesto (a)
requisition	solicitud
responsible relative	pariente responsable
retardation	retardación
mentally retarded	mentalmente atrasado (a)
to revoke	revocar
revoked licence list	lista de licencias revocadas
robbery	robo
roof	techo
search and seizure	registro y embargo
search warrant	orden de registro
scene of the accident	lugar del accidente
screen (noun)	tela metálica
self-defense	legítima defensa; defensa propia
sentence (noun)	sentencia; condena
to sentence	dar sentencia
to set	fijar
settlement	transacción
shift (noun) (e.g., at work)	turno
shoplifter	ratero de tiendas
shoplifting	ratería de tiendas
simple assault and battery	asalto y agresión simple
single	soltero (a)
Social Security Administration	Administración del Seguro Social
spouse	esposo (a)
statement of earnings	estado de cuentas
stay (noun)	suspensión
to stay; to suspend	suspender
to steal	robar; hurtar
stepfather	padrastro
stepmother	madrastra
to still stand; to remain standing	quedar en pie
stipulation	estipulación
subpoena	citación
to sue	demandar; poner pleito
summons	auto de comparecencia; citación; aplazamiento

superintendent	superintendente
support; maintenance	sostenimiento; manutención
Supreme Court	Tribunal Supremo
surrogate	juez del tribunal testamentario
to sustain an injury	sufrir una herida
to swear	jurar
sworn (statment)	(declaración) bajo juramento
taxpayer	contribuyente
tenant	inquilino (a)
to testify; to give evidence	declarar (bajo juramento); testificar
testimony	testimonio; declaración
theft	robo; hurto
ties	vínculos
timely notice	notificación a tiempo
tort	acto dañoso; agravio
to trespass	meterse
trial	juicio; proceso; causa
unborn child	feto; niño no nacido
unconditional separation	separación absoluta
to become unconscious; to lose consciousness	perder el sentido
under oath	bajo juramento
undersigned	suscrito (a)
unemployment	desempleo
unemployment benefits	beneficios del desempleo
unemployment compensation	compensación por desempleo
unemployment hearing	audiencia sobre la compensación de desempleo
unemployment insurance	seguro sobre el desempleo
to collect unemployment	cobrar desempleo
unified tax	tributo unificado
uninsured	sin seguro
unlawful	ilegal
to uphold	sostener; apoyar
usual occupation	ocupación usual
to vacate	desocupar
verdict	sentencia; decisión
victimless crime	crimen sin víctima
waiting period	período de espera
to waive	renunciar
waiver of rights	renuncia de derechos; abandono
warning	advertencia
warrant	autorización
warrant of arrest	orden de arresto; auto de detención
welfare	bienestar público (American- "el welfare")
whereas	por cuanto
will (noun)	testamento
with prejudice	sin derecho de nuevo juicio; con perjuicio

to withdraw	retirar
witness (noun)	testigo
work (noun)	trabajo
worker	obrero; trabajador
writ	mandamiento; decreto

GLOSSARY OF WORDS AND TERMS USED AT THE DEPARTMENT OF WELFARE

ENGLISH-SPANISH

The following glossary contains many terms used by the Department of Welfare in intake interviews and questionnaires.

WELFARE WORDS AND TERMS

absence	ausencia
absent	ausente
administrative procedure	procedimiento administrativo
to adopt	adoptar
adopted	adoptado (a)
adoption, petition for	petición para adopción
to affect	afectar, conmover
affirmation/oath	juramento
to aid, help, assist	ayudar
amount	suma, cantidad
amount of assistance	cantidad de ayuda/asistencia
analysis	análisis
applicant	solicitante
application	solicitud
to apply (for)	solicitar
attorney	abogado
assistance, aid, help (noun)	ayuda, asistencia
assistance pending the fair hearing	asistencia mientras que se llega a una decisión final, pendiente de
authorization	autorización
to authorize	autorizar
basic need	necesidad básica
basic standard of need	cantidad básica requerida para mantenimiento
both	ambos (ellos dos) (los dos)
budget	presupuesto
case worker, eligibility worker	trabajador de bienestar social
care and support	cuidado y manutención
change(s)	cambio(s)
changes in circumstances	cambio de circunstancias

claimant	reclamante
client	cliente
clothing	ropa
confidentiality	confidencialidad
continually absent	ausencia continuada
contribution	contribución
cost of living	costo de vida
credibility	credibilidad
date	fecha
death	muerte
deceased	fallecido
definition	definición
dependent child	hijo (a) menor de edad
deprivation	deprivación
to be deprived	deprivado
determination	determinación
to determine	determinar
dissatisfied	insatisfecho, descontento
district attorney	procurador, fiscal
earnings	ingresos
educational expenses	gastos educacionales
effect (noun)	efecto
eligibility	elegibilidad
essential person	persona esencial
established	establecido
evidence	evidencia, prueba
exempt	exento
exemption	exención
gross income	ingresos brutos
home	hogar, casa
household	grupo familiar, utensilios de hogar
in kind	en especie
incapacitated	incapacitado
income	ingresos
to indicate	indicar
to investigate	investigar
jail	cárcel
legally responsible	tutor, guardián legal
limit (noun)	límite
mentally	mentalmente
need	necesidad
needy	necesitado
(the parents) never maintained a home together	(el padre y la madre) no están casados y nunca han vivido juntos en la misma casa
oath	juramento
opportunity	oportunidad
parent	padre o madre
per month	al mes
percentage	porcentaje

personal	personal
petition	petición
physically	físicamente
property	propiedad
purpose	propósito
pursuant	de acuerdo
real estate	bienes raíces
receipt of income	recibo de ingresos
to receive	recibir
recipient	recipiente
recognized	reconocido
registration	registración, matrícula
regulations	reglamentos
to remarry	volverse a casar
report	informe
representative	representante
request (noun)	petición
to require	requerir
requirement	requisito
to reside	vivir con, residir
resources	recursos
responsibility	responsabilidad
responsible relative	familiar responsable
right to	derecho a
shelter	albergue
status of the parent	situación del padre o de la madre
step-father	padrastro
to stop	parar
stop (command)	pare Ud.
support and care (nouns)	manutención y cuidado
taken into consideration	tomado en consideración
timely notice	aviso anticipado
transportation	transporte
unemployed	desempleado (a)
value (noun)	valor
waiver (noun)	renuncia
Welfare	Bienestar Social (Público)

REFERENCE MATERIALS

Alfaro, Ricardo J. *Diccionario de anglicismos.* Madrid: Gredos, 1964.

Amercian Hospital Association. *Interpreters' Services and the Role of Health Care Volunteers.* Chicago, 1074.

Anonymous. "Right of the Accused to Have Evidence or Court Proceedings Interpreted." Annotation. 36 *Annotated Law Reports 3d* 276 (1971).*

———. "Breaking the Language Barrier: New Rights for California's Linguistic Minorities." 5 *Pacific Law Journal* 648 (1974).

———. "Interpreters for the Defense: Due Process for the Non-English-Speaking Defendant." Comment. 63 *California Law Review* 801 (1975).

———. "Non-English-Speaking Persons in the Criminal Justice System: Current State of the Law." Note. 61 *Cornell Law Review* 289 (1976).

Arora, Shirley L. *Proverbial Comparisons and Related Expressions in Spanish: Recorded in Los Angeles, California.* Berkeley: University of California Press, 1977.

Arrowsmith, William and Roger Shattuck. *The Craft and Context of Translation.* Austin: The University of Texas, 1961.

Ayala, Francisco. *Problemas de la traducción.* Madrid: Taurus, 1965.

Black, Henry C. *Black's Law Dictionary: Definitions of the Terms and Phrases of American and English Jurisprudence, Ancient and Modern.* 4th ed. St. Paul, Minn.: West Publishing Co., 1968.

Bomse, Marguerite D. and Julián H. Alfaro. *Practical Spanish for Medical and Hospital Personnel.* New York: Pergaman Press, 1973.

———. *Practical Spanish for School Personnel, Firemen, Policemen and Community Agencies.* New York: Pergaman Press, 1973.

Bower, William W. *International Manual of Linguists and Translators.* Scarecrow Press, 1959.

Breslin, Richard W., Editor. *Translation: Applications and Research.* New York: Gardner Press, 1976.

Brower, Reuben A. *On Translation.* New York: Oxford University Press, 1966.

California, State of. *State Hearings Handbook for Interpreters With Glossary of Select Welfare Terms.* Health and Welfare Agency, Department of Benefit Payments, 1977.

Carbajo, Antonio. *Spanish for Police Officers.* Miami Springs, Fla.: Language Research Press, 1963.

Cooper, George, et al. *Cases and Materials on Law and Poverty.* St. Paul, Minn.: West Publishing Co., 1968.

Caveney, James and Julian Amey. *Glossary of Spanish and English Management Terms. Léxico de términos de gestión español-inglés.* Harlow and London: Longman Group Ltd., 1978.

De Vries, Henry P. *The Law of the Americas: An Introduction to the Legal Systems of the American Republics.* Dobbs Ferry, New York: Oceana Publications, 1965.

Eder, Phanor J. *Comparative Survey of Anglo-American and Latin American Law.* New York: New York University Press, 1950.

Fernández García, Antonio. *Anglicismos en el español.* Oviedo: Gráficos Lux, 1972.

Finlay, Ian F. *Language Services in Industry.* London: Lockwood, (1973).

———. *Translating.* London: St. Paul's House, 1971.

Frankenthaler, Marilyn and Herbert L. McCarter. "A Call for Legislative Action: The Case for a New Jersey Court Interpreters Act." 3 *Seton Hall Legislative Journal* 125 (1978).

Freeman, Roger L. *English-Spanish, Spanish-English Dictionary of Communications and Electronic Terms. Diccionario de terminología electrónica y de telecomunicaciones inglés-español, español-inglés.* (London): Cambridge University Press, 1972.

Fuentes, Dagoberto and José A. López. *Barrio Language Dictionary: First Dictionary of Caló.* La Puente: Calif.: El Barrio Publications, 1974.

Fuller, Frederick. *A Handbook for Translators.* London: Colin Smythe Ltd., 1973.

*Citations to legal journals are given according to the standard form for legal citations: Volume Number, *Name of Periodical,* Page Number, Year of Publication.

Gámez, Taha de, Editor. *Simon and Schuster's International Dictionary. Diccionario internacional Simon and Schuster. English-Spanish, Spanish-English.* New York: Simon and Schuster, (1973).

García-Pelayo y Gross, Ramón, Micheline Durand, et al. *Diccionario moderno español-inglés.* Paris, New York: Larousse, 1976.

García Rodríguez, Mariano. *Diccionario matemático: español-inglés, inglés-español. Mathematics Dictionary: Spanish-English, English-Spanish.* New York: Hobbs, Dorman, (1965).

Goldberg, Morris. *Spanish-English Chemical and Medical Dictionary. Comprising Terms Employed in Medicine, Biochemistry, Surgery, Dentistry, Veterinary, Biology, Pharmacy, Allied Sciences, and Related Scientific Equipment.* New York: McGraw Hill, 1952.

Halse, Edward. *A Dictionary of Spanish, Spanish-American, Portuguese and Portuguese-American Mining, Metallurgical and Allied Terms.* London: C. Griffiths, 1926.

Hendry, J.F. *Your Future in Translating and Interpreting.* New York: Richards Rosen Press, Inc., 1969.

Hippchen, S. "Development of a Plan for Bilingual Interpreters in the Criminal Courts of New Jersey." 2 *Justice System Journal* 258 (1971).

Holmes, James, Editor. *The Nature of Translation.* Paris: Publishing House of the Slovak Academy of Sciences, 1970.

International Federation of Translators. *Quality in Translation: Proceedings of the IIIrd Congress of the International Federation of Translators.* New York: Macmillan, 1963.

Iribarren, José María. *El porqué de los dichos: sentido, origen y anécdota de los dichos, modismos y frases proverbiales de España, con otras muchas curiosidades.* Madrid: Aguilar, 1974.

Karst, Kenneth L. *Latin American Legal Institutions: Problems for Comparative Study.* Los Angeles: University of California, Latin American Center, 1966.

————. *Law and Development in Latin America: A Case Book.* Barkeley: University of California Press, 1975.

Kay, Margarita A. with J. Meredith, et al. *Southwestern Medical Dictionary: Spanish-English, English-Spanish.* Tucson: University of Arizona Press, 1977.

Kelly, Louis G. *The True Interpreter: A History of Translation Theory and Practice in the West.* New York: St. Martin's Press, 1979.

Kelz, Rochelle K. *Conversational Spanish for Medical Personnel: Essential Expressions, Questions, and Directions for Medical Personnel to Facilitate Conversation with Spanish-Speaking Patients and Co-Workers.* New York: Wiley, 1977.

Kingsborough Community College. *Spanish for Nurses and Allied Health Science Students.* New York: Arco, (1977).

Milner, Neal A. *The Court and Local Law Enforcement: The Impact of Miranda.* Beverly Hills, Calif.: Saga Publications, 1971).

Murray, William S. "The Use of Interpreters in Court." 30 *North Dakota Law Review* 304 (1954).

Moll, Aristedes. *English-Spanish Medical Dictionary.* Chicago: American Medical Association, 1926.

New Jersey Courts. *Revision of the Rules Governing the Courts of the State of New Jersey. Effective September 9, 1953.* Newark, New Jersey: Gann Law Books, (1953).

Nida, Eugene A. *Language Structure and Translation.* California: Stanford University Press, 1975.

————. *Toward a Science of Translating.* Netherlands: E.J. Brill, 1964.

Palacios, Bartolomé, José Luis Jiménez Osorio and José Orozco Ruiz. *Curso práctico de oficinas. Libro segundo. Organización de oficinas,* 12a ed. Pamplona, Spain: Editorial Gómez, 1974.

Payne, Alfred S. *Secretary Handbook of Useful Commercial Terms. Spanish-English, English-Spanish.* Madrid: Fragua, 1973.

Pina Vara, Rafael de. *Diccionario de derecho.* México, D.F.: Editorial Porrúa, S.A., 1980.

Radin, Max. *Law Dictionary.* Dobbs Ferry, New York: Oceana Publications, 1970.

Rivera García, Ignacio. *Diccionario de términos jurídicos.* Orford, New Hampshire: Equity Publishing Corp., 1976.

Robb, Louis A. with the collaboration of Tomás I. Nido, et al. *Dictionary of Legal Terms. Spanish-English and English-Spanish.* New York: John Wiley and Sons, Inc., 1955.

————. *Engineers' Dictionary, Spanish-English and English-Spanish.* New York: J. Wiley and Sons, Inc. London: Chapman and Hall Ltd., 1946.

Rochin Zazueta, Fernando. "Attorneys' Guide to the Use of Court Interpreters, With an English and Spanish Glossary of Criminal Law Terms." 8 *University of California at Davis Law Review* 471 (1975).

Savory, Theodore. *The Art of Translating.* Boston: The Writer, Inc., 1946.

Seleskovith, Danica. *Interpreting for International Conferences.* Washington, D.C.: Pen and Booth, 1978.

———. *Langage, lengues et mémoire: étude de la prise de notes en interprétation consecutive.* Paris: Lettres Modernes, 1975.

Sissons, Peter L. *The Hispanic Experience of Criminal Justice.* Monograph No. 4. Bronx, New York: Hispanic Research Center of Fordham University, 1979.

Tsuzaki, Stanley M. *English Influences on Mexican Spanish in Detroit.* The Hague: Mouton, 1970.

United States Army Map Service. *Glossary of Spanish Terms Commonly Appearing on Maps and Charts.* Provisional edition prepared under the direction of the Chief of Engineers. Washington, D.C., 1943.

Vanson, N. George and Marilyn R. Frankenthaler. *Spanish-English Legal Terminology / Terminología español-inglés en el área legal.* Cincinnati: South-Western Publishing Co., 1982.

Vázquez-Ayora, Gerardo. *Introducción a la traductología.* Washington, D.C.: Georgetown University Press, 1977.

Various Authors. *The World of Translation:* Papers delivered at the Conference on Literary Translation. New York: P.E.N. American Center, 1971.

Yeldell, Stanley B. *Guide to New Jersey Courts and Related Departments in the Use of Bilingual Court Interpreters.* Prepared for the Administrative Office of the Courts of New Jersey, 1974. (Spanish Translation by Florentino C. Martínez, entitled *Manual de preceptos para intérpretes bilingües en los tribunales de New Jersey. 1975.)*

PART III

TRANSLATING FOR LEGAL PERSONNEL

Jo Anne Engelbert

INTRODUCTION

These materials are intended to provide a basic introduction to legal translation for legal personnel serving the Hispanic community. They may be used in a self-teaching program by persons having good writing skills in both Spanish and English. It should be stressed that these materials provide preparation only for the simplest types of legal translation, that of personal documents (birth and marriage certificates and the like) and of routine agency or office correspondence. Progress beyond this level demands, as we shall discover, not only additional linguistic training but a deeper understanding of the principles and procedures of the law and of the peculiarities of the legal systems of the various countries. Legal translation cannot be done successfully by simply looking up words in a dictionary. Actually, dictionaries are of surprisingly little value in legal translation. Look at the following examples:

Cancelaron el cheque.	They *cancelled* the check.
Cancelarán el giro.	*They will honor* the draft.
Se ha cancelado la reclamación.	The claim *has been settled.*
Se ha cancelado la audiencia.	The hearing *has been suspended.*

Like "*cancelar,*" many words occurring frequently in legal discourse have a variety of meanings. "*Testimonio*" may mean "testimony," "evidence," "affidavit," "certified copy," "transcript" or "excerpt." It is the context in which words are used, of course, that determines what they mean and how they should be translated. This observation is considerably more important for legal translation than for other types of translating (see Chapter 4 of this part of the text, "Characteristics of Legal Discourse").

In learning to do legal translation it does little good, therefore, to memorize lists of isolated words and their equivalents; one must study the meaning of words as they are used in a given context. For this reason, the materials that follow contain many passages of legal discourse with the corresponding translations given immediately afterward. Getting the most out of these passages requires some active work on the part of the student.

STUDY SUGGESTIONS

Read each passage and translation several times, aloud if possible. Use file cards to make note of new words and words whose translation varies according to context. Use an English/English or Spanish/Spanish dictionary to learn more about these words. After studying a passage carefully, test your ability to translate it. Correct your errors and try the exercise again in a few days. As you come across new meanings of the words on your cards, make additional notations, including enough additional words to give the context clearly.

> hábil
>
> hábil — competent, capable, qualified
>
> días hábiles — working days
>
> testigo hábil — competent witness
>
> sello hábil — valid stamp

You may also find it useful to note the source of your findings.

TEXT FORMAT

This text is divided into the following chapters:

What Is Translation?
Ethical Considerations
Some Practical Rules
Characteristics of Legal Discourse
Translation of Personal Documents
Translation of Legal Correspondence
Appendix

Each chapter is followed by exercises of two basic types: a series of questions for thought and discussion, and passages for translation, followed by model translations. (It should be understood that in many cases alternate translations of a passage may be possible.) The Appendix contains full bibliographical information for all works cited in the text, a list of research tools and reference materials, and examples of various types of personal documents not included in Chapter 5.

Students can continue to practice and to improve their translating skills if they have access to examples of legal discourse *with reliable translations,* such as the series *Leyes de Puerto Rico* published by Equity (Orford, New Hampshire), each volume of which has a companion volume containing an excellent translation into English. There are many United Nations publications, available in the United Nations Bookstore, that would lend themselves to the same type of study since they are published both in Spanish and in English. Another series of books useful in a self-teaching program is *Formularios de Equity* by Roberto Alonso and Bernardo Figueredo (Equity Publishing Company, Orford, New Hampshire, 1970). These books contain the formulas —standard headings, citations, statements, oaths— which are the basic components of various types of legal instruments. A perusal of these volumes would provide a thorough understanding of the conventions of this type of writing and should be an aid to accurate translation.

An excellent resource tool for checking the meaning of legal terms *in context* is the book *Spanish-English Legal Terminology* by George N. Vanson (South-Western Publishing Company, Cincinnati, Ohio, 1982). Marilyn Frankenthaler, General Editor.

* * *

I should like to acknowledge the generous help provided in the preparation of these materials by Mr. Luis Aguayo and Mr. George Vanson, whose advice and encouragement have been of inestimable value, and to the C.E.T.A. staff of the Montclair State College Hispanic Community Program Internship in Law, working at Essex-Newark Legal Services of New Jersey, who under Dr. Marilyn Frankenthaler's supervision prepared the series of form letters included in Chapter 6.

I should also like to acknowledge the contribution of Professor Milton Schwartz of New York University School of Law, Member of the New York Bar, who, together with Dr. Marilyn Frankenthaler prepared materials for sections dealing with the protocolization and legalization of documents.

Jo Anne Engelbert

Montclair State College

CHAPTER 1

WHAT IS TRANSLATION?

Etymologically, translating means "carrying across"; meaning is transported out of one language and into another:

Source Language:[1] Cuatro ojos ven más que dos.
Target Language:[1] Two heads are better than one.

Look at the examples above. At what level is meaning "carried across"? Has the translator translated words or ideas?

The mental processes involved in translation are extraordinarily complex and as yet are not fully understood. Linguistic scientists believe that the transfer of meaning takes place at a fairly deep level they call the "kernel" level. The mind, after analyzing the message in the original, or source language, seems to search for an appropriate place at which to make the "crossing." Eugene Nida likens the process to a hiker looking for a place to ford a stream: he may have to travel a considerable distance upstream or downstream to find the place where the crossing can be made most efficiently. In another analogy, Nida describes the process of transfer as packing for a trip:

> One does not really translate words but bundles of componential features. The words may be regarded essential as vehicles for carrying across the component of meaning. In fact, the words may be likened to suitcases carrying various articles of clothing. It really does not make much difference which articles are packed in which suitcase. What counts is that the clothes arrive at the destination in the best possible condition, i.e., with the least damage. What matters is not the particular words which carry the componential features, but the fact that the correct componential features are lexically transported.
>
> *Language Structure and Translation,p. 91*[2]

An idea that travels comfortably in one language in a suitcase called "noun" may travel more comfortably in another in a suitcase called "adjective," and so forth:

S.L. (Source language): Tenía hambre.
T.L. (Target language): He was hungry.

---

[1]The "source" language is the language of the original statement or text. The "target" language is the language into which the translation is being done.

[2]The complete bibliographic reference for all works cited in the text is found in "Reference Tools" at the end of this part of the text.

S.L. Me quedan veinte dólares.
T.L. I have twenty dollars left.

Can you think of additional examples to illustrate this idea? How can we decide what to put in which "suitcase"?

TRANSLATION IS FOR THE READER

A distinction is often made between translating, which is usually done in writing, and interpreting, which is done orally. But let us use the term translating in its broader sense for a moment in order to consider what is actually occurring during the process of transfer of meaning. In a general sense, we could say that everyone is a translator of sorts. Octavio Paz reminds us that "learning to speak is learning to translate: whenever a child asks his mother for the meaning of a word, he is really asking her to translate the term into his language" *(Traducción y literalidad, p. 7)*.

If she tells him that *pachyderm* means *elephant* or *He pulled the wool over her eyes* means *He fooled her*, and he understands, the translation has been successful. We are all familiar with this type of translation within a language, and it is a useful model for us to look at as we begin to analyze the process of translation between languages. When the mother "translates" for the child, she adjusts her language to his. She anticipates the impression her words will have on the child and finds equivalents for terms he might not understand. In the same way a teenager might "translate" words like "wasted" or "crashed" when these are used in ways unintelligible to parents. An important axiom of translating is in evidence in these examples: *translation is for the reader*; it exists for the reader —not for the author, not for posterity, certainly not for the translator. If the reader understood the language of the original statement, there would be no need for the translation. The test of the translation, then, is not the perfection of the written text so much as the reader's response to it. Accordingly, translators must constantly try to anticipate the reader's responses so that they can make all appropriate adjustments.

WHAT IS A FAITHFUL TRANSLATION?

We make a very wide range of adjustments even when we are translating within a language. Your doctor may tell you have "hives," rather than "urticaria," which is the precise technical term he or she would use in speaking to another doctor. Your English friends may remember to say "gas" instead of "petrol," or "baby carriage" instead of "pram," when speaking to Americans. Argentines may say "abrigo" and "falda" instead of "tapado" and "pollera" when speaking to non-Argentines, just as Mexicans remember that "tortilla" means something quite different to a Spaniard and to a Chilean.

North Americans when speaking Spanish may remember to prefix *Don* or *Doña* to the first name of a respected older person in a way that is not common in English. These common-sense adjustments for variations in knowledge, experience, regional usage and social custom are also part of the translation process. The final test of a translation, as we have said, is the total effect it has upon the reader. The American Translators Association defines the translator's duty in the following way:

> It shall be the duty of every translator to translate with the greatest fidelity and accuracy he can command, endeavoring always to give his readers and audience the impression they would have if they could hear or read the original.
>
> *A.T.A. Code of Ethical Practices*
> (See next chapter.)

There can be no absolute definition of a "faithful translation"; the concept can only be defined with respect to its effect upon the prime or intended reader.

WHO IS THE PRIME READER?

Some types of legal texts have a number of readers of varying levels of knowledge and experience. Which reader should the translator keep in mind? Whose needs take precedence, the client's for example, or the attorney's? Think this over very carefully, for it has an important bearing on your work: *technical materials,* such as legal documents, are, first and foremost, *communications between experts:* they are written by professionals and directed to other professionals. The prescription your doctor writes for your medication is fundamentally a communication between himself and the pharmacist. It is written in a specific way, according to rigidly established formula, to guarantee an absolute minimum of confusion with regard to the composition and preparation of the medication. If you as patient happen to be able to understand the prescription, well and good. But you are not the prime reader of the prescription; the pharmacist is, and his need to understand specific directions takes precedence over your curiosity to know what the prescription "says." Your medical needs are better served when the communication between physician and pharmacist takes place with maximum safeguards, and this often means that sophisticated, technical language must be used.

The prescription is analogous to a legal instrument such as a contract, a will or a birth certificate. These are essentially communications between professionals —they were written by attorneys or experts in the law *for others similarly prepared.* They are written in language that is extraordinarily precise, formulaic and exact, for the purpose of protecting the individuals involved. The prime reader of professional, technical communications, then, is *not* ordinarily the layman (the holder of the prescription or the birth certificate) but *another professional equipped to understand technical language.* The translator's duty is to give *this reader* the same impression he would have if he could read the original in his own language. A Spanish word like "urticaria" should be rendered *urticaria* —not "hives"— in a technical translation.

Obviously, the client's need to know what a document "says" is also very great and should by no means be overlooked. Explaining the meaning of legal terms in simple language so that clients can understand them clearly may be an important part of your work in a legal environment. But in translating documents, the translator should remember that the prime reader is another member of the legal profession, not the client; precision and accuracy are top priorities.

Not all the translations you will do in a legal environment are of legal documents. You will be frequently called upon to translate letters, newspaper articles, brochures, materials for tenants associations and the like. The prime readers of these materials are not likely to be legal experts; to facilitate communication, you may have to make a number of adjustments. Correctly identifying the prime reader and keeping that person's responses constantly in mind are prime requisites for faithfulness in translation.

TRADUTTORE, TRADITTORE: GAINS AND LOSSES

How close can we actually come to "giving the reader the same impression he would have if he could read the original in his own language"? The answer to this question is enormously complex, quite beyond the scope of this introduction, but even the beginning translator must begin to think about all that is implied by the phrase "the same impression." This "impression" is so difficult to achieve that many languages have a formula similar to the Italian "Traduttore, tradittore" — "Translator, traitor." What is "lost" in translation is lamentable; and what is unintentionally gained is every bit as worrisome. Even at the level of the single word, it is so difficult to find exact equivalents that some loss or gain of meaning is almost inevitable. If we translate "siesta" as "nap," have we lost or gained meaning? Examine the following pairs of "equivalents" for meaning loss or gain:

SOURCE LANGUAGE	TARGET LANGUAGE
hobby	pasatiempo
girlfriend	novia
pet	mascota
sobremesa	tabletalk
patio (Sp.)	patio (Eng.)
plaza (Sp.)	plaza (Eng.)
niñera	baby sitter

It is rare that the so-called equivalents the dictionaries give us coincide exactly. Different cultures structure experience differently, and these differences are reflected directly in language. *Novia,* since it also means *fiancée* eand *bride,* inevitably says more than the English *girlfriend.* The consequences of this phenomenon are obvious: if serious misunderstandings are not to occur, the translator must tax his or her ingenuity to correct, to compensate for these gains and losses.

CONNOTATION

The *connotation* of a word (the feelings we associate with it) is an important part of its meaning. Sometimes the denotative range (what the word refers to) of each of a pair of "equivalents" is very similar, but the connotation is so different that their effect is entirely different in the two languages. What are the differences in *connotation* in the following pairs?

SOURCE LANGUAGE	TARGET LANGUAGE
¡Jesús!	Jesus!
entrañas	entrails
Christmas	Navidad
siesta	nap
sereno	night watchman

Unlike the scientific, technical vocabulary, everyday language is charged with emotional association, and these associations often defy translation; the translator does not translate words, but ideas, feelings, desires and the intentions that lie behind these, as Vázquez Ayora explains in *Introducción a la traductología* (p. 55).

NATURALNESS OF EXPRESSION

Another factor that affects the overall impression created by the translation is the naturalness of expression. The native speaker through long experience with the language has acquired a set of expectations with respect to usage. Notice the various small adjustments the translator of the following passage has made in order to insure a natural-sounding translation:

SOURCE LANGUAGE

ALIMENTOS, DEFINICIÓN DE

Se entiende por alimentos todo lo que es indispensable para el sustento, habitación, vestido y asistencia médica, según la posición de la familia.

Los alimentos comprenden también la educación e instrucción del alimentista, cuando es menor de edad.

Leyes de Puerto Rico
(*Código Civil,* 1930, #142)

TARGET LANGUAGE

SUPPORT, DEFINED

Support is understood to be all that is indispensable for maintenance, housing clothing and medical attention, according to the social position of the family.

Support also includes the education and instruction of the person supported when he is a minor.

Laws of Puerto Rico
(*Civil Code*, 1930, #142)

"Alimento" obviously means "support," rather than "food"; accordingly "maintenance" is a better choice than "sustenance," which comes first to mind; "housing" is more natural than "habitation," "medical attention" more natural than "medical assistance," and so on. "Social" is inserted before "position" to round out in English a concept that was clear enough in Spanish: we are left with the slightly redundant "education and instruction" because there is no English equivalent for the broader meaning of "educación." When choices like these are made carefully, with an eye to natural usage, the resulting translation should sound *as if it had been originally written in the target language.*

SET PHRASES

Every language is a storehouse of ready-made forms, whole strings of words already linked up by habit and usage, phrases that lie ready to be used for certain specific purposes.

Compare the following translations of a proverb:

S.L. Adonde fueres, haz lo que vieres.
T.L. (a) Wherever you go, do what you see.
T.L. (b) When in Rome, do as the Romans do.

Which is the best translation? Word for word, (a) is certainly very close to the original, but it fails to give us the impression the original gives: we need and expect a *proverb* here. Since (b) satisfies this *formal requirement,* we prefer it to (a); even though the words are different, we feel that the meaning is the same, and, more importantly, that the meaning is expressed in the same way —in the form of proverb— as in the original. Set phrases or *frases hechas* —greetings, closings, stock comparisons, clichés, proverbs, sayings— since they "preexist," so to speak, in the source language, need to be rendered by such preexisting forms in the target language.

S.L.	T.L.
Son iguales como dos gotas de agua.	(a) They are as similar as two drops of water. (b) They are as alike as two peas in a pod.
En boca cerrada no entran moscas.	(a) Flies do not enter a closed mouth. (b) Silence is golden.
Llovió a cántaros.	(a) It rained by the pitcherful. (b) It rained cats and dogs.

In each of the above, (a) is more similar to the original on a word basis, but (b) comes closer to conveying the impression given by the original because of the translator's identification and use of preexisting forms. As you can see, these "formal" demands are very strong and often take precedence over other considerations.

REGIONAL DIFFERENCES

An area of special concern to the English/Spanish translator is the question of regional differences in vocabulary. What shall be the translation of a simple word like "peas," for example, which is "guisantes" in Spain, "chícharos" in Mexico, "arvejas" in Argentina, "petits pois" in the Caribbean, etc.? Obviously, it may be of some help to think of the possible readers of the translation, but it is rare that a translation from English into Spanish, written in the U.S., will have readers of only one national group. A legal notice to the Hispanic community, an article for a Spanish-language newspaper, a form letter, etc., will be read by Mexicans and Puerto Ricans, Uruguayans and Chileans. Most regional differences, however, occur at the lexical rather than the morphological level; that is, they usually affect only the names of things, rather than the structure of the language. Moreover, *most speakers know the standard as well as the regional names of things;* i.e., Mexicans know that in most places *camión* means "truck," even if for them it means "bus," just as Americans know that "gas" is "petrol" in England. In general, unless a translation is exclusively for readers of one particular national group, *it is better to aim at a standard Spanish that is as free from regionalisms as possible.*

ANGLICISMS

Closely related to the problem of regional differences is the question of the use of anglicisms, words like "relevante" for "relevant" and "nursa" for "nurse." The Spanish spoken in the United States is constantly bombarded by the English language, and it is inevitable, probably even desirable, that certain words be officialy adopted. But this is a long, slow process, and there is a long period during which the status of certain words is indefinite. In a given region where people may use words like "rufo" (roof) and "liqueando" (leaking) in conversation, there is a temptation to use them in writing also.

It is imposible to make a blanket statement that would cover all situations, but there are two things that should be kept in mind in deciding whether to use anglicisms or standard Spanish expressions. First, people of every culture make a distinction betwen spoken and written language; the written language is nearly always more conservative, slower to admit borderline forms and phrases. Anglicisms are more alarming in print than they are in everyday speech. Many people are offended by them because they feel that the Spanish language ought to be respected and that existing Spanish words ought not to be displaced by formations from English. The second point to consider, then, is that the translator who peppers his work with anglicisms may be sending several erroneous messages: that he thinks his readers are incapable of understanding standard Spanish; that the Spanish language is not worth preserving in its original form; that he, the translator, is incapable of making a proper distinction between spoken and written language.

Anglicisms are justified when they accurately identify an object or idea for which there exists no equivalent in the other language (such cases are extremely rare), and also when they are used with obvious stylistic intent — to express irony, outrage, frustration, to make a joke, etc.

In routine texts, however, the ends of communication are usually better served by accuracy and precision of expression, in standard Spanish, than by a folksy attempt to write "like people talk."

Note: when you are not certain whether a word is standard Spanish or an anglicism, consult a bilingual dictionary or the *Diccionario de dudas* (see Reference Tools, Appendix.)

STYLE AND TONE

The style and tone of a written text are an integral part of its meaning. Far more than a mere accessory veneer, they offer important clues as to the writer's seriousness, sincerity, mental state, ability to organize and express ideas, ability to deal with abstract concepts, and the like. The translator, then, in order to fully render the meaning of the original, must try to match its style and tone as closely as possible.

Is the translator ever justified in "improving" the style of a badly written original? If the original is incoherent, contains contradictions, grammatical errors, ambiguous references, etc., should it not be "corrected" by the translator? This is not a simple question to answer. In general, the translator's role is to facilitate communication; normally, communication is improved by judicious editing. However, great care must be exercised in making editorial changes in certain kinds of style-sensitive materials. When the style of a text relays insights of the type just mentioned, the translator should remember that these can be significant in a legal setting. Confusion and incoherence in the text of a deposition, for example, reflect to some extent the mental state of the deponent: a clear and coherent translation of such a text deprives the reader of certain of the essential features of the original.

How should the translator handle obscenities and abusive language? In an actual case, a woman giving a deposition in Spanish cited three or four obscene epithets her husband had hurled at her during an altercation. The translator, not wishing to offend anyone, substituted much milder words for these terms. Needless to say, the translator did the woman a great disservice in making such changes. Instead of improving communication between attorney and client, the translator effectively impeded it.

The texts you will be dealing with vary enormously as to their sensitivity in this respect. You will have to consider each example individually to determine the aspect of the message which is being conveyed by the style and tone of the passage. In all probability it will be helpful to keep the needs of the prime reader clearly in mind.

CULTURAL ADJUSTMENTS

Perhaps the trickiest fine-tuning of all is that which must be done because of cultural differences. Strange and erroneous impressions can be conveyed when the translator attends only to the words of the text and not to its cultural overtones. An English business letter may close with a simple "Very truly yours"; a conventional Spanish closing might be "Hago uso de esta oportunidad para saludar a Vd. muy atentamente y expresarle el testimonio de mi alta y distinguida consideración." The English writer expresses respect for the recipient of the letter by "not wasting the person's time" with "unnecessary" verbiage. The Hispanic writer, in contrast, may express deference for the person by spending additional time composing a suitably elaborate closing, making specific mention of the individual and of the writer's esteem.

Both closings are logical expressions of the cultures' unique ways of looking at personal relationships and of their attitudes towards time.

If the Spanish closing were to be rendered into English as "I take advantage of this opportunity to send you my most cordial greetings and to tell you of my high esteem for you," erroneous messages are conveyed — insincerity, servility, fuzzy-mindedness and inability to think are a few that come to mind. A translator must be sufficiently aware of the expectations and conventions of both cultures to be able to anticipate misunderstandings and to make necessary adjustments. In the example cited, the translator might match the formality of the conventional Spanish closing with the English equivalent: "Very truly yours." Though all the words are different, the feeling of respectful formality is the same.

CONCLUSION

We have touched very briefly on just a few of the many factors that influence what we have called the reader's impression. The process of translation can be seen to involve extremely difficult decisions based on linguistic, cultural, psychological and aesthetic judgments, requiring sensitivity on the part of the translator to the total number of ways in which the various aspects of the text may affect the reader. The subject is "difficult and ill-defined"; perhaps the age we live in, which has been called "the age of translation," will develop a scientific approach to translating that will be more reliable than the present seat-of-the pants approach that relies so heavily on the intuition and life experience of the individual translator. Regarding the possible translation into English of Chinese philosophical concepts, I.A. Richards said, "We have here what may very well be the most complex type of event yet produced in the evolution of the cosmos" (quoted by George Steiner in *After Babel,* p. 48).

We can take some comfort in Octavio Paz's observation that translation is after all possible, no matter how difficult it may be to do it well, because "en lenguas distintas los hombres dicen siempre las mismas cosas" (*Traducción: literatura y literalidad,* p. 7).

QUESTIONS FOR DISCUSSION

1. What is the difference between interpreting and translating? In what ways do the qualifications of interpreter and translator differ? Discuss the relative difficulty of the two activities.

2. What is a faithful translation? What factors must be taken into account to produce a faithful translation?

3. Eugene Nida has written, "The appropriate response to the question 'Is this a correct translation?' must be another question, 'Correct for whom?'" Explain.

4. Explain whether an attempt should be made to rationalize obviously confused or garbled statements in translating the following:

   Ransom note
   Bomb threat
   Instructions to client to appear in court
   Excerpt from a diary to be used in evidence
   Medical examiner's report
   Transcript of statement made by mental patient

5. Explain the approach you would use in translating the following. Can you find equivalents?

   Rome wasn't built in a day.
   It's an ill wind that blows nobody good.
   It's time to throw in the sponge.
   She was born with a silver spoon in her mouth.
   El hábito no hace al monje.
   Metiendo muchas cucharas, se echa a perder la sopa.
   Le canté las cosas claras.
   No te dejes dar gato por liebre.

6. Give some examples of anglicisms. Explain whether or not you would use them in writing a newspaper article in Spanish.

7. Explain why it is difficult to translate the following:

   baby sitter
   suburb
   singles' bar
   Boston baked beans
   Las Posadas
   ¡Que sea enhorabuena!
   caudillo
   guayabera
   minister (of a church)
   asopao
   Oficialía de Estado Civil

CHAPTER 2

ETHICAL CONSIDERATIONS

Like members of other professions, translators have an extraordinary responsibility to their clients. Like doctors and lawyers, translators can bestow enormous benefits or inflict incalculable harm upon the people they serve. Their responsibility is particularly grave, since in the majority of cases the translator is the sole arbiter of meaning. Under normal conditions, even in a legal setting, no one else is monitoring the process, and both client and attorney are totally dependent upon the translator's words.

Lack of precision in the use of language can have disastrous consequences in a legal context. Inaccurate translations cause more serious problems than no translations at all; people have been deprived of their rightful property, even of their freedom because of a translator's carelessness. Consider the following actual case:

> A man walking home from work tripped over a length of pipe a local industry had discarded and left lying across the sidewalk where it became covered with snow during the afternoon. In making his statement in Spanish, the man, permanently disabled as a result of the injury, explained "Tropecé y me caí," which the translator rendered, rather vaguely, "I slipped and fell." The insurance company eagerly seized upon the word "slipped" and used it to make its entire case: the man had not *tripped* over the pipe, but had *slipped* on the snowy sidewalk; the company, therefore, was not liable. The man, unable to work and unable to collect anything from the negligent industry, eventually lost his home.

In this case, the real *desliz,* we can all agree, was the translator's.

There have probably been countless cases like this one. It is chilling to consider that countless others go undiscovered because no one realizes that a translation error has been made. After all, who is going to discover it? It could only be detected by someone who knows both languages, and in most cases this is the translator himself. *The importance of cross-checking an important translation cannot be overemphasized. Having a second, fully competent translator with experience in a legal setting check each translation is the only safeguard against errors that can have grave consequences for all concerned.*

Few laymen have the practicing attorney's extraordinary sensitivity to language. This sensitivity is acquired through years of experience and stems from a direct understanding of the legal implications of all aspects of language. There is no substitute for this knowledge, and the serious translator will want to consult frequently with members of the legal profession to ascertain exactly which word, phrase or formula is most suitable in a given context. Mere fluency in two languages is not sufficient preparation for legal translation. A person may have a very extensive vocabulary in both English and Spanish, for example, and still be totally unaware of the special or restricted meanings of words in legal parlance. It is especially dangerous to take familiar-looking words at face value and give them a conventional or "common-sense" translation; the results can be comical — or very serious.

How many of the following can you translate *accurately* without doing any special research?

(I.) TRANSLATE INTO ENGLISH: (ANSWERS FOLLOW.)

a. Hurto de menor cuantía
b. Violación
c. Rapto
d. Exposiciones deshonestas
e. Las actas del registro civil
f. El registro demográfico
g. Las disposiciones de la ley vigente
h. Los ingresos, rentas o sueldos percibidos
i. Bienes inmuebles

(ANSWERS)

a. Petit Larceny
b. Rape
c. Abduction
d. Indecent exposure
e. The records of the civil register
f. The registry of vital statistics
g. The provisions of the law in force
h. Income, earnings or salary received
i. Real estate

(II.) TRANSLATE INTO SPANISH: (ANSWERS FOLLOW.)

a. Rights allowed to remain dormant
b. Commercial paper
c. Beneficial owner
d. The judicial authority, however, will not entertain the complaint . . .

(ANSWERS)

a. Derechos dejados inmobilizados
b. Documentos mercantiles
c. Dueño útil
d. La autoridad judicial, puede, sin embargo no estimar la demanda . . .

Learn to be extremely skeptical of familiar-looking words; their meaning in a legal context may be *totally different from their every day meaning*. This meaning cannot be improvised; by the very nature of the law, legal language has developed in a very long, very conservative tradition which allows very little flexibility. It will be necessary for you to use specialized dictionaries (see Appendix), dictionaries of legal terminology, in order to find proper equivalents for many terms. Do not be content with your translation of a new term until you have found a way of verifying it. Do not hesitate to ask others for help, but be absolutely sure that the people you ask are really qualified to answer authoritatively. Mere fluency is no guarantee of the specialized knowledge needed for legal translating. Under no circumstances should you guess about the meaning of a word. The most valuable words in a translator's vocabulary are *"I don't know what this means." An inaccurate translation can cause for more problems than no translation.*

The translator, then has an *ethical* responsibility to be as accurate as is humanly possible; this implies a duty on his part to develop effective research skills and to use them conscientiously.

CODE OF ETHICAL PRACTICES

The following code of ethics has been adopted by the American Translators Association as a guide to all members of the profession. Study the points carefully and consider which of them have special application to the translator in a law office or legal services agency.

IT SHALL BE THE DUTY OF EVERY TRANSLATOR

1. To translate with the greatest fidelity and accuracy he can command, endeavoring always to give his readers and audience the impression they would have if they could read or hear the original.
2. To maintain professional discretion and in particular to respect the rights of his client or employer by divulging nothing he may have learned in his professional capacity that is harmful to their interests; and to derive no personal profit or advantage from any confidential information he may have acquired in his professional capacity.
3. To accept no assignment for which he knows himself to be less than well qualified in either language or understanding of the subject, except with the prior knowledge of his client or employer; and to refuse any assignment which he believes he cannot properly complete within the time allowed.
4. To share professional knowledge with colleagues on a reciprocal basis.
5. To refrain from any action likely to discredit the profession, and in particular to abstain from engaging in unfair competition.
6. To seek or accept no work on terms that are humiliating to him or the profession.
7. To refuse any assignment that he believes to be intended for illegal or dishonest purposes, or against the public interest.
8. To be loyal to his colleagues and to his profession and to agree to settle professional differences by arbitration whenever possible.

CARE OF PERSONAL DOCUMENTS

Many of the documents a legal translator handles contain personal information of a sensitive nature. It is vitally important that great discretion be exercised in caring for such documents. Birth certificates, adoption papers, divorce proceedings and the like contain sensitive information that should under no conditions be divulged. It is particularly important that such documents be cared for in an orderly way. The original document should in most cases be retained by the client rather than the translator, who can work with a photocopy. It is literally impossible for natives of some countries to replace original documents should these be lost.

Documents and copies of them should be kept under lock and key and not removed from the premises. Follow scrupulously the procedures used in your office for recording and filing documents.

The translator's obligation to respect confidentiality is as binding as that of the psychologist, priest or physician. Be sure that you do not unintentionally violate this obligation by carelessly leaving photocopies of documents around for others to see. Destroy your scrap paper and put your translations away as soon as you finish them; do not take them home with you. Do not discuss the contents of documents with colleagues.

It is so easy to make copies of papers that we tend to become very casual about the process. Take a moment to think of the possible consequences of having extra copies of documents like adoption papers, immigration papers professional credentials, etc., fall into the hands of unscrupulous persons. Be sure you can account for each and every copy of a personal document given to you to translate. Do not make extra copies of documents unless absolutely necessary and do not retain extra copies of any document without the *explicit* permission of the client.

CERTIFIED TRANSLATIONS

A certified translation is one that ends with a pledge written by the translator or other individual qualified to certify stating that the translation is a faithful rendition of the original; the pledge is signed in the presence of a notary, who affixes a seal. A sample pledge or oath might read as follows:

> This is to certify that the (above/attached) translation of (here identify the type of document, name of individual, date, identification numbers, etc.) is a faithful and accurate rendition of the original (Spanish).
>
> Signed ....
> (Title)
> (Institution)

Note that different types of documents require different types of certification. Some require the use of specific adjectives in the oath —patents, for example, must stipulate that the translation is "literal" (if it were really "literal," it would probably be a terrible translation!). Professional credentials, such as the transcripts of physicians, pharmacists, etc., can only be certified by certain individuals— the faculty of university foreign language departments, for example. A routine pledge that might be affixed to a translation of a birth certificate, etc., might read "This is a true and accurate translation of the attached photocopy of an original document." The document should be identified in the pledge in order to prevent the pledge being removed and affixed to a falsified document.

"TRANSLATION AGAINST MISUNDERSTANDING"

The distinguished translator Gyorgy Radó, editor of *Babel* magazine, has written an eloquent statement of the mission of the translator which, if we read between the lines, has special significance for the translator working with the Hispanic community in a legal environment. Although the quotation is rather long, it may serve to remind us of the important trust that rests with an interpreter or translator:

"The word understanding is not only the name for a psychological process; it is also an historical notion. Ever since men of different tongues have been meeting each other, translating has been the basic guarantee of understanding...

"There is a French saying, 'Tout comprendre c'est tout pardonner.' To understand, to forgive, to live in peace. Translation eliminates misunderstanding; consequently it is an antidote to the passion called hatred.

"I quote the Bible: '... let us go down, and there confound their language, that they may not understand one another's speech,' so said the Lord. And in this way the Tower of Babel represents the symbol of the confusion of languages, a source of wars, revenge and hatred, becoming hereditary through the generations.

"And again in the Bible, the proclamation of love as a religion was followed by Whitsuntide when '... there appeared unto them parting asunder, like as of fire; and it sat on each one of them. And they were all filled with the Holy Spirit and began to speak with other tongues, as the Spirit gave them utterance.'

"Whether we believe this as a fact or regard it as a symbol, the beginning of our era represents a change in the course of human history.

"At the same time that national languages began to acquire respectability in Europe, European culture began to extend to the Americas and Siberia; but the European style of war extended there too. Wars were caused by the lust to possess; their spiritual background was misunderstanding, and misunderstanding can be dissipated by translation.

"That is why, at the beginning of modern history, translation from biblical languages satisfied national ambitions, but no longer in the XVIII century. Translation from one modern language into another had to begin.

"It began slowly. Its first valuable achievements are noticeable in the XIX century, but only in our age did it become significantly extensive, chiefly after World War II . . . I make bold to say that beside the fear of atomic devastation, the continuous growth of translation is connected with the fact that in 31 years no large-scale war has broken out. Fear of the atom has a military character, but translation affects minds and souls; it dissipates misunderstanding. The translator's task is a noble one."

Excerpt from Dr. Radó's address, "Translation Against Misunderstanding" in *Translating, a Profession*, Proceedings of the International Federation of Translators (FIT), Edited by Paul A. Horguelin, Quebec, 1978.

QUESTIONS FOR DISCUSSION

1. What is a profession? Does translating have the characteristics of a profession? Explain.

2. List some of the methods by which a translator can check a translation for accuracy. Can one rely entirely upon dictionaries in checking the meaning of a word in a given context? What kind of professional preparation should be required for a career in legal translation?

3. Does fluency in two languages guarantee competence in legal translation? Explain your answer.

4. What safeguards should be taken in caring for the personal documents of clients? Why are these precautions necessary? Explain why it is essential to use special discretion in dealing with the following types of documents: adoption papers; immigration papers; professional credentials; divorce proceedings. Can you think of other materials that might contain especially sensitive information?

5. Explain the ethical considerations one should keep in mind when making or retaining photocopies of personal documents.

6. Assume that you have been asked to make a translation of a technical document such as a patent; you attempt the translation and find that it is much too difficult for you. What is the ethical thing to do?

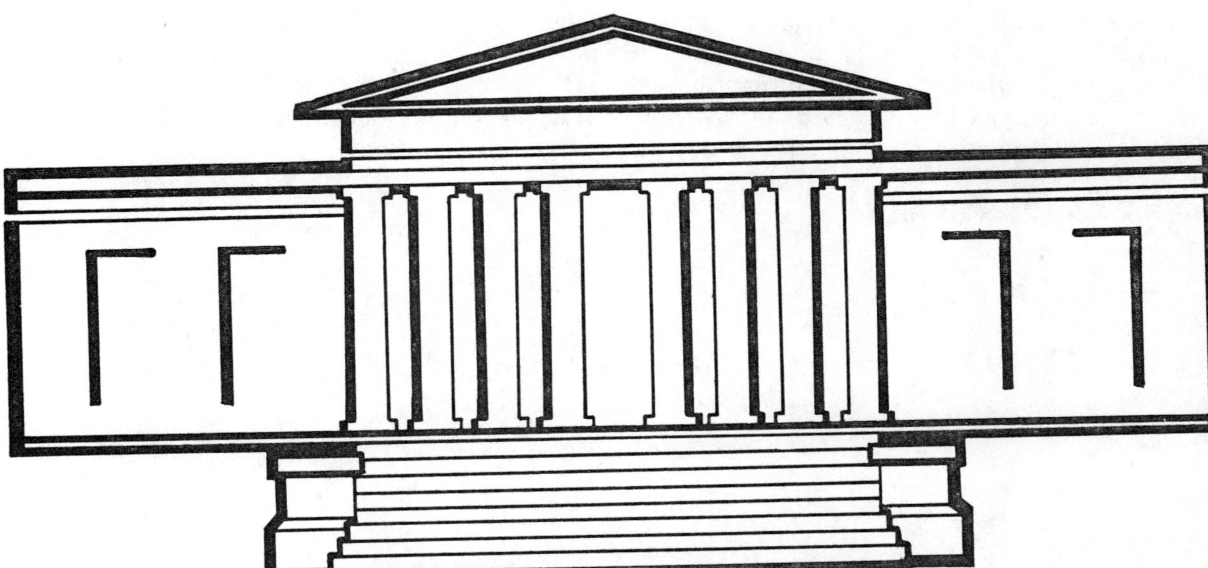

PRACTICE

Read each of the following passages throughly. Translate each passage.

EXERCISE A

Legally speaking, the terms "residence" and "domicile" are not synonyms. Id. The term "residence" is used to designate the place where a person dwells or resides temporarily, whether it be as a result of work, studies or pleasure. Id. Even though a person can have only one domicile, he can have one or more residences.

TRANSLATE INTO SPANISH:

EXERCISE B

En el Registro de la Propiedad de Puerto Rico se anotarán, inscribirán y archivarán los mismos documentos y se harán las mismas operaciones y en igual forma que hasta el presente se han efectuado bajo autoridad de ley en los actuales registros de la propiedad; disponiéndose, que el Secretario de Justicia podrá implantar sistemas fotográficos mecánicos o cualquier otro sistema moderno para la anotación, inscripción y archivo de los documentos en el Registro de la Propiedad que facilite el funcionamiento administrativo del mismo.

TRANSLATE INTO ENGLISH:

CHAPTER 3

PRACTICAL CONSIDERATIONS

"'Cada traducción es un acto de aproximación, de leve pérdida o falla para acercarse al centro ..."

George Steiner

A. PREPARATION

Every translation involves an infinite number of choices, and difficult ones at that. If the translation is good, these choices are not made *arbitrarily* but with reference to a set of conscious priorities. If you have to translate "The ship was anchored a mile from shore," how will you render "a mile from shore"? Will you write "a 1,852[1] kilómetros de la costa" or "a dos kilómetros de la costa" or "a una milla de la costa"? Each of these might be appropriate in a given context. The solution you choose will depend on your priorities. In a report of a crime at sea, accuracy might be the first priority: "a distance of 1,852 kilómetros". In a novel such accuracy would be a distraction; expressing the actual distance might be less important than maintaining a smooth narrative flow: "dos kilómetros" might be a good solution. "Una milla" might be appropriate in some contexts, while in others it might sound like a foreign intrusion.

Part of the necessary preparation for translation is making a brief analysis that will assure a sound order of priorities. Here is a series of basic considerations that may help you in your analysis:

1. Begin by identifying in your own mind the prime or intended reader of the translation. Keeping this reader clearly in mind — his level of understanding, his special needs, his national origin, his familiarity with the subject under discussion — will be of enormous help as you decide what level or register of language to use, what lexical difficulties must be explained, what compensations must be made, etc.

2. The next step is to analyze the function of the text you are translating: is it essentially expressive (subjective, creative, like a poem); informational (like a report or a legal document); or communicative (persuasive, emotive, like an advertisement or political harangue)? Again, your analysis of function will help you order priorities and make consistent choices as you translate.

3. Next, spend a few minutes analyzing the way the original text "works"; the more you can observe about the use of language in the original, the closer you can come to giving the same impression as the original in your translation. In the next chapter we shall outline some of the characteristics of legal language as an aid to your making a textual model for translation.

4. Consider what kind of translation is actually needed. Full translation is only one possibility. Sometimes a paraphrase may be more helpful than a translation. (A paraphrase is a free rendition, often in simpler language, of the meaning of a passage, text or work.) If you decide to write a paraphrase, *be sure to indicate that it is a paraphrase and not a full translation.* A précis or abstract may be sufficient in some cases: the translator reads the material and writes a brief summary of the essential points.

---

[1] A nautical mile represents a longer metrical distance than a terrestrial mile.

(In many busy offices routine correspondence received is rarely translated in full. The translator reads a letter and makes a note at the bottom: "Mr. X needs additional copy of agreement"; "Mrs. Y requests info. on status of case.")

5. By all means *read the whole of the original text before you begin to translate it.* Make sure that your copy is legible from beginning to end, that no pages are missing and that the pages are in the right order. This reading yields important insights about how the text works, how the various parts are related, and what preliminary research has to be done. Never begin the translation of a text until you thoroughly understand what you are reading. *If you do not understand the text in the source language, you should under no circumstances attempt to translate it.* The idea that you can translate material you do not understand is absolute nonsense.

6. Check to see whether your office has in its files a translation of a document similar to the one you are working on. This move might save you hours of unnecessary work!

7. Last, assemble the necessary reference tools (see Appendix for list of titles) and make a list of special words and phrases that will be needed.

8. After you have completed a rough draft of the translation, it is a good idea to read it aloud to yourself before you type the final copy. It should read smoothly and naturally, as if it were originally written in the target language. Your ear should tell you when it is necessary to depart from the word order and grammatical structure of the original. The novice has a difficult time deciding how much leeway — how much freedom — he or she has to depart from the original. There is no hard and fast rule, but Gregory Rabassa, the translator of García Márquez, Cortázar and Vargas Llosa, offers the following good advice:

> "I take my text from Johnny Cash: 'I've walked the line.' What the translator must do first off is walk the line. And in keeping with that image, he must always be aware that in a very deep sense he is the prisoner of his author, convicted on a number of counts. But at the same time he must be a model prisoner, a trusty, walking willingly at the mercy of the text he is rendering and of all the turns it might take...
>
> "Ear is important in translating because it really lies at the base of all good writing. Writing is not truly a substitute for thought, it is a substitute for sound...
>
> The translator with a tin ear is as deadly as a tone deaf musician."
>
> "The Ear in Translation," in *The World of Translation* P.E.N. American Center, 1971.

B. NUTS AND BOLTS: A FEW PRACTICAL GUIDELINES

1. WHAT NOT TO TRANSLATE

Knowing what to leave unchanged is every bit as important as knowing how to find equivalents. In the type of translation you are likely to be doing, remember to

LEAVE UNCHANGED:

a. NAMES OF INDIVIDUALS

S.L. un niño de sexo masculino a quien se le ha dado el nombre de Ricardo
T.L. a male child who was given the name Ricardo (Not "Richard"!)

S.L. Guillermo Rodrigo de la Nuez, Notario
T.L. Guillermo Rodrigo de la Nuez, Notary

Exceptions: Historical figures of great renown (i.e., Aristotle, Aristóteles; Alexander the Great, Alejandro el Magno.)

LEAVE UNCHANGED

b. NAMES OF STREETS, CITIES, TOWNS

S.L. el pueblo de Esperanza
T.L. the town of Esperanza (Not "Hope"!)

S.L. la avenida Arenales
T.L. Arenales Avenue

LEAVE UNCHANGED

c. NAMES OF PARISHES, CHURCHES, HOSPITALS, BANKS, AND OTHER LEGALLY CONSTITUTED ENTITIES.

S.L. En la Parroquia del Niño Jesús de Bogotá
T.L. In the Parish of Niño Jesús, Bogotá

S.L. La Iglesia de Nuestra Señora de la Esperanza,
Provincia Las Villas, Diócesis de Cienfuegos
T.L. The Church of Nuestra Señora de la Esperanza,
Las Villas Province, Diocese of Cienfuegos

LEAVE UNCHANGED

d. FOREIGN WORDS AND PHRASES

With few exceptions, these should be left in the original language. Note, however, that you must understand what the phrase means in order to use it properly in a sentence. Most of the foreign phrases you will encounter in your work will be in Latin; a good legal dictionary will help you determine the meaning.

S.L. aquel que alegue que los pagarés e hipotecas son simulados, fraudulentos y nulos, tiene el *onus probandi**
T.L. the person alleging that the note and mortgages are simulated, fraudulent and void, has the *onus probandi**

S.L. y firmo fecha *UT SUPRA*†
T.L. and I sign on the date *UT SUPRA*†

2. DATES

In some documents, dates are written out in words rather than in numbers. This is done to insure clarity and to make it difficult to falsify a document by altering the numbers. In translating, *follow the format of the original:* if dates are written in words, use words; if in numbers, use numbers.

S.L. el trece de septiembre de mil novecientos cuarenta y dos
T.L. September thirteenth, one thousand nine hundred forty-two

---

**onus probandi:* burden of proof.

†*UT SUPRA:* as (indicated) above.

S.L. el 3 abril, 1956
T.L. April 3, 1956

SLASH-STYLE DATES: In most countries of Europe and Latin America, the day is usually given *before* the month when dates are expressed slash-style:

2/4/67 might mean April 2, 1967, or it might mean February 4, 1967, the meaning which it would have here in the United States.

Sometimes Roman numerals are used to give the month and Arabic, the day:

VI/8/78 means June 8, 1978.

Double check dates that are expressed with slashes.

3. ABBREVIATIONS

Remember that abbreviations and acronyms must be translated; since they allude to words in the source language, they make absolutely no sense in the target language.

S.L. 200 TM de azúcar
T.L. 200 MT of sugar

Suppose the translator had carelessly left the Spanish abbreviation "TM" (toneladas métricas) unchanged in the English translation: "200 TM of sugar"; instead of "metric tons" we would have "tons per minute" (TM is a standard English abbreviation for this phrase).

Sometimes no corresponding abbreviation exists in the target language; in this case the word is simply written out:

S.L. fdo. Carlos Castel R.
T.L. signed Carlos Castel R.

S.L. Santo Domingo, R.D.
T.L. Santo Domingo, Dominican Republic

S.L. Bogotá, D.E.
T.L. Bogotá, Special District

In general, however, when dealing with very common abbreviations, follow the lead of the source language in deciding whether to abbreviate or write words in full.

However, when the abbreviation or acronym is non-standard or not likely to be understood by the reader, supply the help necessary to insure understanding:

S.L. los miembros del CGT
T.L. the members of the CGT (Congreso General de Trabajadores; General Congress of Workers).[2]

Having given the full meaning of CGT in both Spanish and English, you may now go on to use the Spanish abbreviation in the rest of the article; this makes more sense than creating a new abbreviation in English ("GCW") unlikely to be found anywhere else and certain to cause confusion.

NOTE:

When the abbreviation stands *for an international organization or institution,* a different procedure is followed: el último período de sesiones de la O.N.U.; the last session of the U.N.

[2] Some publications omit the foreign words entirely: the members of the CGT (General Congress of Workers).

The United Nations (la Organización de las Naciones Unidas) is well known in both languages, and it is customary to refer to it with an abbreviation. Similarly, the IDB (Inter-American Development Bank) is the BID (Banco Interamericano de Desarrollo) in Spanish.

A good bilingual dictionary such as *Simon and Schuster's International Dictionary Spanish/English, English/Spanish* can be of enormous value in translating abbreviations and acronyms.

The following entry from this dictionary will serve as an example:

"WHO abbreviation for World Health Organization,
Organización Mundial de la Salud (OMS)" (p. 865, [1973 edition]).

The list of research tools in the Appendix includes several specialized dictionaries of abbreviation and acronyms.

4. CONVERSION

In deciding whether to convert kilos to pounds or inches to centimeters, the principal consideration must be the needs of the prime reader.

If the conversion does not have to be exact, it may be sufficient to add an explanatory phrase:

S.L. El tipo pesaba tal vez cincuenta kilos.
T.L. The guy weighed maybe fifty kilos (about a hundred pounds).

In general, it would be better to leave the units unchanged rather than risk an inaccurate conversion. If you must do conversions, be sure to check them carefully.

If your work requires you to do a great deal of conversion, you might find a small calculator useful. Some calculators are especially designed to do conversions.

The list of research tools in the Appendix includes several books that contain conversion tables.

MONETARY UNITS:

Be especially careful with monetary units. Under no circumstances substitute the word "dollar" for "sol", "quetzal", and the like. "Peso" is often used for "dollar" in the U.S.; however, it may mean *peso*. Be sure you know the speaker's intention when you translate this word.

In translating foreign correspondence, do not assume that the sign $ necessarily means American dollars; it is used to represent many forms of foreign currency.

Here is a partial listing of currencies and symbols.

Country	Monetay Unit	symbol
Argentina	Peso	m$n
Bolivia	Peso	B$
Chile	Peso	$
Colombia	Peso	Col. $
Costa Rica	Colón	C ₵
Cuba	Peso	$
Ecuador	Sucre	S/.
El Salvador	Colón	C.

Spain	Peseta	Ptas.
Puerto Rico	Dólar	US$
Philippines	Peso	P
Guatemala	Quetzal	Q
Mexico	Peso	$
Nicaragua	Córdoba	C$
Panama	Balboa	B/
Paraguay	Guaraní	₲s.
Peru	Sol	S/.
Dominican Republic	Peso	$
Uruguay	Peso	Ur$
Venezuela	Bolívar	Bs.

NOTE:

The abbreviation MN ("moneda nacional") is sometimes used to indicate "national currency."

5. NUMBERS

It is difficult to imagine that numbers could cause problems in translation, but they do. Here are a few points to bear in mind:

a. In some Spanish-speaking countries it is customary to use a period rather than a comma to separate thousands.

S.L. 1.000.890 habitantes
T.L. 1,000,890 inhabitants

b. In some Spanish-speaking countries a comma is used instead of the decimal point.

S.L. el 1,25 por ciento de los empleados
T.L. 1.25 per cent of the employees

S.L. 5.825 miles
T.L. 5,828 millas

In the United States, the word "billion" means 1,000,000,000 (one thousand million). The Spanish equivalent of this number is *mil millones.* "Un billón" in Spanish means 1,000,000,000,000 — *one thousand times an American billion:* Americans call this a "trillion".

The U.S. conception of "billion" is exceptional; in Great Britain, France, Germany as well as most countries of this hemisphere, there is an intermediate step called "milliarde" (one thousand millions) between a million and a billion. Be sure to think of the system *the reader has in mind* in making these translations.

S.L. (U.S. English): a trillion dollars
T.L. (British English): a billion dollars

6. UNTRANSLATABLE WORDS

There are items that defy translation. The word "untranslatable" gives one an uncomfortable feeling; there is probably some equivalent for everything under the sun. But sometimes the resulting phrase is so long or peculiar-sounding or unwieldy as to justify leaving the term in the original language, perhaps with a clarifying note.

A phrase like "common law," for example, has much more meaning than the Spanish "ley común." Notice how the translator handles this difficulty in the following example:

S.L. Common Law. The Common Law has never been in force in Puerto Rico...
T.L. Ley Común. El "Common Law" nunca ha regido en Puerto Rico.

The translator makes an explicit reference to the English "Common Law," charging the inadequate "Ley Común" with the necessary associations. This done, he can now go on to use "ley común" or "derecho común," knowing that the reader understands the concept referred to:

"Comete error el tribunal al acudir al derecho común anglosajón para resolver situaciones que... están reguladas por el derecho civil..."

Leyes de Puerto Rico, Supplement to Vol. 30, p. 23.

Notice that the adjective "anglosajón" gives additional enrichment to the concept "derecho común."

Variations of this technique must often be used to compensate for loss or gain in meaning:

S.L. Se apoyó contra un mezquite (*Los de abajo).*
T.L. He leaned against a mezquite tree *(The Underdogs).*

Here the translator has deftly kept the flavor of the original while informing the reader that *mezquite* is a tree and not cactus, a mosque or an insect.

7. FALSE FRIENDS — FAUX AMIS

False friends or *faux amis* are false cognates, words like "actual" (English) and "actual" (Spanish, meaning "present-day"). Legal materials contain an unusually high percentage of such words. LEARN TO BE EXTREMELY SKEPTICAL OF THE MEANING OF FAMILIAR-LOOKING WORDS. In all probability, they are waiting for the chance to betray you. Take particular care not only to look them up but to see how their meaning *changes* according to context. The dictionary may not help you very much in dealing with these words.

For example, "Presidente" does mean President in certain contexts, but in the context "Presidente de la Audiencia" the translation should be "Presiding Judge."

As a "sensitizing" experience, try to translate the following phrases, then compare your answers to those listed.

Terms

a. Convenio de las partes
b. Alegaciones
c. Acumulación con acción de nulidad
d. Sellos de rentas internas
e. Colegio de abogados
f. Operaciones de Bolsa
g. Transacción
h. Dispongo de capital
i. Ratificó su declaración

Translations

a. Agreement of the parties
b. Pleading
c. Joinder with action for Annulment
d. Internal Revenue Stamps
e. Bar (Law)
f. Stock Exchange
g. Settlement (rarely, "Transaction")
h. I have capital at my disposal
i. He confirmed his testimony.

j.	Todos están complicados en el crimen	j.	All are implicated in the crime.
k.	Mi sincera adhesión a su política.	k.	My sincere adherence to his policy.
l.	Esta obligación rinde el cuarto por ciento.	l.	This bond yields 4 per cent.
m.	Autor de un crimen.	m.	Perpetrator of a crime.
n.	Delito menor (falta leve)	n.	Misdemeanor.
o.	Esto me compensa de las penalidades sufridas.	o.	This compensates me for the inconveniences I suffered.
p.	Copia expedida	p.	Copy issued.
q.	Recursos contra distintas resoluciones de los registradores deben registrarse	q.	Appeals from distinct decisions of the registrars should be filed
r.	Una resolución dictada en un recurso gubernativo	r.	A decision rendered in an administrative appeal
s.	Las pretensiones del recurrente	s.	The demands of the appellant

The above are merely a few examples chosen at random and by no means constitute an exhaustive list of false cognates. It should be apparent, however, that the dangers of relying on the face value of a word are very great. Learn to be wary of cognates, particularly those of Latin derivation; chances are that over the centuries usages have determined a different denotative range for each of the words in the pair.

8. CAPITALIZATION AND PUNCTUATION

Always be scrupulously careful to observe *the conventions of the target language with respect to capitalization and punctuation.*

S.L. On Monday, April 5, we met Mr. Gómez and General Blanco on the corner of Fifth Avenue and Forty-fifth Street. Mr. Gómez said, "I have received an important letter."

T.L. El lunes, 5 de abril, encontramos al Sr. Gómez y al general Blanco en la esquina de la Quinta Avenida y la calle Cuarenta y cinco. El señor Gómez dijo, — He recibido una carta importante.

C. EDITING YOUR OWN COPY

The truly critical stage of your translation will be the transition from first or draft version to final copy. It is at this point that the work of rewriting takes place: sentences are joined together or broken apart; all internal relations within the sentence are clarified; words are added or deleted to insure smooth narrative flow.

In short, the translator makes all necessary changes to insure that the final version reads as if it had been written in the target language. The following page has been keyed to indicate some of the adjustments that had to be made as the final draft was developed:

(A fragment of a State of the Union Message given by Antonio Guzmán, President of the Dominican Republic.)

S.L. Fue firmado un convenio de cooperación técnica con el Banco Interamericano de Desarrollo, BID,[1] mediante el cual[2] se hará un estudio de la Educación de Adultos[3] en la República Dominicana[4] que permita un adecuado reforzamiento de la misma en los programas de educación nacional. Por otra parte,[5] el número de escuelas de capacitación de adultos fue elevado de nuevo a veinte en todo el País con el consecuente número aumento de la matrícula de adultos de 2 mil 90 a 4 mil.[6]

T.L. Through an agreement signed with the Interamerican Development Bank, IDB, providing for technical asistance, a study will be undertaken of present facilities for adult education in the Dominican Republic; this study will make it possible to strengthen these facilities within the country's educational programs. In this connection, I should also like to point out that the number of adult training schools throughout the country has increased from nine to twenty, raising the number of students enrolled from 2,090 to 4,000.

NOTES:

1. *Banco Interamericano de Desarrollo.* An international entity such as this will in all probability have a standard translation in all major languages. English translation: Interamerican Development Bank, IDB. (Source: *Simon & Schuster's International Dictionary* under "BID.")

2. *Mediante el cual.* If we follow the lead of the original Spanish, our first draft of this translation might read as follows: "An agreement for technical assistance was signed with the Interamerican Development Bank, IDB, under the provisions of which a study will be made of Adult Education in the Dominican Republic..." Part of the awkwardness of this rendition stems from the use of the relative pronoun "which"; since "which" is uninflected (does not show gender or number) in English, it will always be harder for the reader to comprehend than an inflected form like the Spanish "el cual." If a solution can be found that eliminates such relative constructions, it is generally to be preferred. Simply starting this sentence with "Through" eliminates the need for the awkward "under the provisions of which": "Through an agreement signed with the Interamerican Development Bank, IDB, providing for technical assistance, a study will be undertaken of present facilities for adult education in the Dominican Republic..."

3. *Educación de Adultos.* Render this "adult education," not "education of adults." In English nouns are often used to modify other nouns: "summer vacation"; "paper hat." Remember to turn Spanish adjective phrases like "de Adultos" into simple noun-adjectives whenever possible:

Examples:

S.L. escuelas de capacitación de adultos
T.L. adult training schools

The Spanish "de' phrase can often be rendered by an English possessive:

S.L. Los programas de educación del país
T.L. the country's education programs

4. *en la República Dominicana que...*

The fairly rigid word order of English together with its lack of inflected forms places certain natural limits on the structure of sentences. It is sometimes easier to render a complex Spanish sentence by breaking it into smaller segments. Here the translator has used a semicolon after "Dominican Republic" and restated the subject ("this study") in order to write a more English-sounding sentence.

5. *por otra parte.* This phrase occasionally means "on the other hand," but quite frequently it is a mere linguistic crutch signifying very little. Since many speakers abuse this phrase, be ready to render it in a variety of ways so that its meaningless repetition does not deaden your text: "in this connection"; "similarly"; "additionally"; "I should also like to point out"; "with respect to this matter," "in this context", etc. (In formal legal discourse "por otra parte" may mean "party of the second part.")

6. *de 2 mil 90 a 4 mil.* Follow the English convention in giving these figures: 2,090; 4,000.

QUESTIONS FOR DISCUSSION

1. Explain the preparatory steps that should be taken before a translation is begun.
2. Why should names of individuals be left untranslated in legal documents? Names of churches and hospitals? Banks?
3. Explain how you would deal with abbreviations and acronyms in a translation.
4. Should Latin phrases occurring in a Spanish text be translated into English or left in Latin? Why?
5. What are "faux amis"? Why do they cause particular difficulty in legal translation? Give ten examples that you have observed in these materials.

PRACTICE 1

Translate or otherwise adjust the following for inclusion in a Spanish text:

1. 11.67% of the students	1.
2. 1,234 houses	2.
3. $1,000,000	3.
4. 7,892 centimeters	4.
5. 1,000,000,000 light-years	5.
6. 5.6 minutes	6.
7. 98.6 degrees Farenheit (convert to Centigrade)	7.
8. *carpe diem; joie de vivre*	8.
9. William Tower	9.
10. Carlos Muñoz y Hnos., S.A.	10.
11. the inhabitants of Friendship, Maine	11.
12. a billion dollars	12.
13. at 2 P.M., ET	13.
14. March first; April second	14.
15. 3/10/82	15.
16. The Interamerican Development Bank	16.
17. ECLA	17.
18. F.O.B.	18.
19. in the year 200 B.C.	19.
20. Finland	20.

PRACTICE 2

EXERCISE A

Read the following passage until you understand it thoroughly, comparing the original Spanish to the English translation. Then on succeeding pages, you are asked to:

(1) Mark in the English text all *adjustments* that the translator has made.
(2) Make a list of all words or phrases that are new to you or that were translated in ways you did not expect.
(3) Translate the passage yourself. Compare your work to the translation given here and correct your errors.

PERSONAS Y PERSONALIDAD

El Artículo 29 del Código Civil español indica que: "El nacimiento determina la personalidad; pero el concebido se tiene por nacido para todos los efectos que le sean favorables, siempre que nazca con las condiciones que expresa el artículo siguiente".

El Artículo 30 continúa, expresando que: "Para los efectos civiles sólo se reputará nacido al feto que tuviese figura humana y viviere[3] veinticuatro horas enteramente desprendido del seno materno". Y el Artículo 32 informa además que: "La personalidad se extingue por la muerte de las personas".

(TRANSLATION)

PERSONS AND PERSONALITY

Article 29 of the Civil Code of Spain indicates that: "Birth determines personality; but a child conceived shall be considered born for all purposes favorable to it, provided that it is born meeting the conditions set forth in the following section."

Article 30 goes on to say that: "For purposes of the law, only that fetus shall be held to be born that has a human form and lives twenty-four hours entirely separated from its mother's womb." And Article 32 further states that: "Personality is extinguished by the death of persons".[4]

* * *

(1) Mark in the English text all adjustments that the translator has made.

(*Note:* The passage is repeated here so that you can note the adjustments in the passage itself.)

PERSONAS Y PERSONALIDAD

El Artículo 29 del Código Civil español indica que: "El nacimiento determina la personalidad; pero el concebido se tiene por nacido para todos los efectos que le sean favorables, siempre que nazca con las condiciones que expresa el artículo siguiente".

El Artículo 30 continúa, expresando que: "Para los efectos civiles sólo se reputará nacido al feto que tuviese figura humana y viviera veinticuatro horas enteramente desprendido del seno materno". Y el Artículo 32 indica además que: "La personalidad se extingue por la muerte de las personas".

(TRANSLATION)

PERSONS AND PERSONALITY

Article 29 of the Civil Code of Spain states that: "Birth determines personality; but a child conceived shall be considered born for all purposes favorable to it, provided that it is born meeting the conditions set forth in the following article."

Article 30 goes on to say that: "For purposes of the law, only that fetus shall be held to be born that has a human form and lives twenty-four hours entirely separated from its mother's womb." And Article 32 further states that: "personality is extinguished by the death of persons."

* * *

[3]The form "viviere" is from the future subjunctive of the verb *vivir*. The future subjuntive appears fairly frequently in legal language in Spanish. If the tense is unfamiliar to you, review its formation. (See Reference Tools for list of grammar books.)

[4]Materials prepared by George N. Vanson.

(2) Make a list of all words or phrases that are new to you or that were translated in ways you did not expect.

....

....

....

....

....

....

....

....

....

....

....

* * *

(3) Translate the passage. Compare your work to the translation given at the beginning of this exercise and correct your errors.

PERSONAS Y PERSONALIDAD

El Artículo 29 del Código Civil español indice que: "El nacimiento determina la personalidad; pero el concebido se tiene por nacido para todos los efectos que le sean favorables, siempre que nazca con las condiciones que expresa el artículo siguiente".

El Artículo 30 continúa, expresando que: "Para los efectos civiles sólo se reputará nacido al feto que tuviese figura humana y viviere[2] veinticuatro horas enteramente desprendido del seno materno". Y el Artículo 32 informa además que: "La personalidad se extingue por la muerte de las personas".

EXERCISE B (CONTINUATION OF THE TEXT BEGUN IN A.)

Read the following passage until you understand it thoroughly, comparing the original Spanish to the English translation. Then, on succeeding pages, you are asked to:

(1) Mark in the English text all *adjustments* that the translator has made.

(2) Make a list of all words or phrases that are new to you or that were translated in ways you did not expect.

(3) Translate the passage yourself. Compare your work to the translation given here and correct your errors.

(CONTINUATION OF THE TEXT)

Antes de seguir leyendo el código citado en cuanto a lo que se refiere al tema de personas, debemos analizar y aclarar el significado de las palabras "persona" y "personalidad".

En su sentido jurídico, la persona se define como "todo ser capaz de derechos y obligaciones", mientras en su acepción jurídica, la personalidad puede definirse como la aptitud para ser sujeto de derechos y obligaciones. Se desprende entonces que, aunque la persona nace con la capacidad para tener derechos y obligaciones, no se le concede la personalidad a menos que se cumplan los requisitos expresados en el Artículo 30 demostrando la aptitud, o sea; tener figura humana (para ser considerado apto para obrar en la vida social y legal) y vivir 24 horas enteramente desprendido del seno materno (para establecer la presunción que sea apto para seguir viviendo).

(TRANSLATION)

Before continuing to read on in the aforesaid code regarding the subject of persons, we must analyze and clarify the meaning of the terms "person" and "personality."

In its legal sense, a person is defined as "any being capable of rights and obligations," while in its legal acceptation, personality may be defined as "the fitness for being the subject of rights and obligations." It follows, therefore, that although a person is born with a capacity for rights and obligations, personality is not conferred upon him unless the requirements, set forth in Section 30 are met, demonstrating his fitness, namely, "that he have a human form (in order to be considered fit to act legally as a member of society) and that he live for 24 hours entirely separated from his mothers' womb (so as to establish a presumption that he is fit to continue living).

* * *

(1) Mark in the text all *adjustments* that the translator has made.

(Note: The passage is repeated here so that you can note the adjustments in the passage itself.)

Antes de seguir leyendo el código citado en cuanto a lo que se refiere al tema de personas, debemos analizar y aclarar el significado de las palabras "persona" y "personalidad".

En su sentido jurídico, la persona se define como "todo ser capaz de derechos y obligaciones", mientras en su acepción jurídica, la personalidad puede definirse como la aptitud para ser sujeto de derechos y obligaciones. Por ello, entonces, aunque la persona nace con la capacidad para tener derechos y obligaciones, no se le concede la personalidad a menos que se cumplan los requisitos expresados en el Artículo 30 demostrando la aptitud, o sea, tener figura humana (para ser considerado apto para obrar en la vida social y legal) y vivir 24 horas enteramente desprendido del seno materno (para establecer la presunción que sea apto para seguir viviendo).

(TRANSLATION)

Before continuing to read on in the aforesaid code regarding the subject of persons, it is necessary to pause for a moment to clarify the meaning of the terms "person" and "personality."

In its legal sense, a person is defined as "any being capable of rights and obligations," while in its legal acceptation, personality may be defined as "the fitness for being the subject of rights and obligations." It follows, therefore, that although a person is born with a capacity for rights and obligations, personality is not conferred upon him unless the requirements set forth in Section 30 are met, demonstrating his fitness, namely, "that it have a human form (in order to be considered fit to act legally as a member of society) and that he live for 24 hours entirely separated from his mother's womb (so as to establish a presumption that he is fot to continue living).

* * *

(2) <u>Make a list of all word or phrases that are new to you or that were translated in ways you did not expect.</u>

....

....

....

....

....

....

....

....

....

....

....

* * *

(3) Translate the passage. Compare your work to the translation given at the beginning of this exercise and correct your errors.

Antes de seguir leyendo el código citado en cuanto a lo que se refiere al tema de personas, debemos analizar y aclarar el significado de las palabras "persona" y "personalidad".

En su sentido jurídico, la persona se define como "todo ser capaz de derechos y obligaciones", mientras en su acepción jurídica, la personalidad puede definirse como la aptitud para ser sujeto de derechos y obligaciones. Por ello, entonces, aunque la persona nace con la capacidad para tener derechos y obligaciones, no se le concede la personalidad a menos que se cumplan los requisitos expresados en el Artículo 30 demostrando la aptitud, o sea; tener figura humana (para ser considerado apto para obrar en la vida social y legal) y vivir 24 horas enteramente desprendido del seno materno (para establecer la presunción que sea apto para seguir viviendo).

PRACTICE 3

TRANSLATE INTO ENGLISH THS FOLLOWING
EXCERPT FROM A VENEZUELAN TEACHER'S CONTRACT:

Entre ————————————, que en lo sucesivo y a los efectos de este documento se denominará EL CONTRATANTE, por una parte, y por la otra ——————————, quien se denominará en lo adelante EL CONTRATADO, se ha covenido en celebrar el contrato contenido en las cláusulas siguientes:

PRIMERA: EL CONTRATADO se compromete a prestar sus servicios profesionales a EL CONTRATANTE como ——————————. Para la realización de dichas funciones, EL CONTRATADO deberá cumplir un horario de ————— horas semanales, de ——————.

SEGUNDA: La duración del presente contrato será en el lapso comprendido del ——— ——————————————— de 19——.

TERCERA: EL CONTRATANTE cancelerá a EL CONTRATADO por la prestación de sus servicios profesionales la cantidad de ———BOLíVARES (Bs. ————) mensuales.

CUARTA: EL CONTRATADO se obliga a: a) Presentarse antes de hacerse cargo del curso para planificar el programa que se propone enseñar con señalamiento de metodología a emplearse, bibliografía y de la dosificación de la actividad docente.

TRANSLATION OF PRACTICE 3

CHAPTER 4

CHARACTERISTICS OF LEGAL DISCOURSE

Legal discourse is a highly specialized use of language requiring a special set of habits. Obviously, translating legal texts requires painstaking attention to detail and sensitivity to the consequences of subtle contextual changes. This kind of writing is such a departure from our everyday use of language that it is worthwhile to consider some of the specific characteristics of legal language which the translator should keep in mind. Understanding why legal language is the way it is can help the translator to develop a kind of textual model, a sense of how language functions in legal discourse.

As you consider the selections presented for comparison, you will note how sensitive legal terms are to changes in context—the specific "setting" in which they are used. For this reason, dictionaries and lexicons are of limited usefulness in translating legal terms. A good translation requires both a through understanding of the subject under discussion and familiarity with similar models in the target language, i.e., the same kind of documents or instruments.

Here are a few general characteristics of legal language:

1. Legal language is conscious of precedent; conservative; slow to change; formulaic.

Underlying legal discourse is the idea that the law is a unified system developing organically from generation to generation. We believe that there is continuity in the law, that it has continued to grow and develop in a consistent way throughout a very long tradition. Legal language reflects these conceptions; a keen consciousness of precedent affects every choice of word, every turn of phrase in legal discourse. For this reason, legal language tends to be quite conservative. It is slow to change and tends to retain phrases and formulas that have fallen into disuse in everyday language. Legal language relies heavily on standard formulas of expression because the meaning of these phrases has been sanctified through long use. Our need for legal language to be as reliable and as consistent as possible from generation to generation is of very high priority.

Can you detect any of the abovementioned characteristics of legal language in the following passage? Read the translation which follows. Has the translator of the passage been sensitive to these values, in your opinion?

TESTAMENTOS

Citación del cónyuge y familiares

Para la práctica de las diligencias expresadas en la sección anterior, serán citados con la brevedad posible, el cónyuge sobreviviente, si lo hubiere, los descendientes y los ascendientes legítimos del testador, y en defecto de unos y otros, los hermanos.

Si estas personas no residieren dentro del distrito judicial o se ignorase su existencia, o siendo menores o incapacitados carecieren de representación legítima, se hará la citación al fiscal.

Los citados podrán presenciar la práctica de dichas diligencias y hacer en el acto, de palabra, las observaciones oportunas sobre la autenticidad del testamento.

Código Civil, 1930, art. 642.

WILLS

Citation of Spouse and Relatives

For carrying out the proceedings mentioned in the preceding section, the surviving spouse, if there be one, the descendants and the ascendants of the testator shall be summoned as soon as possible, and in the absence thereof, his brothers and sisters.

If the said persons do not reside within the judicial district or if their existence be unknown, or if they be minors or incapacitated persons without legitimate representation, the prosecuting attorney shall be cited.

The persons cited may be present at the time such proceedings are carried out and may make, at the time, verbally, such observations as they may deem proper with regard to the authenticity of the will.

Civil Code, 1930, art. 642.

2. Legal language is definite, precise and technical.

"The lawmaker sends his message over wide reaches of space, and he hands it down through indefinite stretches of time. These facts require that the lawmaker, above all speakers, transmit his message in a form which cannot miscarry or be lost to view" (Burke Shartel, *Our Legal System and How It Works,* p. 288).

The message must be transmitted in language that is extraordinarily definite and precise. Words must be used in strict accordance with definitions understood by all concerned. Members of the legal profession make careful distinctions between words that seem nearly interchangeable to the layman: the difference between residence and domicile, dictum and decision, privilege and right, may be of little consequence in everyday language, but in a legal context these distinctions are critical. Inevitably a large number of technical words must be used; popular language simply lacks the necessary consistency and precision. "The degree of definiteness (needed for legal discourse) can usually be obtained only by employing technical legal words whose meaning has been brought out and fixed by long experience and use," Burke Shartel explains (p. 295). Technical words, once we understand their meaning, are not only precise but *economical.* Imagine how the following passage would sound if we took out the underlined technical terms and substituted the equivalent phrases listed below. Would the passage be easier or harder to understand if we used "shorter" words?

"*Holographic wills*[1] shall be placed in a *protocol*[2] being presented for this purpose to the part of the Superior Court of the last *domicile*[3] of the *testator*[4] . . ." (*Laws of Puerto Rico*)

1. *Holographic will:* "A will which the testator writes in his own hand in the form and with the requisites mentioned in section 2161 of Art. 627, the Civil Code of 1930" *(Laws of Puerto Rico).*
2. *Protocol:* "Original record kept by a notary of documents or transactions from which he certifies copies" *(Webster's Third International Dictionary).*
3. *Domicile:* "The place with which a person has a settled or established connection for important legal purposes as determination of his civil status, jurisdiction to impose personal judgments

or taxes on him, or determination of the succession to his personal property on his death" *(Webster's Third International Dictionary).*

4. *Testator:* "A person who leaves a will or testament in force at his death" *(Webster's Third International Dictionary).*

3. Legal language tends to spell things out with painstaking attention to minute detail.

In everyday language, we ordinarily try to leave the obvious unsaid; we take it for granted that people know what we are thinking and understand what we mean. In legal discourse, *nothing can be taken for granted: every significant detail must be stated explicitly.* We often feel that legal language is unnecessarily wordy, even redundant, and we often feel tempted, while translating, to try to reduce the number of "unnecessary" words. This can have dangerous consequences, because the apparent redundancy usually is serving and important function. Consider the following example:

(From a Mexican Promissory Note)

"Los intereses que causa este Pagaré, deberán ser pagados el último día de cada período de seis meses contados a partir de la fecha de suscripción, sin perjuicio del derecho que tiene el Beneficiario de cobrar los intereses devengados a la presentación de este Pagaré, a pesar de que no hubiere transcurrido el período de seis meses.

"La Suscriptora se obliga a efectuar todos los pagos tanto de los intereses como de la suerte principal en dólares, moneda de los Estados Unidos de América, con fondos federales, en las oficinas de ...., y a efectuarlos sin deducción alguna, por o a cuenta de todos o cualesquier impuestos, exacciones fiscales, gravámenes, contribuciones, derechos, retenciones y cargos presentes o futuros, impuestos, establecidos, cobrados o gravados por o a cuenta de los Estados Unidos Mexicanos o cualesquier subdivisión política o autoridad impositiva de ellos, todos los cuales serán por cuenta exclusiva de la Suscriptora."

(Translation)

"Interest on this Promissory Note shall be paid on the last day of each six-month period counted from its date of issuance, without thereby limiting the right that the beneficiary has to collect the interest accrued to the presentation of this Promissory Note notwithstanding that a six-month period has not elapsed.

"The Maker obliges itself to make all payments of principal and interest in U.S. dollars in federal funds at...................................... without deduction for or on account of any and all future taxes, levies, imposts, charges, duties or withholdings whatsoever imposed, assessed, levied, or collected by or for the account of the United Mexican States or any political subdivision or taxing authority thereof or therein, all of which shall be for the sole account of the Maker."

Note the series in line 14 of the Spanish, "impuestos, exacciones fiscales, gravámenes, contribuciones, derechos, retenciones y cargos presentes o futuros, impuestos, establecidos, cobrados o gravados . . . " Explain why the apparent redundancy is justified here (why we cannot simply say "all taxes").

4. Legal language is characterized in all its aspects by formality.

Formality in legal language is the expression of the formality of the legal process itself. Berman and Greiner define formality as follows:

"If . . . a *legal* solution is sought to . . . problems, then *time* must be taken for *deliberate* action, for *articulate definition* of the issue, for a decision which is subject to *public* scrutiny and which is *objective* in the sense that it reflects an explicitly personal judgment. These qualities of legal activity may be summed up in the word *formality;* formality in this sense inheres in all kinds of legal activity, whether it be the making of laws (legislation), the issuing of regulations under the law (administration), the applying of laws to disputes (adjudications), or the making of private arrangements intended to be legally binding (negotiation of a contract, drawing of a will, etc.)" *(The Nature and Functions of the Law,* p. 26).

Study the following excerpt from the Spanish Foreign Investment Law of 1974 and compare the English translation to the original.

(Law)

Dispongo:

Art. 1. Las personas señaladas en el número 1 del art. 1 de la Ley de Inversiones Extranjeras podrán transferir a España sus capitales en moneda extranjera, admitida a cotización en el mercado español de divisas, con objeto de invertir su contravalor, sin limitación en cuanto al porcentaje de participación, en la creación o su posterior amplificación de sociedades nuevas dedicadas al desarrollo de alguna de las actividades que se indican en el art. 5 de este Decreto.

La presente autorización no exime de la obtención de las autorizaciones administrativas que pudieran ser precisas según la legislación vigente, con independencia de que exista o no participación extranjera en la sociedad.

En todo caso, las inversiones que se efectúan al amparo de lo dispuesto en el presente Decreto deberán ser declaradas en el Registro de Inversiones del Ministerio de Comercio, estando sometidas a lo previsto en el capítulo VII del Reglamento de Inversiones Extranjeras a efectos de poder gozar del derecho de transferencia.

Art. 2. Para poder acogerse a lo dispuesto en el presente Decreto, las personas interesadas en realizar inversiones deberán remitir a la Dirección General de Transacciones Exteriores la transcripción del objeto social de la empresa, a fin de que dicho Centro directivo verifique la inclusión o no del mismo en los supuestos contemplados en este Decreto.

Francisco Franco

(Translation)

Be It Enacted As Follows:

Art. 1. The persons listed in Article 1, number 1, of the Foreign Investment Law may transfer capital to Spain, in foreign currency admitted to quotation as the Spanish currency market, for the unrestricted investment of the counterpart thereof, without any limitation whatsoever as to the percentage of participation, in the creation or subsequent expansion of new companies engaging in any of the activities specified in Article 5 hereof.

This authorization shall not relieve the parties concerned from obtaining any government permissions that may be required under the legislation in force, independently of whether or not there is foreign participation in the company.

In any event, investments made under the provisions of this Decree must be declared to the Investments Register of the Ministry of Commerce, and shall be subject to the provisions of Chapter VII of the Registration on Foreign Investments, in order to enjoy the right of transfer.

Art. 2. Persons interested in making investments under the provisions of this Decree shall forward to the Directorate General of Foreign Transaction a transcription of the corporate purpose of the company, in order that the said Directorate General may check as to whether or not the said purpose is included in the cases contemplated in this Decree.

Francisco Franco

5. **The complexity of certain legal concepts demands a corresponding complexity in sentence structure.**

A great many qualifying phrases and dependent clauses may be required in order to express a concept with the necessary precision.

Study the following excerpt from the Spanish Foreign Investment Law of 1974.

(Law)

Art. 5. Se encuentran liberadas por el presente Decreto las inversiones en Empresas cuyo objeto social sea, única y exclusivamente, la fabricación en España de unos o varios de los bienes de equipo comprendidos en la Lista Apéndice del Arancel de Aduanas, salvo que expresamente se haya determinado lo contrario en el momento de inclusión.

(Translation)

Art. 5. The benefits of this Decree shall be applicable to investments in companies whose corporate purpose is solely and exclusively the manufacture in Spain of one more of the items of capital equipment included in the Appendix List of the Customs Tariff(providing the contrary has not been expressly stipulated at the time of their inclusion).

Reread the example given in Section 4 of this chapter for additional illustrations of the same characteristic.

QUESTIONS FOR DISCUSSION

1. List the characteristics of legal language that the translator should keep in mind. Explain the rationale behind these characteristics (i.e., why does legal language tend to be slow to change, etc.?)

2. Look up the following terms in a bilingual legal dictionary. Take note of the equivalents listed for each:

   a. orden
   b. testimonio
   c. demanda
   d. cesión
   e. hábil
   f. cancelar

   In light of the above, comment on the importance of *context* in legal translation.

3. Review the formation and translation of the Spanish future subjunctive. In the texts given in Sections 1-5 of this chapter, find four examples of the future subjunctive.

What characteristic of legal discourse is illustrated by the persistence of future subjunctive, a tense which has all but disappeared from everyday usage?

PRACTICE

Translate into English the following excerpt from a Mexican Promissory Note. A sample translation follows.

> El presente Pagaré se regula por las leyes aplicables de los Estados Unidos Mexicanos y la Suscriptora se somete expresamente para todo lo relativo al cumplimiento y ejecución de este Pagaré, a los Tribunales competentes del Estado de............................y los Estados Unidos de América y a los Tribunales competentes del Primer Partido Judicial de la Ciudad de México, Distrito Federal, en los Estados Unidos Mexicanos a la libre elección del tenedor, renunciando a cualquier otra jurisdicción que por cualquier causa le pudiere corresponder.

(Sample Translation)

> This Promissory Note is governed by the applicable laws of the United Mexican States and the Maker expressly submits itself as to all matters pertaining to compliance and execution of this Promissory Note to the competent Courts of the State of................... and the United States of America and to the competent Courts of the City of Mexico, Federal District, United Mexican States, at the sole election of the holder, hereby waiving any other jurisdiction to which it might be otherwise entitled.

CHAPTER 5

TRANSLATING PERSONAL DOCUMENTS

For obvious reasons, the translation of personal documents such as birth, baptismal and marriage certificates, divorce and adoption decrees, professional credentials and the like must be done with extreme care. In this type of work the translator's difficulties are nearly always those arising because of discrepancies between differing legal systems. If translations are to be accurate and consistent, the translator must have a sound understanding of the process by which such documents are formally prepared in both the Hispanic and North American legal traditions. As preparation for the translation of the model documents given in this chapter, therefore, we shall first consider some key aspects of this process, giving special attention to some of the differences between the two systems. Without this preparation, the translator might make some erroneous assumptions.

It is rare that a translation problem has such grave consequences as to attract the attention of legislative bodies. Such is the case, however, with a pair of words that have caused considerable difficulty because of the very different meanings they have within the legal traditions of which they are a part: *notario* and notary. The legislatures of California, Texas and Illinois have recently enacted laws prohibiting the translation of the term "Notary Public" into Spanish in advertisements. This rather drastic step was deemed necessary to alleviate the confusion that arises when Spanish speaking people living within the United States assume that a "Notary Public" has the broad powers the "Notario" has in Latin American countries.

> "South of the Río Grande, the *notario* operates under the Latin notarial system with broad powers to prepare legal documents. North of the border, however, the notary's comparatively narrow powers do not allow him to draft legal papers, but only to identify signers and administer oaths; in the United States, only an attorney is authorized to prepare legal papers for someone else.
>
> "This difference between *notario* and notary is often not understood by (Spanish-speaking) visitors and immigrants to the United States, who approach notaries for tasks . . . that are only the province of U.S. attorneys . . . U.S. citizens, too, suffer from the misunderstanding. Many Americans planning travel in Mexico are assured by ill-informed sources that, in the absence of documentary proof of U.S. citizenship (passport, birth or baptismal certificates, voter registration or military, discharge papers) an affidavit *prepared by a notary* suffices to get a Mexican tourist visa.
>
> "American notaries are not empowered to draft such citizenship documents and numerous would-be travelers who have waited until the last minute to pick up their bogus affidavit from a notary must postpone or cancel their trip to Mexico."
>
> (*National Notary*, March/April 1980, p. 32).

In his role as cultural intermediary, the translator must anticipate possible misunderstandings; persons with little or no experience in the legal environment are almost certain to assume that the familiar-looking word has the meaning it would have in their country of origin. In translations destined for the layman such as advertisements, etc., an explanatory note might be added if there is any possibility that the words "notary" or "notario" might be misunderstood. (The abovementioned laws prohibiting the translation of "Notary Public" into Spanish in advertisements also mandate the inclusion of the disclaimer "I am not an attorney and cannot give legal advice" as a further protection for the Spanish-speaking public.) In formal documents, however, "notario" should be translated as "notary," and vice-versa; such documents are destined for members of the legal profession who are conversant with both legal traditions.

This example may serve to point up the necessity of looking closely at the differences between the two legal traditions. The following sections on protocolization and legalization are intended to provide a background for understanding these procedures in a general way, but it must be remembered that certain procedures vary somewhat from country to country and that these differences must be also taken into account.

PROTOCOLIZATION OF DOCUMENTS

ROLE OF THE ATTORNEY

The protocolization of a document refers to the process by which a document must be formally consigned to a public notarial instrument and entered in the book of protocol of a *notario público* so that the document will be recognized as legal and binding for the parties involved in a given transaction as well as for any third parties who may be required to have notice of the transaction. Any consideration of the process of the protocolization of documents in Spain or Latin America must begin with the roles of the lawyer and of the *notario público* within the legal system. For the sake of simplicity, we shall limit this discussion to Latin America.

A lawyer in Latin America is someone who is learned in the law. This differs markedly from the lawyer in the United States, who is considered to be an officer of the court. An attorney in the United States can go to court and say: "I represent Mr. Jones in the following legal matter." An attorney in Latin America must obtain a formal power of attorney, called a *poder*, before a court will acknowledge that the attorney is the legal representative of a client. The requirement of the power of attorney for the initiation of legal proceedings is an integral part of the formality associated with the code-based civil law legal systems. See Chapter 3 of Part I, Cultural Fluency, for a detailed description of the differences between the common law legal system of the United States and the civil law code-based system which is in force in most Latin American countries.

DISTINCTION BETWEEN NOTARY PUBLIC AND NOTARIO PÚBLICO

The *notario público* is the central figure in the protocolization of documents in the countries of Latin America. He has a unique and very important status, far more official than that of the notary public in the United States. The *notario público* is, first of all, a lawyer, and must often meet the qualifications of a judge. At times the position is passed from father to son, subject to eligibility requirements; at times it is purchased, again subject to the same requirements. The qualifications for the position, in all cases, are high. For example, in certain countries, a test is required before an attorney can become a *notario público.*

The *notario público* is a public official. As such, he cannot choose clients, and must accept all who come before him. His fees are governed by statute and vary according to the type and length of document with which he is dealing.

The formality involved in the notarial system is illustrated by the existence of the voluminous *Reglamento de Notarías Públicas,* the Notarial Regulations, which govern all actions by notaries. A notary can function in two distinct ways:

(1) He can merely authenticate the signatures of the persons coming before him. The resulting document is said to be *auténtico de firma* (having signature authenticated). In this case, the notary does not enter the document in his book of protocol or keep the original, both of which he does do in carrying out his other notarial function. This first function is not unlike that of the notary public in the United States.

(2) The second and more important way in which a notary can function is in the creation of documents which are called "public notarial instruments." A public notarial instrument requires much more than the mere authentication of signatures. It is an instrument executed before a notary public which follows the legal formalities of execution.

To illustrate, let us assume that Señor Pérez and Señor Menéndez wish to execute a contract which is required by law to be a public notarial instrument. The attorneys for both parties can prepare a draft or *minuta* of the contract. It is the notary, however, who prepares the final version of the contract. It is the notary, not the parties, who speaks in the final document. Thus, the document may begin with the following words of the notary: "Herein came before me Señores Jorge Pérez López and Pedro Menéndez González to conclude the following contract. . . ." The final version of the document is written on official imprinted paper. Note that the complete names of the parties are stated in the instrument. The original of this final version, called the *protocolo,* bears the signatures of the parties. It remains in the possession of the notary. A certified copy of the document, called a *testimonio,* can be obtained from the notary. It will contain the signature of the notary, but the names of the parties will be found in typewritten form where they had signed in the original. Much of the procedural predictability and regularity of the Latin American legal system is based upon the assurance that one can go back and check the notarial archives if it is necessary to verify something from the original document for evidentiary purposes. In some countries, after a certain number of years, all notarial documents will pass to a central registry, where they will remain forever.

EXECUTION OF PUBLIC DOCUMENTS

There are several degrees of formality in the execution of public documents. The applicable code will specify the kind and manner of formality required for a given type of document. If the requisite degree of formality is not followed, then the documents will still be recognized and legally enforceable between the parties who voluntarily agreed to such a document. Such documents may not, however, be legally binding against third parties. The reasoning behind this is related to the notice requirements of code law. If the code says that a certain kind of document has to be in the form of a public notarial instrument, then anyone who might want to refer to that document has the right to expect the document to be in that form. If it is not the proper form or is not "raised" to public instrument form by one of the parties, then no one except persons knowingly and voluntarily agreeing to the arrangement can be held responsible for knowing about it.

THE PUBLIC REGISTRY

Some public notarial instruments must additionally be filed at the appropriate registry if they are to be binding against third parties. The requirement that a document be registered is a separate and distinct one from the requirement that a document be prepared as a public notarial instrument. The Public Registry Office serves an additional purpose in Latin America. It should be noted that there are various kinds of registries in different Latin American countries, for example, separate civil and commercial registries. The purpose of this recording of the document is to insure that someone seeking information can check the appropriate archives to verify necessary information.

PUBLICATION OF DOCUMENTS

Only a few types of documents require the additional and final step of "publication". For example, a deed of mortgage usually does not require publication, but if a corporation is dissolved, the document of dissolution must usually be publicized. The reason is apparent: it is so much more important to the creditors of the corporation that they know if the corporation is going out of business. If it is required that a document be publicized, then that document will not be effective against third parties if it is simply formalized as a public notarial instrument. Once again, the required degree of formality must be adhered to if the document is to be legally binding.

LEGALIZATION OF DOCUMENTS

THE CHAIN OF AUTHENTICATING SIGNATURES

While certain documents must be protocolized if they are to have legal effect, a different process, called "Legalization" is involved in *authenticating the signatures* on a document. We have already seen that one function of a notary public, in both the United States and in Latin America, is to authenticate signatures. *A chain of authenticating signatures is necessary if a document coming from the United States is to be acceptable for process of protocolization within a Latin American country.*

The process of document legalization is an exacting one. There are only certain designated persons who are authorized to authenticate the signatures of certain other persons. In each individual case, the question must be asked: Who is the proper individual who can certify the signature of a given person? The chain of authentication may be different for different kinds of documents. For example, if we deal with the authentication of a deed of sale by a corporation, then the chain of authentication will begin with the question: Who is the authorized person in the corporation who can sign the required papers? This is followed by the question: Who is the authorized person who can authenticate the signature of the authorized individual within the corporation?

If the process of document legalization is not properly and precisely followed, then a given document cannot even begin the process of protocolization within the Latin American country of destination.

LEGALIZATION ILLUSTRATED: THE POWER OF ATTORNEY

Let us take the example of a Chilean businessman currently residing in the United States who must do business in Chile and does not wish to return home to complete his transactions. The businessman has designated an attorney in fact *(apoderado)* in Chile to act for him. He contacts an attorney in the state where he is residing, in order to prepare the required power of attorney. That attorney contacts a correspondent attorney in Chile, in order to protocolize and record the power of attorney. It should be noted that a power of attorney is simply an authorization which empowers one person to act on behalf of someone else. Except in the case of litigation powers of attorney, the recipient of the power need not be a lawyer.

The power of attorney prepared by the attorney in the United States must meet all of the requirements of a Chilean power of attorney, or else it cannot be protocolized in Chile according to the requirements of Chilean law. The power of attorney is drawn up by the American attorney-notary following the Latin American notarial style. Typically, it will begin with: "Herein came before me . . ." The document is then signed in public instrument form by the parties in the presence of the attorney-notary. It should be remembered that attorneys in the United States are generally permitted by law to act as notaries, although not all attorneys have so qualified. Once the document is signed in this manner, the process of legalization in the United States can begin. This involves the authentication of signatures in a chain which ultimately reaches Chile. The first signature to be authenticated is that of the attorney in the United States (functioning as notary), which is authenticated by the County Clerk. From here on the requirements for authentication will differ, depending upon the existence of a consular representative of Chile in the state where the attorney practices. Thus, in New York, where there is a Chilean consul, the process of legalization would involve the following chain:

- The signature of the County Clerk is authenticated by the Chilean consul located in New York.
- The signature of the Chilean consul from New York is then legalized by the Foreign Ministry in Chile.
- The document is now ready to begin the process of protocolization in Chile. This may involve registration and publication, depending upon Chilean rules relating to the particular kind of document.

If the Chilean businessman and his attorney were carrying out this same process in the State of New Jersey, the chain of legalization might be different if there is no Chilean Consulate in New Jersey, and the New York consular office has no jurisdiction. The chain would follow the sequence illustrated below:

- The signature of the County Clerk is authenticated by the Secretary of State of the State of New Jersey.
- The signature of the Secretary of State of the State of New Jersey is authenticated by the Secretary of State of the United States.
- The signature of the Secretary of State of the United States is then authenticated by the Chilean Embassy in Washington, D.C.
- Once in Chile, the process of legalization by the Foreign Ministry and protocolization is the same as in the prior example.

Examples of actual documents illustrating steps in the processes of legalization and protocolization are found in Section III of the Appendix of this part of the text.

SEALS AND STAMPS

Most official documents bear a number of seals and stamps that must be accounted for in the translation. If the document has been drawn up on *papel sellado* or imprinted paper, this should be indicated. The seal normally appears in the upper left hand side of the paper. In the corresponding space, the translation might state, for example:

Republic of Colombia
Imprinted Paper
National Tax Stamp
Six Pesos

The translation should also include any identification numbers given in the original; these often appear in the upper right hand corner of the paper.

All signatures, initials and handwritten marks on the original should be indicated in the translation. If a signature is not legible, write "Signature illegible."

The color, relative position and content of the various stamps and imprints should be given as well. The birth certificate translated as "B" in the Sample Documents section of this chapter might have the following notation at the end describing the stamps:

"In the bottom portion of the document, the following can be found: One blue stamp that reads:

REPUBLIC OF COLOMBIA
FIVE PESOS
NATIONAL TAX STAMP
Q 840391

One blue imprint canceling the stamp that reads:

SECOND NOTARY
PEREIRA
JULY 13, 1958
CANCELLED

One imprinted stamp that reads:

REPUBLIC OF COLOMBIA
SECOND NOTARY PEREIRA
Pedro Cuadro"

SAMPLE DOCUMENTS

The sample documents included in this section are all from Colombia. They reflect the following events in the life of a single family, the Sueros:

A. The marriage of Dolores Sánchez Amador on January 3, 1955 in Buenaventura.
B. Birth of daughter, Marta Isabel, on October 11, 1956 in Pereira.
C. Baptism of Marta Isabel en October 30, 1956.
D. Education of Dolores Sánchez Cantú (fragment of transcript).
E. Graduation of Dolores Sánchez Cantú from the Colegio de Nuestra Señora del Rosario.

For examples of various types of documents from countries other than Colombia, see Section II of the Appendix of this part of the text.

A short list of words and abbreviations often found in such documents is given at the end of this chapter.

NOTES — NOTAS

A. Marriage Certificate

NOTARÍA ÚNICA

Circuito de B/ventura

Dr. Alfredo Gómez Padilla

Notario

El suscrito Notario Único del Círculo de Buenaventura,

HACE CONSTAR:

Que revisados detenidamente los Libros de Registro Civil de MATRIMONIOS que se llevan en esta Notaría aparece a folio #145 del Libro respectivo la siguiente partida que dice:

ADALBERTO SUERO AMADOR

DOLORES SÁNCHEZ CANTU

en la República de Colombia, Depto. del Valle del Cauca, Municipio de Buenaventura, el 3 del mes de enero de mil novecientos cincuenta y cinco (1,955) contrajeron matrimonio católico en la Pquia. Ntra. Sra. del Carmen. La ceremonia la celebró el R. P. Ignacio Aristizábal. En constancia se firma esta acta hoy 5 de enero/55. Esta partida fue enviada por la parroquia, el día 4 de enero de 1,955. El Notario (fdo) ALFREDO GÓMEZ PADILLA. Exenta de timbre y papel sellado.
En fe de lo cual se expide la presente copia en Buenaventura, a 4 de julio de 1,955.

Dr. Alfredo Gómez Padilla

NOTARIO ÚNICO DE B/VENTURA

(Translation)

SOLE NOTARIAL OFFICE

Buenaventura Circuit

Dr. Alfredo Gómez Padilla

Notary

The undersigned Sole Notary of the Buenaventura District,

CERTIFIES,

Having duly examined the Books of the Civil Register of MARRIAGES that are kept in this office, that there appears in Folio #145 of the respective Book the following entry that states:

ADALBERTO SUERO AMADOR

DOLORES SÁNCHEZ CANTU

in the Republic of Colombia, Department of Valle del Cauca, Municipality of Buenaventura, the 3rd day of the month of January of one thousand nine hundred fifty-five (1955) contracted Catholic matrimony in the Parish of Nuestra Señora del Carmen. The ceremony was celebrated by the Reverend Father Ignacio Aristizábal, in faith of which this certificate is signed today the 5th of January/55. This certificate was sent by the Parish, on the 4th day of January, 1955. They Notary (signed) ALFREDO GÓMEZ PADILLA. Exempt from seal and imprinted paper. In faith of which the present copy is issued in Buenaventura, the 4th day of July, 1955.

Dr. Alfredo Gómez Padilla

SOLE NOTARY OF BUENAVENTURA

B. Birth Certificate

El SUSCRITO NOTARIO SEGUNDO DEL CíRCULO DE PEREIRA-RDA

CERTIFICA:

Que en el folio 3408037 del Registro de Nacimientos
está inscrito el nacimiento de Marta Isabel Suero
de sexo femenino ocurrido en
Pereira el día 11 del mes de octubre de mil novecientos
cincuenta y seis (1,956), hija de Adalberto Suero y
de Dolores Sánchez.
Pereira Julio 13 de 1,958

Pedro Cuadro
Notario Segundo

(Translation)

THE UNDERSIGNED SECOND NOTARY OF THE DISTRICT OF PEREIRA-RISARALDA

CERTIFIES:

That in Folio 3408037 of the Register of Births
there is inscribed the birth of Marta Isabel Suero
of female sex, born in Pereira, the 11th day of the
Month of October of one thousand nine hundred fifty-six
(1956), daughter of Adalberto Suero and Dolores Sánchez.

Pereira, July 13, 1958.

Pedro Cuadro
Second Notary

C. Baptismal Certificate

DIOCESIS DE CARTAGO, PARROQUIA DE VERSALLES V. ....
El Suscrito Párroco de Versalles a veinte de noviembre de mil
novecientos cincuenta y seis. CERTIFICA: Que en el libro
19 de bautismos, folio 117 se halla la siguiente Partida: ....
En la Parroquia de Versalles a treinta de octubre de mil novecientos
cincuenta y seis el Pbro. Andrés Prieto Suárez bautizó solemnemente a
una niña nacida el once de octubre de mil novecientos cincuenta y
seis a quien llamó Marta Isabel, hija de Adalberto Suero y Dolores
Sánchez. Abuelos Paternos: Carlos Suero y Clara Rosa Amador.
Abuelos Maternos: Tomás C. Sánchez y Ana Cantú. Padrinos: Jesús
Muñoz y María Torres. Doy Fe. Carlos Pimental Rodríguez Pbro.
Sin Nota Marginal. Es fiel copia del original. ....

(Translation)

DIOCESE OF CARTAGO, PARISH OF VERSALLES V. ....
The undersigned Parish Priest of Versalles, November twentieth,
of nineteen hundred fifty-six, CERTIFIES: That in Book 19 of
Baptism, Folio 117 there is found the following entry: ....
In the Parish of Versalles, October thirtieth, nineteen hundred
fifty-six, the Parish Priest Andrés Prieto Suárez did solemnly
baptize a girl born October eleventh, nineteen hundred fifty-six,
who was named Marta Isabel, daughter of Adalberto Suero and Dolores
Sánchez. Paternal Grandparents: Carlos Suero and Clara Rosa Amador.
Maternal Grandparents: Tomás C. Sánchez and Ana Cantú. Godparents:
Jesús Muñoz and María Torres. I Certify: Carlos Pimentel Rodríguez,
Parish Priest, Without marginal notes. This is a true and faithful
copy of the original. ....

C. Fragment of Transcript

REPÚBLICA DE COLOMBIA
COLEGIO DE NUESTRA SEÑORA DEL ROSARIO

Religiosas Dominicas de Santa Catalina de Sena
Calle 2a., No. 6-43 — Teléfono: 46-35-38
Bogotá, D. E.

Aprobado por el Ministerio de Educación Nacional
Mediante Resoluciones Nos. 1,362 (Oct. 28/42) y 2,957 (Jun. 30/71)
Para el Ciclo Básico de Enseñanza Media y Bachillerato.

Resolución No. 001574 (Jun. 23/52) para Primaria.

CERTIFICADO No. 0304/73

(CONTINUACIÓN)

DOLORES SÁNCHEZ CANTÚ

ASIGNATURAS	H.S.	CALIFICACIONES	
Educación Religiosa y Moral	2	4.51	cuatro cinco uno
Filosofía	3	3.99	tres nueve nueve
Sicología	2	3.66	tres seis seis
Español y Literatura	3	3.32	tres tres dos
Francés	3	3.06	tres cero seis
Inglés	2	1.70	uno siete cero
Trigonometría y Geometría An.	3	3.01	tres cero uno
Física	4	3.20	tres dos cero
Química	4	3.28	tres dos ocho
Cooperativismo	1	4.42	cuatro cuatro dos
Ahorro Escolar	1	4.58	cuatro cinco ocho
Dibujo	1	4.52	cuatro cinco dos
Música y Canto	1	4.12	cuatro uno dos
Educación Física	3	4.12	cuatro uno dos
Urbanidad	1	4.50	cuatro cinco cero
Actividades Co-programáticas	4	4.66	cuatro seis seis
CONDUCTA	—	4.8	cuatro ocho

NOTA: Presentó habilitación con el siguiente resultado
INGLÉS, calificación 3.0 (tres cero) Diciembre 6/49

Dado en Bogotá a los 6 días del mes de Agosto de 1,951.

La Directora,

....
Sor
C.C. No. de Bogotá

La Secretaria,

....
Sor
C.C. No. de Bogotá

(Translation)

REPUBLIC OF COLOMBIA
SCHOOL OF NUESTRA SEÑORA DEL ROSARIO

Dominican Order of Santa Catalina de Sena
Calle 2a., No. 6-43 — Telephone: 46-35-38
Bogotá, Special District

Approved by National Ministry of Education

Resolution Numbers 1362 (Oct. 28/42) and 2957 (Jun. 30/71)
for Basic Cycle of Intermediate Education and High School
Resolution No. 001574 (Jun. 23/52) for Primary,

CERTIFICATE NO. 0304/73

(CONTINUATION)

DOLORES SÁNCHEZ CANTÚ

SUBJECTS	SEM HRS	GRADES	
Religious and Moral Education	2	4.51	four five one
Philosophy	3	3.99	three nine nine
Psychology	2	3.66	three six six
Spanish and Literature	3	3.32	three three two
French	3	3.06	three zero six
English	2	1.70	one seven zero
Trigonometry and Analytical Geometry	3	3.01	three zero one
Physics	4	3.20	three two zero
Chemistry	4	3.28	three two eight
Cooperation	1	4.42	four four two
School Savings	1	4.58	four five eight
Drawing	1	4.52	four five two
Music and Singing	1	4.12	four one two
Physical Education	3	4.12	four one two
Etiquette	1	4.50	four five zero
Extracurricular Activities	4	4.66	four six six
CONDUCT	—	4.8	four eight

NOTE: Took proficiency examination with the following result:
ENGLISH, Grade 3.0 (three zero) December 6/49.

Given in Bogotá the 6th day of the month of August of 1951.

The Director,

....
Sister
National Identification No. of Bogotá

The Registrar,

....
Sister
National Identification No. of Bogotá

E. Diploma

DIPLOMA

REPÚBLICA DE COLOMBIA

COLEGIO DE NUESTRA SEÑORA DEL ROSARIO

Dirigido por Religiosas Dominicas de Santa Catalina de Sena

Bogotá, D. E.

Aprobado por el Ministerio de Educación Nacional mediante

Resoluciones Nos. 1362 de Octubre 28 de 1942

y 1738 de Junio 30 de 1971

teniendo en cuenta que:

Dolores Sánchez Cantú

terminó satisfactoriamente los estudios correspondientes a la Educación Secundaria y fue aprobada en todos los exámenes y pruebas reglamentarios, le confiere el título de

B A C H I L L E R

La Directora, La Secretaria,

....

Bogotá, D. E., Noviembre 23 de 1950

Gobernación de Cundinamarca

Anotado al Folio 11-C del Libro de Registro No. 2

El Gobernador del Departamento, El Secretario de Educación,

....

(Translation)

DIPLOMA

REPUBLIC OF COLOMBIA

SCHOOL OF NUESTRA SEÑORA DEL ROSARIO

Directed by the Dominican Order of Santa Catalina of Sena

Bogotá, Special District

Approved by Ministry of National Education by means of

Resolutions Numbers 1362 of October 28, 1942, and 1738 of June 30, 1971

Considering that

Dolores Sánchez Cantú

has satisfactorily completed the studies corresponding to Secondary Education and has passed in all examinations and required tests, confers upon her the title of

B A C H I L L E R

The Director, ...

The Registrar, ...

Bogotá, D. E., November 23 of 1950

Government of Cundinamarca

Noted in Folio 11-C of Registry Book No. 2

The Governor of District, ...

Secretary of Education, ...

WORD LIST

The following words occur with some frequency in the type of documents considered in this chapter. The translations given are intended to be helpful only in this limited context; most of the words listed have many additional meanings.

acta, f.	certificate, record
actas de juicio	court record
actor, m.	plaintiff
autentificar	to authenticate
cancillería	chancery
comparecer	to appear (as in court)
compareciente, m.	person appearing (in court, before a magistrate, etc.)
confrontar	to check, compare
contrayente	contracting party (esp. marriage)
constar	to be evident to be recorded, to show
hace constar	to certify
dactilograma, m.	fingerprint, dactylogram
dar fe	to certify
demandado	defendant
demandante, m./f.	plaintiff
domiciliado en	domiciled in
expedir	to issue
extender	to draw up (ex: *"extendido en papel común"* — "drawn up on plain paper")
fe, f.	testimony; credence; assertion; validity
en fe de lo cual	in witness thereof
fecha de asiento	date of entry
fehaciente	evidencing, certifying, attesting, authentic
infraescrito	undersigned
legalizar (often)	notarize, authenticate
legitimar	to legitimate, to legalize
mayor de edad	of legal age
natural	native
oficialía del estado civil	bureau of vital statistics
papel sellado	imprinted paper
partida	entry, certificate
referido	abovementioned
revisar	to examine, check; to audit; to review; to revise
rubricar	to sign and seal
sentencia (de divorcio)	(divorce) decree
vecino	resident

ABBREVIATIONS

The following are abbreviations that have been observed in actual documents; it should be noted that many of them are not standard abbreviations; do not use them without first checking a good dictionary to see whether they are in common use.

Art.	artículo
B/ventura	Buenaventura
bto.	bachillerato
C.C.	Código Civil
C.C.	cédula civil (national identification card)
D.E.	Distrito Especial
Depto.	Departamento
D.F.	Distrito Federal
fdo.	firmado
Hno.(s)	hermano(s)
H.S.	horas/semestre
Nos.	números
Ntra.	nuestra
Of.	Oficio
Ord.	ordenanza (statute, ordinance)
Pbro.	presbítero (priest)
p.p.	por poder (by power of attorney)
R. Civil	Registro Civil
Pquia.	parroquia
R.D.	República Dominicana
R.P.	Reverendo Padre
S.R.I.	Sello de Renta Interna
Test. de	Testamentaría de
Vda.	viuda
Vdo.	viudo

EXERCISE 1

Translate into English. Assume all phrases to be taken from the type of documents dealt with in this chapter.

1. profesión u oficio ....
2. declaración jurada ....
3. Nació una criatura de sexo femenino. ....
4. Profesión: HOGAR ....
5. Nombres y apellidos del padre ....
6. una partida que a la letra dice: ....
7. Copia expedida en Bogotá ....
8. a quienes advertí el parentesco ....
espiritual y obligaciones ....

9. padrinos ....
10. notas marginales: no consta ....
11. con fines de unirse por el ....
vínculo de matrimonio ....
12. una hoja de papel sellado ....
del valor de cinco colones ....
13. ambas de emisión del año ....
mil novecientos cincuenta y dos ....
14. la ceremonia fue presenciada por ....
15. contraer nuevas nupcias ....
16. Of. domésticos ....

EXERCISE 2

Explain in English the meaning of the following terms as they apply to legal documents:

a) protocolización ....
b) minuta ....
c) testimonio ....
d) registration ....
e) publication ....
f) chain of authenticating signatures ....
g) notary public ....
h) notario público ....

EXERCISE 3

Translate the sample documents included in Section II of the Appendix at the end of this part of the text. Check your work.

CHAPTER 6

TRANSLATING LEGAL CORRESPONDENCE

Like hats and songs and novels, letters are cultural artifacts that reflect the values and attitudes peculiar to a certain cultural group at a particular moment in history. The total message a letter conveys reflects these values and attitudes; the appearance, style, tone, length and formal qualities of a letter are often as critical to the communication process as the letter's actual text. These aspects of a letter transmit ideas and impressions over and above the explicit contents of the message. People's expectations regarding letters undergo subtle but often critical changes from decade to decade, and, of greater consequence to us here, from country to country. As a result, any type of letter writing is far more complicated than it may appear at first glance, and formal legal correspondence that must bridge not only different cultures but different legal systems is certainly no exception.

Letters, no matter how routine, are never really impersonal, as we might wish them to be, and they inevitably reflect the sender's cultural conditioning — which may or may not coincide with that of the receiver. When letters cross cultures, a number of adjustments may have to be made to provide for these differences in expectations. In addition to the specific problem of translating the text of the letter, the translator must be aware of the larger message, the additional signals being sent by the unusually sensitive type of text we call a letter.

Both North American and Latin American business letters, for example, reflect the cultural value that time is precious; but the way in which this value is signaled may be quite different. In showing courtesy, for example, the North American has tended to focus on the receiver's time, reasoning more or less as follows: "You are an important person whose time is very valuable; by sending you the shortest letter posible, I render maximum tribute to you as a busy, influential individual." In Latin America, particularly in the past, the process tended to work in reverse: "I have high regard for you; I can give a graphic demonstration of my conception of your worth by expending much of my precious time in drafting a letter of size and substance, long enough to suggest the extent of my esteem for you." Such different approaches were bound to disappoint expectations and produce unfortunate misunderstandings. The North American letter, so carefully edited, too often seemed crass, insultingly curt; the Latin American letter, so carefully edited, appeared inconsiderate in its seemingly pointless inclusion of extraneous information. In recent years the two systems have adjusted admirably to each other, the North American letter becoming increasingly courteous, in Latin terms, and the Latin letter, increasingly streamlined. It should be noted that this process of evolution is at different stages in different countries; the best indication of the recipient's formal expectations with regard to letters is still the file of letters that person has written to you.

Space does not permit a detailed treatment of all the different types of letters that may have to be translated in a legal environment. However, legal correspondence is not essentially different from other types of formal correspondence, and excellent manuals, containing models of all types of letters, are readily available (see *Appendix* for suggested titles).

Both Spanish and English business letters are comprised of the following elements: letterhead (name of organization and location); date; inside address; name and address of the person to whom the letter is directed; greeting; introduction; text; closing; signature; initials (of the person who dictated the letter and of the person who typed it); list of enclosures. A subject or reference line ("Asunto" or "Referencia" in Spanish; "Subject" or "Re" in English) may also be included. The disposition of these elements is fixed by convention and seldom varies. The following letter may serve as an example:

1. LAW OFFICES
STEPHEN A. MOSER
STEPHEN A. MOSER
STANFORD A. SCHWARTZ
HARRY WILSON

1975 HEMPSTEAD TURNPIKE
EAST MEADOW, N. Y. 11554
TEL: (516) 794-1766

2. June 6, 1980

3. Metropolitan Life Insurance Company
25 Madison Avenue
P. O. Box 833
Madison Square Station
New York, N.Y. 10010

4. Re: Estate of
Policy #51 967AB

5. Gentlemen:

6. A notice of claim was filed for the above policy number which was an annuity policy as well as for an ordinary life policy #637230271A.

7. I have received the check made payable to the beneficiary for the ordinary life policy but I have heard nothing to date regarding the annuity and the payment that is due the beneficiary pursuant to same. Would you please be good enough to check the progress of this matter and advise me as to whether or not the lump sum benefit will be paid or if it must be paid out on an annuity basis. In addition, please advise when payment can be anticipated.

8. Very truly yours,

9. *Stephen A. Moser*
STEPHEN A. MOSER

10. SAM:jb
11. Enc.

1. letterhead
2. date
3. inside address
4. subject line (often typed two spaces after the salutation)
5. salutation
6. introduction
7. text
8. closing
9. signature
10. initials
11. enclosures

Style and Tone

What does a letter communicate over and above the explicit information it contains? Think carefully about this point, because the quality of communications between attorney and client is an essential element in the development of a sound relationship. Letters are critical precisely because they affect that relationship. If clients are to develop a feeling of trust and confidence, they must feel that the people who are handling their affairs are competent and efficient and have genuine respect for them as individuals as well as a personal concern for them as human beings facing a difficult situation. It is obvious that letters to clients have the potential to either enhance or inhibit the development of this essential feeling of trust.

The style of the letter, the manner in which information is presented, may denote competence — or the lack of it. The sense that reliable, efficient procedures are being followed will be conveyed if the letter:

1. is written in the correct format
2. includes all necessary facts, double-checked for accuracy
3. is specific and to the point
4. reflects proper attention to the mechanics of writing (spelling, capitalization, punctuation, paragraphing)
5. has been carefully proofread and corrected
6. reflects the cultural adjustments discussed above.

A carelessly written letter can undermine the client's confidence in the ability of an attorney or legal agency to provide effective help; this lack of confidence could materially affect the outcome of the case. Safeguard against error by emulating good models and by carefully reviewing all translations before and after final typing.

The subjective qualities mentioned above, the sense of respect and personal concern for the client as an individual, are closely related to what might be called the tone of the letter. While letters to clients resemble business letters in style and format, the tone must be somewhat less formal and more cordial if letters are not to sound cold and impersonal.

The following observations may be helpful in this context:

(1) Keep the reader clearly in mind as you write; use a more natural form of address than you would use in a business letter. Humanize phrases like "Acusamos recibo de su grata del 6 del corriente" which, while appropriate in a business office, make the client feel like a name on a mailing list. Write instead, "Quisiéramos informarle que hemos recibido su carta del 6 de (octubre) y . . ."

(2) The greater sensitivity to hierarchical structures in Hispanic culture is reflected in the forms of address used in formal correspondence. Titles such as "Licenciado," "Ingeniero," "Profesor," and "Doctor" are highly regarded and should be used whenever appropriate. The choice of salutation should reflect sensitivity to status as well as to the level of formality desired. Consider the following alternatives:

Estimado señor García:
Distinguido profesor:
Muy estimado colega:
Respetable doctor Muñoz:
Honorable señor juez:
Apreciado amigo:

In writing to ecclesiastical dignitaries, you may use the following forms of address:

Sacerdote — Reverendo padre:
Monseñor — Muy Reverendo Padre:

Obispo — Su Ilustrísimo:
Cardenal — Su Eminencia:
El Papa — Su Santidad or Santo Padre:

In writing to consuls, ambassadors, governors, presidents or kings, you may use:

Honorable señor:
Excelentísimo señor:
Ilustrísimo señor:

(3) Spanish formal correspondence is slightly more ceremonious, for want of a better word, than English correspondence of the same type. In general, Spanish letters have a higher percentage of courteous formulas and conventionalized, formal phrases than do English letters. Additional phrases must often be added in translating English letters into Spanish in order to avoid conveying an erroneous impression of brusqueness or lack of civility. The only certain method for developing good letter-writing skills is to observe good models and try to emulate them.

(4) The closing of the letter is another point at which the level of formality or familiarity may be indicated. In an earlier era extravagantly elaborate closings were used in Spanish letters; until well into this century such closings as "Quedamos de Vds. afms. ss. ss. q.e.s.m. (ustedes afectuosísimos seguros servidores que estrechan su mano)" were not unusual. Such closings now sound old fashioned. But the expectation of a rather substantial closing phrase lingers on, even though nowadays a simple "Atentamente" is considered a courteous and fully adequate closing throughout the major part of the Hispanic world.

The following alternatives are provided for variety's sake:

Respetuosamente,
Con la mayor consideración y respeto,
Atentamente a sus órdenes,
Les reiteramos nuestra gratitud y nos ofrecemos muy atentamente,
Reciba Vd. la sincera estimación de . . . .
Sin otro particular, lo saludamos atentamente,
Lo saluda atentamente...
Quedamos a la espera de sus gratas noticias,
En espera de su respuesta,
Cordialmente,

LETTERS FOR RECURRING SITUATIONS

Offices of all kinds make use of form letters for dealing with routine correspondence needed for recurring situations. Such letters have a number of obvious advantages for office personnel, but they are often cold and impersonal. Consider the following examples of form letters used in an actual legal services agency and suggest specific ways in which each might be made more cordial or courteous.

A. LETTER TO NEW CLIENT

TO ALL NEW CLIENTS:

Now that we haven taken your case, we will do everything we can to provide you with the best possible legal representation. However, to do this we must have your complete cooperation. We ask that you observe the following:

1. Always be completely truthful with your lawyer, so that he can best assist you in the preparation of your case. Anything you tell your lawyer is confidential.

2. If you are asked to obtain certain information or to be in court or in the office at a certain time, please do so. If you cannot comply, please call the lawyer in advance and explain why.

3. Please advise this office of any change in your address or telephone number so that you can be reached when there are new developments in your case.

4. If court proceedings have been started for you, and you change your mind and no longer wish to continue, please let your lawyer know, by mail or phone, as soon as possible.

5. Do not discuss your case with anyone or sign anything unless you check with your lawyer first. If you are approached by persons on the other side, explain politely that you have a lawyer and that they should discuss the case with your lawyer and not with you.

(Translation)

A TODO NUEVO CLIENTE:

Queremos comunicarle que, siendo ahora sus representantes legales, haremos todo lo posible para proporcionarle el mejor servicio posible. Sin embargo, para poder hacerlo, necesitamos toda su cooperación. Le pedimos que siga las siguientes instrucciones:

1. Su abogado es la persona que mejor le puede ayudar en su caso; por esto, debe conocer todos los hechos y aspectos relacionados con su situación. Su información es de carácter confidencial y solamente se usarán aquellos elementos que convengan a su caso; de tal manera, no tema decir a su abogado toda la verdad. De esta forma él podrá proporcionarle el mejor servicio posible.

2. Cuando se le pide que entregue ciertos datos, que vaya al tribunal o que venga a la oficina, le rogamos sea puntual en la hora y el día; en caso que no pudiera hacerlo, sírvase avisar con antelación para evitar problemas que pueden afectar su caso.

3. Si usted cambia de domicilio o número de teléfono, le rogamos que nos avise inmediatamente. Recuerde que necesitamos estar en constante comunicación con usted por si acaso se presenta alguna novedad con respecto a su caso.

4. En el caso que Vd. quiera desistir de su queja, y el tribunal ya ha comenzado a tratar su caso, debe hacérselo saber lo más pronto posible a su abogado, por teléfono o por carta; de esta manera se evita todo tipo de problema.

5. Le aconsejamos que no discuta ni en público ni en privado su caso con nadie; tampoco firme papeles o documentos sin antes consultar con su abogado. En el caso que alguien de la parte contraria desee comunicarse con Vd., infórmele cortésmente que Vd. tiene un abogado y que él es la persona a quien debe dirigirse.

B. ASKING CLIENT TO CALL FOR AN APPOINTMENT

Dear

Please call our office as soon as you receive this letter so that we can make an appointment to discuss current developments in your case.

Very truly yours,

(Translation)

Estimado(a)

Recientemente se han desarrollado nuevos hechos en relación a su caso. Le rogamos que se comunique con nuestra oficina a la brevedad posible y que fije una hora para una mayor información.

Atentamente,

C. INFORMING CLIENT OF TIME AND PLACE OF HEARING

Dear

Your case is scheduled for at at which is located at

Please arrange to be present at the above time and place together with any witnesses you may have.

Please also call our office on to ascertain if this matter will go on as scheduled.

Very truly yours,

(Translation)

Estimado( )

Su caso se ha fijado para el a la(s) en localizado en

Haga el favor de hacer los arreglos necesarios para estar presente en el lugar y a la hora indicados junto con los testigos que tenga.

Haga el favor de llamar a nuestra oficina el para asegurarse que su caso va a proseguir de la misma manera en que ha sido fijado.

Atentamente,

D. ASKING CLIENT TO ANSWER INTERROGATORIES

Dear

We enclose herein a set of written interrogatories (questions) which we have received from the other side and which we are required by the rules of court to answer. If they are not answered, you could lose your right to defend this case.

Please prepare answers to the best of your recollection on the enclosed yellow sheets (do not write on the forms) and return them in the enclosed envelope. This should be done as soon as possible since we have a time limit.

If you have any difficulty in answering the questions, please don't hesitate to call our office for assistance.

Very truly yours,

(Translation)

Estimado(a)

Con la presente le adjuntamos una serie de interrogatorios (preguntas) que hemos recibido de la parte contraria y que, según los reglamentos de los tribunales hay que contestar; al no hacerlo, usted podría perder el derecho a defenderse en este juicio.

Por favor prepare las respuestas con la mayor exactitud posible en las hojas amarillas que incluimos (no escriba en los formularios) y devuélvanoslas en el sobre que también incluimos. Usted debe hacer esto lo más pronto posible ya que tenemos un límite de tiempo.

Si tiene cualquier dificultad en contestar las preguntas, llámenos y nuestro personal le ayudará.

Atentamente,

E. REQUESTING CLIENT TO COME TO OFFICE TO SIGN STATEMENT

Dear

This is to let you know that the answers you gave to the interrogatories have been typed up and to request that you come by our office on ....at ....to approve and sign.

Very truly yours,

(Translation)

Estimado ( )

La presente es para informarle que sus respuestas a los interrogatorios han sido escritas a máquina y, por lo tanto, le pedimos que se presente en nuestra oficina el .... a la (s) .... para aprobarlas y firmarlas.

Atentamente,

F. ADVISING CLIENT THAT CASE WILL BE DROPPED IF HE DOES NOT CONTACT AGENCY WITHIN 10 DAYS

Dear

Our records indicate that you failed to keep your appointment scheduled for ....

If you desire our continued services you must contact our office within days of the receipt of this letter.

If you do not contact us within the above specified time we will be forced to close your case.

Very truly yours,

(Translation)

Estimado ( )

Nuestros archivos indican que usted no asistió a la cita fijada para el ....

Si desea continuar con nuestro servicio, debe comunicarse con nuestra oficina dentro de los próximos días a partir de la fecha en que reciba esta carta.

De no recibir notificación suya dentro del tiempo especificado arriba, nos veremos obligados a dar su caso por terminado.

Atentamente,

EXERCISE A

Study the following letter (from *Manual de referencia para la oficina* by Eva S. de García Díaz, South-Western Publishing Company, 1977, p. 103). Identify the parts of the letter; comment on the appropriateness of format, style and tone. Translate the letter into English.

BUFETE SANCHEZ Y ALVAREZ ASOCIADOS

Borinquen 212
Hato Rey, Puerto Rico 00919

7 de julio de 19__

Lic. Jorge Enrique Macías
Apartado 20331
Río Piedras, Puerto Rico 00928

Estimado compañero:

La Compañía Nacional de Seguros me ha referido el expediente relacionado con la reclamación establecida por usted a nombre de Hilda Polanco Viera, beneficiaria en la póliza expedida por la referida corporación sobre la vida de Osvaldo Polanco Viera.

De acuerdo con los documentos en mi poder, el último pago efectuado por el asegurado en esta póliza se hizo el 10 de agosto del año pasado, por lo cual la póliza caducó el 21 de septiembre siguiente. Como el asegurado falleció el 5 de octubre de ese mismo año, es evidente que la póliza en cuestión no estaba ya en vigor.

La Compañía Nacional de Seguros me ha informado de la contención suya en el sentido de que el asegurado hizo un pago adicional al del 10 de agosto, y que el mismo no aparece anotado en su libro de cobros. Si esto es así, y puede usted producir el recibo de dicho pago u otra evidencia fehaciente del mismo, entonces no tendré objeción en recomendar a la Compañía Nacional de Seguros el pago de la póliza. Sin embargo, si no existe documento alguno que acredite el referido pago adicional, me veré obligado a informarle que mi cliente deniega responsabilidad alguna en esta póliza por razón de caducidad.

Cordialmente,

Miguel Sánchez
Director

:mae

EXERCISE B

Write the greeting or salutation you would use in writing to the following persons:

a. Sra. Benítez (a client) ....

b. Sr. Presidente de los Estados Unidos de México ....

....

c. Sr. Embajador de España ....

d. S.E. Francisco Domínguez ....

e. Monseñor José Flores Miranda (Cardenal) ....

....

f. R.P. Angel Guarino Z. (Párroco) ....

g. Sr. Rector de la Universidad del Norte ....

....

h. Dr. Jorge Villarreal (médico) ....

i. Srta. Carmen Mendoza ....

j. Sr. Ministro de Educación ....

KEY:

a. Estimada señora:	b. Excelentísimo señor:
c. Honorable señor:	d. Su Eminencia:
e. Muy reverendo padre:	f. Reverendo padre:
g. Honorable señor:	h. Distinguido señor:
i. Estimada señorita:	j. Honorable señor:

EXERCISE C

Draft the following letters in Spanish, adding details as necessary:

1. To: Mrs. Ana Castro
   15 Tree Street
   Haddon, New Jersey
   07999

Tell Mrs. Castro that you have received her letter of October 4; thank her for sending the documents requested. Remind her not to discuss her case with anyone or sign anything without first checking with her attorney.

Ask her to call the office as soon as she receives this letter so that you can arrange to discuss new developments in her case with her. Closing. Signed, J. Rodríguez, Legal Assistant.

2. To: R.P. Joaquín Sánchez
   Iglesia de la Santa Trinidad
   San Pedro de Macorís
   República Dominicana

Explain that you have received his letter of August 1; thank him for sending the marriage certificate you requested. Tell him that you now realize that an additional document will be needed; the baptismal certificate for the child Ana Ma. Figueroa, born September 12, 1971. Ask him if he can help you obtain a copy; any expenses incurred will be paid by your agency. Closing. Signed, R. Smith, Legal Assistant.

3. To: Mr. Alfredo Méndez
Departamento de Personal
Banco Agrícola e Industrial
San Juan, Puerto Rico

Tell Mr. Méndez that you are writing on behalf of a client, Mrs. Angela Paez; Ask him to send verification of her employment with the bank from October 6, 1967 to November 2, 1971. Closing. Signed, E. Pérez, Legal Assistant.

4. To: Mr. and Mrs. Federico Colón
12-72 Essex Parkway
Fieldmont, New Jersey
07724

Tell Mr. and Mrs. Colón that your records indicate that they failed to keep their appointment scheduled for January 3, 1978 at 2:00 p.m. Inform them that there have been some new developments in their case and that it is essential that they call the office for an appointment. Closing. Signed, R. Picón, Legal Assistant.

5. To: Mr. David Anchoa
17 Saladini Place
Crosscreek, Pennsylvania

Tell Mr. Anchoa that his written answers to the interrogatories have been typed. Ask him to call the office this week for an appointment to approve and sign them. Closing. Signed, H. Hershfeld, Legal Assistant.

APPENDIX

Contents:

I. Dictionaries and Other Reference Works

- A. Dictionaries: General
  - Bilingual
  - Spanish/Spanish
  - English/English
- B. Dictionaries: Specialized
  - Synonyms and Antonyms
  - Abbreviations and Acronyms
  - Law:
    - Bilingual
    - Spanish/Spanish
    - English/English
    - Various
- C. Reference Works
  - Grammar and Usage
  - Translation, Theory and Practice
  - Law
  - Business and Professional Correspondence

II. Samples of Documents with Translations

- A. Proof of Destruction of Birth Record
- B. Baptismal Certificate
- C. Resolution of Abandonment
- D. Divorce Decree

III. Protocolization and Legalization: Sample Texts

- A. Power of Attorney
- B. Registration of Document
- C. Example of Public Notarial Instrument
- D. Title Page of a Public Notarial Instrument
- E. Legalization of Document

I. DICTIONARIES AND OTHER REFERENCE WORKS

(A) DICTIONARIES: GENERAL

Bilingual:

Cassell's Spanish/English, English/Spanish Dictionary. Revised by Anthony Gooch, Angel García de Paredes. London: Cassell Ltd., N.Y.: Macmillan Publishing Co., 1978.

Simon and Schuster's International Dictionary. Spanish/English, English/Spanish. N.Y.: Simon and Schuster, 1973.

Spanish/Spanish:

Diccionario de la lengua española. 19th Edition. Madrid: La Real Academia Española, 1970.

English/English:

Webster's New Collegiate Dictionary. Springfield, Mass.: G. & C. Merriam Co., 1976.

Webster's Third International Dictionary of the English Language, Unabridged. Springfield, Mass.: G. & C. Merriam Co.

(B) DICTIONARIES: SPECIALIZED

Synonyms and Antonyms:

Gili Gaya, Samuel. *Diccionario de sinónimos*. Barcelona: Vox, 1970.

Roget's International Thesaurus. 4th edition. Revised by Robert L. Chapman, N.Y.: Thomas Y. Crowell Co., 1977.

Webster's New Dictionary of Synonyms. Springfield, Mass.: G. & C. Merriam Co., 1968.

Abbreviations and Acronyms:

Acronyms, Initialisms and Abbreviations Dictionaries. 6th edition. 3 vols. Detroit: Gale Research Co., 1978.

Paxton, John. *Dictionary of Abbreviations*. Totowa, N.J.: Rowman and Littlefield, 1974.

Law:

Bilingual:

Robb, Louis A.: *Dictionary of Legal Terms. Spanish/English, English/Spanish*. N.Y.: London, Sydney: John Wiley & Sons, Inc., 1955.

Vanson, George N. and Marilyn R. Frankenthaler. *Spanish-English Legal Terminology / Terminología español-inglés en el área legal*. Cincinnati, Oh.: South-Western Publishing Co., 1982.

Spanish/Spanish:

Rivera García, Ignacio. *Diccionario de términos jurídicos*. Orford, N.H.: Equity Publishing Co., 1976.

English/English:

Black's Law Dictionary. 4th edition. St. Paul: West Publishin Co., 1951.

Cochran, Law Lexicon. 4th edition. By Robert A. Mace. Cincinnati: W.A. Anderson Co., 1956.

The Legal Secretary's Encyclopedic Dictionary. Englewood Cliffs: Prentice-Hall, 1962.

Various:

Blanes Prieto, Joaquín. *Dictionary of Accounting Terms. Diccionario de términos contables*. Spanish/English, English/Spanish, Mexico: Compañía Editorial Continental, S.A. 1978.

Espinosa Pérez, Darío. *Diccionario de cubanismos*. Barcelona: M. Pareja, 1972.

Diccionario médico (traducido del italiano por Rafael Ruiz Lara). Barcelona: Teide, 1976.

Manual de pesos, medidas y monedas del mundo. Edited by Frederico Beigbeder Atienza. Madrid: Ediciones Castilla, 1959.

(C) REFERENCE WORKS

Grammar and Usage:

Alonso, Martín. *Gramática del español contemporáneo.* Madrid: Ediciones Guadarrama, 1968.

Hodges, John C. *Harbrace College Handbook.* N.Y.: Harcourt Brace.

Follett, Wilson. *Modern American Usage: A Guide.* Edited and completed by Jacques Barzun. N.Y.: Hill and Wang, 1966.

Sallese, Nicholas and Oscar Fernández del Valle. *Repaso: Gramática moderna.* 2nd edition. N.Y.: D. Van Nostrand, 1978.

Schmidt, Conrad. *Spanish Gramar.* (A Self-Teaching Manual). Schaum's Outline Series, N.Y.: McGraw Hill, 1972.

Seco, Manuel *Diccionario de dudas y dificultades de la lengua española.* Madrid: Aguilar, 1966.

Stockwell, Robert P. and J. Donald Bowen. *The Gramatical Structures of English and Spanish.* Chicago: University of Chicago Press, 1965.

Wonder, John P. and Aurelia Espinosa. *Gramática analítica.* Lexington, Mass., Toronto and Lndon: D.C. Heath, 1976.

Translation, Theory and Practice:

Finlay, Ian F. *Translating.* London: The English Universities Press, Ltd., 1971.

Horguelin, Paul A., editor. *La Traduction, une Proféssion/Translating, A Profession.* Proceedings of the Eighth World Congress of the International Federation of Translators. Montreal: The Canadian Translators and Interpreters Council, 1977.

Levy, Bernard. *Present-Day Spanish.* N.Y.: Dryden Press, 1954.

Nida, Eugene A. *Language Structure and Translation.* Stanford, CA: Stanford University Press, 1975.

Paz, Octavio. *Traducción, literatura y literalidad.* Barcelona: Tusquets, 1971.

Steiner, George. *After Babel: Aspects of Language and Translation.* London and New York: Oxford University Press, 1975.

Sykes, J.B., editor. *Technical Translator's Manual.* London: ASLIB, 1971.

Vázquez Ayora, Gerardo. *Introducción a la traductología.* Washington, D.C.: Georgetown University Press, 1977.

The World of Translation. Papers delivered at the conference on literary translation held in New York City in May 1970 under the auspices of the P.E.N. American Center. P.E.N. American Center, 1971.

Law:

Berman, Harold J. and William R. Greinea. *The Nature and Functions of the Law.* Brooklyn: The Foundation Press,1966.

Leyes de Puerto Rico, Anotadas/Laws of Puerto Rico, Annotated. Orford, N.H.: Equity Publishing Co., 1967.

Mack, William, Editor-in-Chief and Donald J. Kiser, Managing Editor. *Corpus Juris Secundum.* A Complete Restatement of the Entire American Law. 97 vols. St. Paul, Minn.: West Publishing Co., 1936. (Contains definitions of many Spanish legal terms.)

Pollack, Ervin H. *Fundamentals of Legal Research.* Brooklyn: The Foundations Press, 1967.

Shartel, Burke. *Our Legal System and How It Operates.* N.Y.: Da Capo Press, 1971.

Business and Professional Correspondence:

Añoraga Larralde, Joaquín. *Correspondencia comercial.* 2nd edition. N.Y.: Minerva Books, 1970.

Harvard, Joseph. *Bilingual Guide to Business and Professional Correspondence/Guía bilingüe de correspondencia profesional y de negocios.* Oxford, N.Y.: Pergamon Press, 1970.

Krey, Isabella. *Principles and Techniques of Effective Business Communication.* N.Y.: Harcourt Brace Jovanovich, 1976.

Lawrence, Nelda R. *Writing Communications in Business.* Englewood Cliffs, N.J.: Prentice-Hall, 1964.

Montano, García Agustín. *Correspondencia de los negocios: Método objetivo para secretariado bilingüe inglés/español.* México: Trillas, 1974.

Reid, James M., and Robert M. Wendlinger. *Effective Letters: A Program for Self-Instruction.* 2nd edition. N.Y.: McGraw Hill, 1973.

Stewart, Marie M. *Business English and Communication.* 2nd edition. N.Y.: Gregg Publications Division, 1961.

II. DOCUMENTS

A. PROOF OF DESTRUCTION OF BIRTH CERTIFICATE (COLOMBIA)

República de Colombia
Papel Sellado
Timbre Nacional
Seis Pesos

EL SUSCRITO NOTARIO ÚNICO
DEL CÍRCULO DE SANTUARIO,
RISARALDA,

CERTIFICA:

Que por haberse incendiado el archivo de esta Notaría en el año de mil novecientos cincuenta y tres (1953) no se halló el registro civil de nacimiento de "ARMANDO VILLEGAS PEÑA". Para constancia se firma en Santuario Risaralda, a los ocho (8) días del mes de julio de mil novecientos setenta y ocho (1.978).

EL NOTARIO DEL CÍRCULO

(Firma)

(Translation)

Republic of Colombia
Imprinted Paper
National Tax Stamp
Six Pesos

THE UNDERSIGNED FIRST NOTARY OF THE DISTRICT OF SANTUARIO RISARALDA,

CERTIFIES:

That because the records of this Notarial Office caught fire in the year one thousand nine hundred fifty-three (1953), the civil record of birth of "ARMANDO VILLEGAS PEÑA" was not located. In evidence thereof this certificate is signed in Santuario Risaralda, the eighth (9) day of the month of July of one thousand nine hundred seventy-eight (1978).

THE NOTARY OF THE DISTRICT

(Signature)

B. BAPTISMAL CERTIFICATE (COLOMBIA)

TIMBRE ECLASIÁSTICO
COLOMBIA
DIOCESIS DE ZIPAQUIRA

DIOCESIS DE ZIPAQUIRA
Parroquia de Nemocón

Libro 8
Folio 7
Número 2

DIANA CHÁVEZ MEJILLA

"En Nemocón a veinticinco de agosto de mil novecientos uno bauticé solemnemente a una niña que nació el diez y siete de julio del presente a quien llamé DIANA, hija legítima de los señores .... y...; abuelos paternos los señores............................ y...; maternos, ... y.. Padrinos los señores..y .... a quienes advertí sus obligaciones. .... Rubricado." *SIN ANOTACIÓN MARGINAL.*

Es fiel copia expedida en Nemocón, Cundinamarca, a los veinte y siete días del mes de abril de mil novecientos setenta y ocho, 1.978. Exenta de papel sellado y T. Nal. Ley 2da de 1.976.

....
pbro.

Timbre
Eclesiástico

Diocesis de Zipaquira
Cundinamarca, Colombia
Parroquia de Nemocón

(Translation)

ECCLESIASTICAL STAMP
COLOMBIA
DIOCESIS DE ZIPAQUIRA

DIOCESE OF ZIPAQUIRA
Parish of Nemocón

Book	8
Folio	7
Number	2

DIANA CHÁVEZ MEJILLA

"In Nemocón on the twenty-fifth of August of one thousand nine hundred one I solemnly baptized a female child who was born the seventeenth of July of that year whom I named DIANA, legitimate daughter of the couple .... and .... Paternal grandparents, the couple ....and...................................... Maternal grandparents: ....and...................................... Godparents: ....and.., whom I advised concerning their obligations,.. Signed and sealed." *WITHOUT MARGINAL NOTES.* This is a true copy issued in Nemocón, Cundinamarca, the seventeenth day of the month of April of one thousand nine hundred seventy-eight, 1978. Exempt from imprinted paper and National Stamp by Law 2 of 1976.

....
Parish Priest.

Ecclesiastical
Stamp

Diocese of Zipaquira
Cundinamarca, Colombia
Parish of Nemocón

C. RESOLUTION OF ABANDONMENT (COLOMBIA)

DEFENSORÍA PROMISCUA DE MENORES DE MÁLAGA

RESOLUCIÓN No. 000 de 1.978
(Abril 20)

Por medio de la cual se declara en estado de abandono una menor. La Suscrita Defensora Promiscua de Menores del Círculo de Málaga (S.) en uso de sus atribuciones legales y

CONSIDERANDO:

PRIMERO.— Que la menor...................., de aproximadamente año y medio fue abandonada por sus presuntos padres ....y........................en el hospital de Santo Domingo de esta ciudad.

SEGUNDO.—Que hechas las diligencias al caso no fue posible dar con su paradero.

TERCERO.— Que por medio de la resolución No. 000 de 1.977 (agosto 3) fue ordenado su internamiento en el Hogar Infantil Santa Teresita de la ciudad de Bucaramanga.

CUARTO.— Que han transcurrido más de noventa días, lapso exigido por la ley 5ta de 1.975 para poderse declarar el abandono.

QUINTO.— Que de conformidad con la ley antes citada y resolución 02524 de 1.976 es al Defensor de Menores a quien corresponde dirimir estas situaciones,

RESUELVE:

ARTÍCULO ÚNICO.—Declarar en estado de abandono a la menor ....

PARÁGRAFO. Envíese copia de la presente resolución a la División Legal del ICBF en Bogotá.

Contra la presente resolución son viables los recursos de reposición ante este Despacho y de apelación ante el Director del ICBF en Bogotá.

Dada en Málaga (S.), a los veinte días del mes de abril de mil novecientos setenta y ocho.

COMUNÍQUESE, NOTIFÍQUESE Y CÚMPLASE.

(Translation)

SPECIAL OFFICE OF THE JUVENILE DEFENDER OF MALAGA

RESOLUTION No. 000 of 1978
(April 20)

Wherein the state of abandonment of a minor is declared. The Undersigned Juvenile Defender of the Circuit of Málaga (S.), in exercise of her legal authority,

WHEREAS:

FIRST.— The minor.........................., of approximately one and a half years of age, was abandoned by her presumed parents, ...and.......... .... in Santo Domingo Hospital of this city.

SECOND.— A proper investigation has failed to reveal their whereabouts.

THIRD.— Her placement in the Santa Teresita Home for Infants in the city of Bucaramanga was ordered by Resolution 000 of 1977 (August 3).

FOURTH.— More than ninety days have elapsed, the period stipulated by Law 5 of 1975 as being the period which must elapse before a state of abandonment can be declared.

FIFTH.— Under the provisions of the law previously cited and Resolution 02524 of 1976, it is the responsibility of the Juvenile Defender to act in these situations,

RESOLVES:

ARTICLE ONE: To declare the state of abandonment of the minor...............................

PARAGRAPH: To send a copy of the present resolution to the Division of Legal Assistance of the ICBF (Colombian Institute of Family Welfare).

Let this resolution be made known to the appropriate parties and implemented.

D. DIVORCE DECREE (CUBA)

....Secretario del Juzgado de Primera Instancia del Este/Oeste de la Habana.—

CERTIFICO: Que en los autos del juicio de divorcio radicado al No. 00 de 1962 se dictó sentencia en este Juicio con fecha 11 de marzo de 1962 en la que se declaró disuelto el vínculo matrimonial existente entre ....y..................................a los que se dejó en aptitud de contraer nuevas nupcias entre sí, en cualquier época y en otro caso, si se tratare del hombre en cualquier momento, y si fuera la mujer, después de transcurridos trescientos un días contados a partir de la firmeza de la sentencia, de conformidad con lo dispuesto en el Art. 12 de la Ley de Divorcio.—

Asimismo certifico que la referida sentencia se encuentra firme por no haberse establecido contra la misma recurso alguno dentro del término legal.

Y en cumplimiento de lo dispuesto, se expide la presente a solicitud de parte interesada en la Habana, ... de ...., ...

....
Secretario Judicial

(Translation)

...., Clerk of the Court of the First Instance of Havana, East/West, CERTIFIES: that among the divorce decrees relative to No. 00 of 1962 this judgment, made on the 11 of March of 1962, declared the bond of matrimony existing between .... and .... to be dissolved; the individuals may remarry one another at any time or may marry other individuals: in the case of the man, at any time, and in the case of the woman after a period of three hundred one days has elapsed, counting from the date this divorce becomes effective.

I do also certify that the abovementioned judgment to be definitive insofar as no motion against it has been entered during the period provided by law.

In fulfillment of the above, this copy is issued at the request of the interested party in Havana, ..., ..., ...

....
Court Clerk

III. PROTOCOLIZATION AND LEGALIZATION: SAMPLE TEXTS

A. POWER OF ATTORNEY (FOR BOLIVIAN ATTORNEY TO REPRESENT U.S. FIRM IN LITIGATION; TELEX)

Telex
western union

QUOTE

CONFIEREN PODER ESPECIAL Y SUFICIENTE POR CUAL DERECHO SE REQUIERE, EN FAVOR Y NOMBRE DEL DOCTOR RENE ROJAS PARA QUE ASUMA DEFENSA EN CUALQUIER ACCION O PROCESO QUE POR ANTE LOS TRIBUNALES DE JUSTICIA ORDINARIA DE LA REPUBLICA DE BOLIVIA INICIE YACIMIENTOS PETROLIFEROS FISCALES BOLIVIANOS CONTRA LA EMPRESA MANDANTE, ASI COMO PARA QUE PROSIGA Y FENESCA EN TODOS SUS GRADOS E INSTANCIAS Y USANDO DE TODOS LOS RECURSOS ORDINARIOS Y EXTRAORDINARIOS CUALQUIER CLASE DE ACCIONES Y PROCESOS ANTE DICHOS TRIBUNALES ORDINARIOS. AL EFECTO, LE CONFIEREN LAS FACULTADES GENERALES DEL MANDATO PARA PROCESOS Y ACCIONES Y LAS ESPECIALES DE FIRMAR Y PRESENTAR ESCRITOS, RESPONDER DEMANDAS, RECONVENIR, PROPONER Y HACER PRODUCIR TODA CLASE DE PRUEBAS LITERALES, TESTIFICALES, PERICIALES Y LAS ADMITIDAS POR LOS PROCEDIMIENTOS, TACHAR Y OBSERVAR LA PRUEBA CONTRARIA, HACER RECIBIR DECLARACIONES DE TESTIGOS, FORMULAR CONTRAINTERROGATORIOS, AMPLIAR LA PRUEBA, CONCURRIR A AUDIENCIAS, INSPECCIONES OCULARES, DEBATES Y DILIGENCIAS, INTERPONER Y PEDIR RECHAZOS DE TERCERIAS EXCLUYENTES, COADYUVANTES, DE MEJOR DERECHO Y DE TODA OTRA INDOLE, CONCURSOS Y RECONVENCIONES, DEDUCIR EXCEPCIONES PREVIAS, PERENTORIAS Y PREJUDICIALES, ASI COMO DEFERIR A CONFESIONES DENTRO DEL PROCESO, SOLICITAR INSPECCIONES JUDICIALES Y RECONSTRUCCIONES, DEFERIR A JURAMENTOS, ACUSAR REBELDIAS O DESERCIONES, RESPONDER Y PLANTEAR INCIDENTES, ARTICULOS, DUPLICAR, REPLICAR, TACHAR, ABONAR, ACUSAR, RECUSAR A TODA CLASE DE AUTORIDADES JUDICIALES, CON POTESTAD DE JURAR QUE NO OBRA CON MALICIA Y ANIMO DE PERJUDICAR AL RECUSADO Y DEMAS REQUISITOS INHERENTES A ESTA DEMANDA, SOLICITAR EXCUSAS, PLANTEAR RECUSACIONES, RECURRIR EN QUEJA, INTERPONER RECURSOS DE REPOSICION, APELACION, CASACION DE FONDO Y FORMA, REVISION DE SENTENCIAS, COMPULSA, DECIR Y RECURRIR DE NULIDAD, FUNDAMENTAR Y CONTESTAR RECURSOS ORDINARIOS O EXTRAORDINARIOS, ASISTIR A AUDIENCIAS DE CONCILIACION, DESISTIR, TRANSIGIR, ADMITIR DESISTIMIENTOS, PEDIR ARRAIGOS, APREMIOS, SECUESTROS, ALLANAMIENTOS, DEPOSITOS, RETENCIONES, ADJUDICACIONES, NOMBRAR PERITOS, ACEPTAR PROPOSICIONES DE CONVENIOS, SOLICITAR INSPECCIONES, INFORMES DE TODO TIPO DE PERSONAS Y/O AUTORIDADES, SOLICITAR AUDIENCIAS, DILIGENCIAS, DEBATES, CERTIFICADOS, TESTIMONIOS, COPIAS LEGALIZADAS, RESOLUCIONES, SENTENCIAS, AUTOS, SOLICITAR EMPLAZAMIENTOS, SUSTANCIAR DILIGENCIAS PREPARATORIAS Y PRECAUTORIAS DE DEMANDA, RECHAZAR Y OFRECER FIANZAS DE CUALQUIER NATURALEZA O LAS QUE FUESEN NECESARIAS, SOLICITAR MANDAMIENTOS EN GENERAL, PEDIR ACLARACIONES, COMPLEMENTACIONES Y ENMIENDAS, LIQUIDACIONES, APROBARLAS Y OBSERVARLAS, SOLICITAR ANOTACIONES PREVENTIVAS E INSCRIPCIONES DEFINITIVAS EN LAS OFICINAS DEL REGISTRO DE DERECHOS REALES DE CUALQUIER DEPARTAMENTO DE LA REPUBLICA DE BOLIVIA, PROPUGNAR E IMPUGNAR DICTAMENES O REQUERIMIENTOS FISCALES, SOLICITAR MEDIDAS PRECAUTORIAS DE

1548 EST

AGMCKEECO I DPC

Telex
western union

ANOTACION PREVENTIVA, EMBARGO PREVENTIVO, INTERVENCION, PROHIBICION DE CELEBRAR ACTOS O CONTRATOS SOBRE BIENES DETERMINADOS, Y LAS QUE PUEDAN SER VIABLES FACULTADAS POR EL ART. 169 DEL CODIGO DE PROCEDIMIENTO CIVIL, PEDIR MEDIDAS PREPARATORIAS COMO LAS DE PROPONER CONFESION ANTICIPADA, RECONOCIMIENTO DE FIRMA, EXHIBICION DE COSA MUEBLE, TITULOS DE PROPIEDAD, DOCUMENTOS, SOLICITAR DECLARACIONES ANTICIPADAS DE TESTIGOS, SOLICITAR MENSURA JUDICIAL, FACULTAD PARA CITACION EN MEDIDAS PREPARATORIAS, PRESENTACION DE COMPROBANTES DE PAGO Y CONTABLES Y OTROS SIMILARES, SUSCITAR CONTENCION, PEDIR DETERMINACIONES, PRESENTAR DENUNCIAS, SOLICITAR INDEMNIZACIONES, SOLICITAR ORDENES INSTRUIDAS, EXHORTOS, EXHORTOS SUPLICATORIOS Y PROVISIONES, COMISIONES, SEGUIR PROCESOS DE INCONSTITUCIONALIDAD Y DE INAPLICABILIDAD DE LEYES, DECRETOS O DE CUALQUIER GENERO DE RESOLUCIONES, PRESENTAR HABEAS CORPUS Y AMPAROS CONSTITUCIONALES, RECURSOS DIRECTOS DE NULIDAD, SEGUIR PROCESOS CONTENCIOSOS Y RESULTANTES DE CONTRATOS, NEGOCIACIONES Y CONCESIONES DEL PODER EJECUTIVO, SEGUIR PROCESOS CONTENCIOSOS-ADMINISTRATIVOS A QUE DIEREN LUGAR LAS RESOLUCIONES DEL PODER EJECUTIVO, Y EN SUMA USAR DE TODO GENERO DE RECURSOS ORDINARIOS O EXTRAORDINARIOS, DIRECTOS O INDIRECTOS, DE INCONSTITUCIONALIDAD Y OTROS SIN EXCEPCION, HACER VALER DERECHOS DE PAGO Y PRESCRIPCION, COMO DE COSA JUZGADA, Y OTROS SIMILARES, SEGUIR TODO TIPO DE PROCESOS Y RESPONDERLOS, SEAN ESTOS, ORDINARIOS, SUMARIOS, SUMARISIMOS DE EJECUCION, CONCURSALES, INTERDICTOS, VOLUNTARIOS, ARBITRALES, DE RESPONSABILIDAD EN TODOS SUS GRADOS, FORMAS E INSTANCIAS HASTA SU TOTAL CONCLUSION. TODAS LAS FACULTADES DEL PRESENTE PODER CUALESQUIERA QUE SEAN ELLAS SON OTORGADAS EN FAVOR DEL MANDATARIO CON RELEVO DE GASTOS PROCESALES, COSTAS Y OTROS QUE SERAN DE CUENTA Y RESPONSABILIDAD EXCLUSIVA DE LA SOCIEDAD MANDANTE O PODERDANTE, OTORGANDOLE ADEMAS LA FACULTAD DE SUSTITUIR EN TODO O EN PARTE EL PRESENTE MANDATO, LAS VECES QUE CONSIDERE CONVENIENTE Y REASUMIR Y EN SUMA REALIZAR CUANTA GESTION Y DILIGENCIAS FUEREN NECESARIAS PARA EL MEJOR EXITO Y CUMPLIMIENTO DEL PRESENTE PODER, SIN QUE POR FALTA DE CLAUSULA EXPRESA U OMISION PUEDA SER TACHADO DE INSUFICIENTE POR PERSONA O AUTORIDAD ALGUNA. UNQUOTE.

POWER OF ATTORNEY MUST INCLUDE RELEVANT PARTS OF MINUTES OF STOCKHOLDERS AND BOARD OF DIRECTORS MEETINGS EVIDENCING QUALIFICATION AND CAPACITY OF PERSONS THAT EXECUTE THIS POWER ON BEHALF ARTHUR G. MCKEE AND A. G. MCKEE.

REGARDS

RENE ROJAS

B. REGISTRATION OF DOCUMENT

R/4

I. Que conozco al compareciente, y lo conceptúo legalmente capacitado para la celebración de este acto. - - - - - - - -

II. Que he tenido a la vista los documentos que se citan en esta escritura, a cuyos originales me remito. - - - - - - -

III. Que el compareciente declara bajo protesta de decir verdad que el contenido del acta transcrita y las firmas que la calzan son auténticas y que toma a su cargo la inscripción de este instrumento en el Registro Público de Comercio. - - -

IV. Que le leí íntegramente esta escritura sin explicarle el valor y consecuencias legales de su contenido en razón de su profesión y conforme con ella la firma ante el suscrito que la AUTORIZA de inmediato por no causar el Impuesto del -- Timbre, hoy día de su fecha. - - - - - - - - - - - - - - - - - --

FIRMA: G. G. G. - RUBRICA. - - - - - - - - - - - - - - - -

A. SOBERON A. - EL SELLO DE AUTORIZAR. - - - - - - - - - -

- - - - - - - - - - - - - NOTAS MARGINALES: - - - - - - - - - - -

DERECHOS DEVENGADOS: $80.00. - A.S.A. - - - - - - - - - --

ES PRIMER TESTIMONIO, QUE SE EXPIDE PARA LA INTERESADA , SOCIEDAD ANONIMA DE CAPITAL VARIABLE, ESTA CORREGIDO Y VA EN CUATRO FOJAS ESCRITAS CON TINTA FIJA Y CON LOS TIMBRES DE LEY. - DOY FE.-- MEXICO, DISTRITO FEDERAL, A VEINTIOCHO DE MAYO DE MIL NOVECIENTOS SE--- TENTA Y CINCO.-:-

ORV/ab.

SECCION DE COMERCIO

México, D.F., a 4 de Junio de 1975

REGISTRADO bajo el número 321 a foja 299

del volumen 941 libro 3º

Derechos $ 100.— Boleta Núm 238301 de fecha

4 de Junio de 1975 Registro de Caja

Núm. 45313 de fecha 4 de Junio de 1975

EL REGISTRADOR

EL DIRECTOR

C. EXAMPLE OF PUBLIC NOTARIAL INSTRUMENT (EL SALVADOR)

3949890

CUARENTA CENTAVOS

014989149

V/Morales.—

EL SECRETARIO DE LA CORTE SUPREMA DE JUSTICIA:

C E R T I F I C A : que la firma que calza el documento que antecede, es auténtica del notario doctor ALFREDO ORTIZ MANCIA. Dicho documento es un testimonio de escritura pública otorgada en esta ciudad, a las dieciséis horas del día catorce de febrero de mil novecientos cincuenta y cinco, ante los oficios del mencionado notario, por el cual los señores don , socialmente conocido por , y doña , también conocida por ambos de generales consignadas manifiestan: que confirman la legitimación de derecho del menor en virtud de que en su partida de nacimiento y en la de matrimonio, la madre doña , conocida por aparece con nombres distintos. La escritura pública en referencia está otorgada en una hoja de papel sellado del valor de cinco colones cincuenta centavos número cero cero cuatro mil setecientos veintiocho, tomada razón al número cero cero cuatro mil trescientos veinticuatro, y en otra del valor de quince centavos número cero cuarenta y un mil quinientos setenta y cuatro, tomada razón al número cero cuarenta y un mil cuatrocientos setenta y cinco, ambas de la emisión del año mil novecientos cincuenta y cinco.

San Salvador, a los veinticinco días del mes de febrero de mil novecientos setenta y dos.-Enmendado-ALFONSO- Vale.-

El In–

frascrito Subsecretario de Justicia, HACE CONSTAR: que la firma que antecede y que dice "J. G. Domínguez", ES AUTENTICA y la misma que usa el doctor Jorge Guillermo Domínguez, como Secretario de la Corte Suprema de Justicia.

MINISTERIO DE JUSTICIA: San Salvador, a los veinticinco dias del mes de febrero de mil novecientos setenta y dos.

P. J. ROSALES.

El infrascrito FUNCIONARIO
del Ministerio de Relaciones Exteriores
CERTIFICA: que la firma que antecede
y que dice: __________
es auténtica y la misma que usa el señor
PEDRO JOSE ROSALES, SUBSECRETARIO
DE JUSTICIA.

San Salvador, a los 29 días
del mes de FEBRERO de mil
novecientos SETENTA Y DOS.

El Ministerio de Relaciones Exteriores no se hace responsable por el contenido del presente documento.

ERASMO ANTONIO SERMEÑO MENA
Director de Administración General

D. TITLE PAGE OF A PUBLIC NOTARIAL INSTRUMENT (MEXICO)

LIC. ALEJANDRO SOBERON ALONSO

NOTARIA No. 68

PRIMER **TESTIMONIO** DE LA ESCRITURA QUE CONTIENE: PROTOCOLIZACION EN LO CONDUCENTE DE UNA ACTA DE JUNTA CELEBRADA POR EL CONSEJO– DE ADMINISTRACION DE , SOCIEDAD ANONIMA DE CAPI– TAL VARIABLE. ––––––––––––––––––––––

VOL. 732 –––––––––––– NO. 40,832 –––––––––––– FS. 259.

DE VEINTIOCHO ––––––––––– DE MAYO ––––––––––– DE 1975.

AMAZONAS 57.60 PISO

MEXICO 5, D. F.

TEL. 5 – 66 – 62 – 77

E. LEGALIZATION OF DOCUMENT

$0.50
CINCUENTA CENTAVOS
VALIDO PARA EL BIENIO
1977–78

ces E. Sutherland.- Notario Público en y por el Estado de California, Mi Comisión expira el cuatro de Marzo de mil- novecientos setenta y dos.- Frances E. Sutherland Notary Públic. City & Co. Of. San Francisco State Of. California. A continuación hay una legalización en idioma inglés donde se acredita la autenticidad de la firma del Notario Público don Frances E. Sutherland, otorgado por don Martín Mongan, Country Clerk and Clerk of the Superior Court of the State of California, in and for the City and County of San Francisco, which Court is a Court of Record having by law a- seal, Do Hereby Certify: That, de fecha siete de Marzo de mil novecientos sesenta y nueve.- Al respaldo se lee: Consulado de Chile en San Francisco Cal. Legalizada la firma del Sr. Martín Mongan, Country Clerk y Clerk de la ciudad- y Condado de San Fco. número doscientos veinticuatro Arancel once- treinta y cinco Derechos nueve dólares. San Francisco, Cal, doce de Marzo de mil novecientos sesenta y nueve. H. Burr. Héctor Burr.- Cónsul de Chile. Hay estampillas inutilizadas y timbre Consulado de Chile San Francisco California.- Número seis mil veintidos Legalizada en el Ministerio de Relaciones Exteriores de Chile la firma del señor Héctor Burr Cónsul en San Fco. Eliana R. de García.- Eliana Rodríguez de Garcia.- Oficial de Legalizaciones.- Santiago primero de Abril de mil novecientos sesenta y nueve.- Hay- estampillas inutilizadas y timbre del Ministerio de Relaciones Exteriores de Chile.- En conformidad con la solicitud de fecha primero de Abril de mil novecientos sesenta y nueve, protocolizo el presente documento, agregándolo al final de mis Registros del presente mes, bajo el número cinco.- Santiago, primero de Abril de mil novecientos sesenta y nueve.- S. Rodríguez G.- Conforme con su original esta copia-fiel.- Santiago, primero de Abril de mil novecientos sesenta y nueve.- Hay firma iligible y timbre de don Sergio Rodríguez Garcés.- Notario Público de Santiago".- Conforme.- En comprobante y previa lectura firman los conparecientes en unión de las testigos hábiles de este domicilio doña Alicia Nuñez Espinoza y doña Dionisia Alexópulos Rojas.- La presente escritura está exenta de pago de impuesto en conformidad a los Decretos Leyes números seiscientos y seiscientos diecinueve de mil novecientos setenta y cuatro.- Se da copia en papel competente.- Doy Fé.- Edward B. Olds Easterday.- J. Samaniego G.- A. Nuñez E.- Dionisia Alexópulos.- ANTE MI, R. UNDURRA=GA L. NOT.=

CONFORME CON SU ORIGINAL ESTA SEGUNDA COPIA.= Santiago, 7 de Septiembre de 1977.-

INDEX

F

G

H

I

L

M

N

P

R

S

T

U

W